PRAISE FOR ROB MUNDLE

for *Flinders*

'In skilful prose, Mundle vividly stresses the personal costs of Flinders' ambition: shipwrecks, the loss of good friends and crew to a hostile sea, as well as his decade-long absence from home' *The Australian*

'Rob Mundle is a master of the maritime narrative' *Sunday Age*

'A drama of adventure and shipwreck' *Sun-Herald*

for *Cook*

'Competitive sailor and accomplished writer Rob Mundle puts readers on the quarterdeck as Cook guides his ship through treacherous reefs and swells to solve the mystery surrounding the existence of Terra Australis' *Courier Mail*

'... a thrilling biography for those who love adventure and the intricacies and challenges of sailing' *sail-world.com.au*

'Rob Mundle brings a wealth of navigational and ship-construction detail to Cook's adventures, and his descriptions of the capricious ocean – having been exposed to Cook's perils himself – lend this biography all the suspense of a good thriller' *Weekend Australian*

for *The First Fleet*

'A colourful, well-researched and fascinating account of the unlikely founding of a great nation' *Australian Women's Weekly*

'Mundle's insight into First Fleet diary and journal descriptions of storms and navigation is enhanced by his personal experience of sailing stretches of ocean traversed by Phillip. But it is his sensitive observation of human frailty that gives his work resonance' *Daily Telegraph*

'Wonderful story – useful reading for all Australians' Ian Perkins, *goodreads.com*

'[The author's] seafaring experience, along with his passion for the subject, has produced another extraordinarily compelling book' *Weekend Australian*

ALSO BY ROB MUNDLE

Bob Oatley: A Life Story

Bond: Alan Bond

Fatal Storm: The 54th Sydney to Hobart Yacht Race

Hell on High Seas: Amazing Stories of Survival Against the Odds

Learning to Sail

Jack Joel: My Life Story

*Life at the Extreme: The Volvo Ocean Race Round the World 2005–
2006*

*Ocean Warriors: The Thrilling Story of the 2001–2002 Volvo Ocean
Race Round the World*

Sir James Hardy: An Adventurous Life

Sydney to Hobart: The 1995 Golden Anniversary

Bligh: Master Mariner

Flinders: The Man Who Mapped Australia

Cook: From Sailor to Legend

The First Fleet

Great South Land

UNDER FULL SAIL

Rob Mundle

ABC
Books

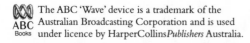The ABC 'Wave' device is a trademark of the Australian Broadcasting Corporation and is used under licence by HarperCollins*Publishers* Australia.

First published in Australia in 2016
by HarperCollins*Publishers* Australia Pty Limited
ABN 36 009 913 517
harpercollins.com.au

HarperCollins*Publishers*
Level 13, 201 Elizabeth Street, Sydney NSW 2000, Australia
Unit D1, Apollo Drive, Rosedale, Auckland 0632, New Zealand
A 53, Sector 57, Noida, UP, India
1 London Bridge Street, London, SE1 9GF, United Kingdom
2 Bloor Street East, 20th floor, Toronto, Ontario M4W 1A8, Canada
195 Broadway, New York NY 10007, USA

National Library of Australia Cataloguing-in-Publication data:

Mundle, Rob, author.
  Under full sail / Rob Mundle.
  978 0 7333 3469 6 (hardback)
  978 1 4607 0559 9 (ebook)
  Includes index.
  Ocean liner passengers–Anecdotes.
  Victoria–Melbourne.
  Clipper ships–Anecdotes.
910.45

Cover design by HarperCollins Design Studio
Cover image: 'The Cutty Sark' by Steven Dews © Felix Rosenstiel's Widow & Son, London.
Typeset in Bembo Std by Kirby Jones
Printed and bound in Australia by Griffin Press
The papers used by HarperCollins in the manufacture of this book are a natural, recyclable product made from wood grown in sustainable plantation forests. The fibre source and manufacturing processes meet recognised international environmental standards, and carry certification.

To the more than one million Australians whose forebears traversed the oceans aboard the mighty clipper ships and fulfilled their dreams of a better life in an exciting new land.

Contents

UNDER FULL SAIL

'Hell or Melbourne'

July 1852. It had been six weeks since the 932 passengers and sixty-man crew aboard the clipper *Marco Polo* had left England bound for Melbourne. They had just crossed the northern latitude of the Roaring Forties, some 350 nautical miles south of the Cape of Good Hope.

Suddenly a fearsome Southern Ocean storm charged in from beyond the western horizon and locked *Marco Polo* in its jaws. In a matter of hours, the moderate seas turned to mountainous breaking combers, accompanied by a howling and callously cold wind, quite possibly laced with flurries of snow.

Abject fear filled the minds of the passengers huddled below deck in an alien world. Many had led sheltered lives in small country villages; now they crouched in the claustrophobic 'tween decks of a giant ship, being pitched and tossed so wildly that tables, chairs and any other loose fixtures were being hurled from one side of their accommodation areas to the other.

But they weren't alone when it came to their anxiety: even members of the crew were unnerved. The end of this nightmare could not come soon enough for all on board.

One of them, however, had a very different reason for wanting to traverse these seas as quickly as possible: the ship's captain, James Nicol Forbes, a thirty-one year old Scotsman more appropriately known as 'Bully' Forbes.

All others aboard *Marco Polo* just wanted to get through this alive. But for Bully Forbes, reputation won out over the fear of death: Forbes had boasted that he would drive the recently launched 184-foot clipper ship to a record-breaking time between Liverpool and Melbourne.

As the storm raged around him, Forbes seemed oblivious to its terrifying nature. His only focus was on driving his charge south-east as hard and as fast as he could, away from the tip of Africa towards iceberg territory in the southern seas: a course that few ships had previously taken.

There was already some justification for Forbes's record-breaking ambition. On her maiden voyage from the builder's yard in Canada in late 1851, *Marco Polo* had crossed the Atlantic to Liverpool in the impressive time of just nineteen days. Now, by harnessing the full force of the storm she was experiencing in the southern seas (today the Southern Ocean), the captain saw the opportunity to prove *Marco Polo* the fastest ship afloat.

Much to his satisfaction, she had so far lived up to expectations – thanks to his determination to maintain maximum speed at all times. But the opportunity to show just how fast she could run had not presented itself until the moment this south-westerly gale had thundered in from astern.

With adrenalin pumping through his veins, and as if goading his ship to sail even faster, a fearless Forbes was said to have been seen standing on the windward side of the deck while holding on to the heavily built, high timber bulwark. It was a location from which he could best absorb the entire scene around him, and really appreciate what it meant to be the master of a ship running hard in what he saw as the ultimate conditions for maximum speed. He could watch his helmsman at the very aft end of the deck battling to hold course, while around him there were the men of the on-watch hanging on for dear life at their respective stations – every one of them hoping they would not be ordered to go aloft to tend the few sails that were still set, all of which appeared ready to burst.

Forbes's seemingly careless attitude towards what others saw as complete mayhem confirmed his confidence in the seaworthiness of his heavily laden ship. He seemed enthralled by the sounds of her being pushed to the absolute limit. Added to the roar of the huge breaking seas was the howl of the wind ripping through the standing rigging, sheets and braces, some of which were stretched to near breaking point. There was also the thunder-like rumble of the churning bow wave that rose up each time *Marco Polo* careered down a wave – a sound that was amplified aft by the curve of the forecourse (the lower square sail on the foremast). For Forbes, it was as if he were listening to Mother Nature's orchestra tuning up for a booming symphony. For just about everyone else, it was a cacophony of terrifying sounds.

Forbes was convinced that no one aboard *Marco Polo*, and possibly no one else in the world, had ever been so fast under sail. This could well be history in the making.

That meant little for the petrified passengers and concerned crew. Apart from the shuddering and vibrations that racked the 2500 tons burthen ship and the horrid sounds they were experiencing, the wildly gyrating motion of the vessel brought additional terror. Each time the powerful press of wind in her sails combined with the force of a large following wave, *Marco Polo* would heel alarmingly to leeward – sometimes around 30 degrees – to the point where the outer end of the main yard on the mainmast appeared destined to touch the water. Then, as she surged forward at nearly 20 knots on what resembled a huge avalanche of churning surf charging down a sheer cliff face – and just before she started to come upright – an immense wave would explode like a dam burst over the leeward bulwark and wash across the flush deck in a seething mass of white water.

Unfortunately, leaks in the deck and companionway hatches meant some of this icy-cold torrent would find its way to the accommodation area below, thus bringing more misery to the ship's inhabitants – the majority of who now expected to die at any moment. Some no doubt knew that in the twelve years prior to *Marco Polo*'s passage, ninety-four ships either had been wrecked or had disappeared sailing to Australia and New Zealand. It was a tally they did not want to add to.

Forbes, it is said, remained on deck unconcerned, but for the passengers, enough was enough. They sent one of their own to confront the captain and plead with him to slow their progress.

After plucking up the much-needed courage, the poor soul emerged from the companionway and stepped onto the deck amid what he could only perceive as a scene of chaos. Then, with the decks awash, and the ship quaking as if in her death throes, he clawed his way to where Forbes stood. Once there he begged the captain to consider the paying passengers, informing him that it was total turmoil below. The majority were certain that the ship would founder and disappear from the face of the planet, simply because of the captain's brazen and irresponsible approach to their safety.

Forbes, cold, soaking wet and with salt water dripping from the peak of his cap, would not have a bar of it. Fixing his steely, dark eyes firmly on the trembling passenger, he waved him away vehemently, and as he did he bellowed: 'It's a case of Hell or Melbourne, I'm afraid, sir.'

Nothing more was said.

Forbes's truculent manner, and his stubborn determination to have every possible stitch of sail set in what were the most challenging of conditions, finally brought the result he desired. This day of discord would prove to be a historic milestone in his relatively short, but spectacular, career as a clipper ship captain. Readings from navigation plots and the log line set from the stern later confirmed that *Marco Polo* had charged across the southern seas at unprecedented speed. She had covered an astonishing 364 nautical miles in one day – an average of nearly 15 knots – and over four successive days she had set a world record by sailing a total of 1344 nautical miles.

Forbes and all aboard his ship could now boast that no one before them had ever been so fast under sail. It could also be stated that *Marco Polo*'s speed was a ground-breaking achievement in British maritime history – one that reflected, for the first time, the true potential of the clipper ship. In today's parlance, passenger ships had just gone from the era of propellers to the age of jets.

Regardless, the passengers had little interest in what was being achieved; they continued to exist on the brink of hell below deck. *Marco Polo* was surging, bucking, tossing, shuddering and shaking so much that countless men, women and children were totally incapacitated through sheer terror, severe cold and seasickness, circumstances made worse by the associated stench. The ship's motion was so violent that many had to crawl along the passageways to get to their sleeping quarters, while others just gave up and lay where they fell.

Yet it was not just the appalling conditions on board that made them anxious to reach Melbourne. The sooner they set eyes on the entrance to Port Phillip and anchored off the town's waterfront, the sooner they could join in the search for the life-changing wealth they expected to find there – with the first major gold find in Victoria made just a year earlier. Ironically, some of the passengers were actually Australian settlers returning home, most empty-handed and disheartened, after joining the rush to California when gold was discovered in the Sierra Nevadas in 1848.

*

Just six months later, on *Marco Polo*'s return voyage, euphoria would have started to replace hope as Forbes navigated her out of the North Atlantic and up St George's Channel towards the Irish Sea. Holyhead, on the coast of Wales, soon loomed up in the distance.

At 3pm on Christmas Day, when the headland was aft of abeam, Forbes called for a course change to the east. From there it was only 75 nautical miles to the docks in Liverpool!

Even James Baines, the owner of *Marco Polo*, had struggled to accept Forbes's claim that she could circle the world faster than all that had gone before her. So Baines would have certainly been sceptical when, on Sunday 26 December 1852, a waterman rushed up to him in a Liverpool street and declared excitedly: 'Sir, the *Marco Polo* is coming up the river!'

'Nonsense, man,' Baines is said to have replied. 'There is no news yet of *Marco Polo* having arrived in Melbourne.'

His response would have been based on the fact that no ship had returned to England with a report that *Marco Polo* had reached Melbourne. But what Baines didn't know was that several ships had left Melbourne bound for England with that news, but *Marco Polo* had passed all of them on the way home!

Baines went towards the century-old Salthouse Dock simply to confirm that the news was not true – but it was! There, before his near-disbelieving eyes, was a magnificent black and white ship, riding easily alongside the pier.

As he stood there incredulous, he noticed something out of the ordinary amid the complex web of rigging that supported the ship's masts. At that moment a wry smile probably spread across his face. Stretched between the foremast and mainmast was a long canvas banner with a message scrawled across it in huge black letters: 'THE FASTEST SHIP IN THE WORLD'.

Minutes later, amid the large and admiring crowd that had already gathered on the dock, Baines was face to face with Forbes, congratulating him wholeheartedly on a remarkable achievement.

Marco Polo had completed her return voyage in seventy-six days. The total circumnavigation had taken her just five months and twenty-one days: an astounding three weeks less than the previous record-holder.

News of this historic passage, and stories relating to the ship's hard-driving captain, spread quickly around the world. Not surprisingly, thousands upon thousands of people from all corners of Britain, and even Ireland, made the pilgrimage to

Liverpool by train, horse-drawn carriage or boat to pay homage to the grand vessel, described by one historian as 'the wonder of the age'. The crowd were enthralled by yarns from proud crew members about highlights of the passage, and gasped when they heard that at times *Marco Polo* had averaged almost 20 knots: an unimaginable speed for a sailing ship.

Baines and his business partner Thomas M. MacKay also enjoyed the adulation; they must have felt as if they were blessed with the Midas touch. For just like that fabled king, their path to prosperity would be paved with gold.

Marco Polo was one of two ships that had left Melbourne carrying £1 million worth of gold back to the Mother Country. Even more importantly, there was a 340-ounce gold nugget on board – a gift for the reigning monarch, Queen Victoria, from the people of the newly declared Australian colony that bore her name. It was also rumoured that one English passenger had returned home with gold worth an impressive £45,000: the result of his efforts in the Victorian goldfields.

Before this, the backbone of all shipping lines offering services to the Antipodes had been emigration – ordinary people migrating to the colonies to start a new life. Now *Marco Polo* had brought tangible evidence of the gold rush in Victoria, and there was no better way to get there than aboard this very ship, the fastest on the seas.

Most satisfying to Baines and MacKay, though, was the knowledge that some passengers were prepared to pay a premium price – £50 each – to make the voyage one-way.

The two men and their associates had found their own goldmine. They could not have hoped for a more satisfying way to launch their newly formed Black Ball Line to the world. Within a decade they would have fifteen ships doing the run to Australia, most of them clippers. The timing of both the Californian and Victorian gold rushes changed the face of commercial shipping, and cemented the clipper even more solidly into maritime history. The speed of these ships was perfect for the gold-rush era, as the treasure hunters were only interested in reaching their destination as quickly as possible. It was *Marco Polo*'s record-breaking circumnavigation – and, around the same time, the big American clipper *Flying Cloud*'s stunning eighty-nine day passage from New York to San Francisco via Cape Horn – that did most to confirm that the swift clipper ships were the only answer to long-haul passenger and cargo transportation to the goldfields.

*

Burgeoning national pride, and a desire to build the world's fastest and most spectacular sailing vessels, led to the beginnings of the clipper-ship era in America in the mid-1840s. These designs were an entirely new concept – hence the reference to them as 'extreme clippers' – and while their heyday lasted a mere thirty years, many American commentators have recognised this period for its profound influence on that country's remarkable history.

The emerging nation of America was ready for such a historic change. As a country of immigrants, it boasted a substantial multinational pool of maritime talent – highly capable ship designers and builders who had gone there from England, Scotland, Wales and many parts of Europe. Neighbouring Canada would also participate in these exciting times.

The ships were unlike anything that had gone before them. They had sweet and sweeping, long and lean lines. They also featured a bow profile that arched up and forward from the waterline, and some were flush-decked. It has been suggested that the shape of the hull was influenced by the form of fast-swimming fish – but whatever its origin, the clipper was far more streamlined than any other ship of its era.

Equally imposing was the sail plan. The towering masts, which were heavily raked, carried acres of sail, thirty or more on some of the larger ships, and they had some romantic names – like the highest of all, which were called skysails or moonrakers. The clipper ships also proved to be amazing sail carriers in strong winds: they could set full sail when their predecessors would have been forced to reef, and their speed was unparalleled. Consequently, they soon acquired the name 'clipper', derived from the verb 'clip', to move swiftly.

The key to their success was their design.

Their predecessors had been created around cargo-carrying capacity, and had hulls that were overly buoyant and far from hydrodynamically efficient. They looked like bulbous-bowed barges that could have been modelled on the shape of a bathtub – and often sailed like them. On the other hand, the slim-lined clippers were designed with an emphasis on passenger numbers and speed, their cargo capacity being secondary.

The design theories that led to the creation of the clipper ship were revolutionary. They were an extension of the design of the considerably smaller but very swift and manoeuvrable 'Baltimore clippers', two-masted schooners that, as the name suggests, originated in Baltimore, on Chesapeake Bay in Maryland. Their pedigree dates back to the Anglo-American War of 1812, when many were built as swift privateers and blockade runners. The design also proved ideal for pilot boats based on America's east coast.

It was the all-round capabilities of these uniquely styled Baltimore clippers that no doubt influenced John Willis Griffiths, a free-thinking naval architect who is credited with creating the first true clipper ship. Named *Rainbow*, she was built at the respected Smith & Dimon yard in New York in 1845, primarily for transporting tea from China. Speed was of the essence in this highly competitive trade: the first ship back into New York with a cargo of the new season's crop could demand a premium price from buyers.

Rainbow's hull shape was unlike that of any other commercial vessel of similar size. Instead of having apple-cheek shaped forward sections that smashed through head seas, her bow sections resembled a long and tapered wedge that knifed through waves with minimal resistance. But this was just one of many innovations that Griffiths included when developing his radical new design. Whereas the latest designs of other naval architects were simply a progression of the thinking around the most recently launched ship, Griffiths's mathematical intellect and 'feel' for a hull shape put him on a completely different tangent. As American maritime historian William H. Thiesen puts it: 'Of all the nineteenth-century American shipbuilders, John W. Griffiths did more than any other builder to champion American shipbuilding methods. An experimenter, an advocate for formal ship-design education, and a working intellectual.'

Griffiths even created a design-testing tank so he could prove his theories by towing small models in it, and study wave patterns and drag readings. It was these endeavours that convinced him that the 'cod's head and mackerel tail' theory behind the shape of existing ships was wrong. His designs were long and lean and had a V-shaped bottom instead of flat floors.

Rainbow was very much the centre of attention while being built on the waterfront in New York. She certainly impressed her backers, Howland & Aspinwall, after she was launched. Her top speed was a remarkable 14 knots, a rare achievement for ships of this time ... and much more was to come. Little wonder that she was classified as an 'extreme' sailing vessel.

Immediately she proved her worth on the China run, but sadly her career was to be short-lived. On 17 March 1848, she sailed out of New York Harbour on her fifth voyage, bound for China via the Chilean port of Valparaiso, and was never sighted again. It was thought that she had foundered off Cape Horn in bad weather with the loss of all hands.

Rainbow would not be the only clipper ship of the era to disappear without trace: over the years an astonishing number of them would depart a port, sail over the horizon and never be seen again. The most common cause of these losses was gung-ho young captains like Bully Forbes, keen to break records and reap rewards, who would drive their ships too hard in extreme conditions. In such circumstances it would take only the combination of high wind strength and a massive rogue wave for the helmsman – or helmsmen, as some ships had twin steering wheels – to lose control.

Almost inevitably, the ship would then broach across the face of a wave, be knocked down to a position where she was beyond her stability point-of-no-return, and be overwhelmed. With her masts in the water and sails flogging wildly, there would be no possibility of her recovery. Instead, within minutes, she would be overwhelmed by the might and brutality of subsequent waves before her hull filled with water and she sank.

Sad as the loss of *Rainbow* was, she would forever be recognised as the foundation and standard-bearer of the remarkable clipper-ship era.

Griffith's next clipper, *Sea Witch*, a 170-foot-long three-master, was launched in 1846, again out of the Smith & Dimon shipyard. Months later, she stunned the New York waterfront when she arrived back in her home port with a cargo of tea from Hong Kong after just seventy-seven days at sea. At the time, the same passage would take a conventional cargo vessel around 160 days to complete.

However, it was two years later that her true potential became undeniable.

On 25 March 1849, a tiny white speck was seen on the distant horizon off the entrance to New York Harbour. Its approach aroused interest for those standing high on the hills at Navesink, just inland from the coast, primarily because its proportions were growing at a rapid rate. In a very little time, discussion centred on what this might be – obviously it was a sailing ship, but never before had one been seen to close on New York so quickly.

This ship had every possible sail aloft, including studding sails set to windward. Lookouts who were in position to semaphore news of any approaching ship to downtown New York struggled to recognise the ship's identity; they agreed she looked like a clipper, and if she was, she could only be returning from China with a cargo of tea, but the first of those was not expected so soon.

A little later, when the ship was close enough to the coast to be identified using a telescope, the lookouts were stunned. This was *Sea Witch* on her return voyage, fully laden with tea.

Her hard-driving master was one of the more colourful characters on the high seas at the time, American Robert 'Bully' Waterman, who had worked closely with Griffiths on the clipper's design. His major contribution had related to the design of the rig and the amount of sail the ship would carry.

Bully Waterman was on his way to achieving what no one thought possible. He was on the verge of completing what was usually a six-month passage from Hong Kong to New York in just seventy-four days, beating by three days the record time he had set two years earlier. To this day, this new mark has never been beaten by a commercial sailing vessel.

*

The birth of the clipper coincided with an era when navigators were developing techniques and equipment that would bring a new dimension to ocean travel.

Matthew Fontaine Maury was an American naval officer who became known as the father of modern oceanography and naval meteorology. As the first superintendent of the United States Naval Observatory, over many decades, Maury gathered and studied the logs and charts of vessels that had traversed the world's oceans, an effort that led him to develop highly detailed data relating to wind and current patterns, the likes of which had never been known. His subsequent publications showed how ships following his course directions between ports, while often covering a substantially greater distance than the direct route, could reduce their time for the passage by days, sometimes weeks.

He also developed a theory about the existence of a north-west passage, his hypothesis being that an area of ocean in the region of the North Pole was on some occasions not frozen over, which meant it would be possible to sail a ship around the top of North America west to east and enter the Atlantic. This conclusion came to him after he analysed the logs he had gathered from old whaling ships. It had been noted in some of those logs that markings on harpoons embedded in whales captured in the Atlantic showed the harpoons had come from ships based in the North Pacific. Recognising that the timeframe was too short for them to have migrated from one ocean to the other via Cape Horn, Maury deduced that those whales must have been able to surface to breathe over the thousands of miles they would have to travel from the Pacific Ocean to the Atlantic. This meant that a north-west passage must exist – probably not every summer season, but certainly during some. His hypothesis was confirmed as fact in 1854, when Irishman Robert McClure crossed the passage partly by ship and partly by sledge. Then, half a century later, Norwegian Roald Amundsen made the first successful transit solely by boat.

On the opposite side of the Atlantic around the same time, John Thomas Towson was developing a separate theory that would revolutionise the art of navigating the world's oceans. Towson started his commercial life as a successful maker of watches and navigational chronometers, but his talents and intelligence were such that history would see him as a contributor to many facets of life. Among his many noted achievements was the invention of a method for taking a photographic picture on glass, and the application of this method to the development of the reflecting camera.

In the mid–1840s Towson turned his attention to navigation, and in particular the 'great circle' route. He devised a set of tables to allow the easy calculation of a great circle course – where by sailing an arc between two points and not along a latitude, the distance to be sailed would be considerably less.

The benefits of this new navigational method were immediately proved on crossings of the Atlantic, and were soon being applied on many passages to and from Australia and New Zealand, in particular on the long legs across the southern seas.

When the great circle route was coupled with the benefits that came from Maury's research into the world's ocean currents and wind patterns, the sailing time between England and the Antipodes by all ships could be reduced by weeks. It meant that the high-speed clippers could now make this journey at unimaginable speeds.

*

It usually took a year to build one of these leviathan vessels. The timber to be used for the ship's construction – usually maple or oak in North America – had been felled up to a year before the build commenced, so that the majority of the sap, which could cause rot, had dried out.

The designer, who was also often the builder, would often start with a 6-foot-long timber block and carve out what was called a half-model – one half of the ship cut lengthwise. Made using a mallet, chisels, saws and fairing equipment, the half-model was created to the hull lines drawn by the designer, with a bit of 'feel' often added to the shape by the builder.

When this model was completed to everyone's satisfaction, templates were taken from it at the proposed frame intervals then expanded to full size. This was achieved with the use of flexible battens and chalk: the battens were bent to the shape of each individual frame then that shape was scribed in full size onto the lofting floor using chalk. Patterns were then taken from these chalked lines so that all the frames and main timbers of the ship could be produced with the highest degree of accuracy. A timber structure that would form the platform for the vessel's construction was erected at the edge of a waterway; this would also serve as a launching slipway. While some carpenters built the full-sized, horseshoe-shaped frames that would form the ship's hull, others lifted completed frames into place with the assistance of large derricks, the cables of which were attached to work horses that plodded across the yard.

Slowly but surely, the frames took on the shape of a giant ribcage, until all stood in place from bow to stern. The planks that would cover the hull were steamed in large ovens so that they became pliable enough to be bent around the frames.

They were attached using treenails (pronounced 'trunnels'): short lengths of dowel that were wedged into holes bored through the plank and the frame using an auger.

When the ship-building industry was at its zenith in north-eastern America, some 10,000 craftsmen – carpenters, joiners, dubbers, caulkers, riggers, mast-makers and the like – were employed by the yards in New York, Boston and elsewhere. From sun-up to sun-down the air along the waterfront was filled with the sounds of hammering, sawing and cussing as the workers went about their task, creating another maritime masterpiece from more than 1000 tons of timber.

These industrious endeavours also provided great interest for the public: the construction of each clipper ship was monitored by enthusiastic spectators, thousands of whom would often be on hand for the launching ceremony.

One regular visitor to the yards was noted American poet Henry Wadsworth Longfellow, who was so captivated by the genesis of these majestic clipper ships that he dedicated a poem to them. It was titled 'The Building of the Ship', and described the entire procedure, starting with the making of the half-model:

And first with nicest skill and art,
Perfect and finished in every part,
A little model the Master wrought,
Which should be to the larger plan
What the child is to the man,
Its counterpart in miniature …

Then, as the grand size and shape of the vessel became apparent, he wrote:

> Day by day the vessel grew,
> With timbers fashioned strong and true,
> Stemson and keelson and sternson-knee,
> Till, framed with perfect symmetry,
> A skeleton ship rose up to view!
> And around the bows and along the side
> The heavy hammers and mallets plied,
> Till after many a week, at length,
> Wonderful for form and strength,
> Sublime in its enormous bulk,
> Loomed aloft the shadowy hulk!

With their ships continually left in the wake of the fleet-footed new 'Yankee clippers', the ship owners of Britain had change forced upon them. Eventually they would respond with their own versions of the American design, but in the meantime, if they were to be competitive, the shipping companies had no option but to buy vessels from America and Canada.

The clipper ship design concept also influenced the shape of many sailing vessels built for pleasure in the mid-nineteenth century. The most famous of these was the 101-foot schooner *America*, which sailed across the Atlantic to Cowes, England, in 1851 and promptly trounced the best vessels the English could muster for a race around the Isle of Wight. The trophy she won would soon take the winning yacht's name: it became the America's Cup. Her victory in England was the start of what would become the longest winning streak in international sporting history: 132 years. After surviving twenty-four international challenges for the trophy, the New York Yacht Club finally lost the America's Cup to the Australian contender *Australia II* in 1983.

The actual impact that the clippers had on international maritime trade during their dominance is seen in the numbers. Their chubby-cheeked and cumbersome predecessors struggled to exceed 6 knots under full sail; the captain and crew would brag about covering 150 nautical miles in a day over pints of warm beer in the dimly lit and smoke-filled dock-front bars when they reached port.

But in the early 1850s the newfangled clippers were leaving a frothing white wake streaming behind them while covering 250 nautical miles in a day. In 1854 *Champion of the Seas* – the second-largest clipper ever to sail the passenger service between England and Australia – covered an astonishing 465 nautical miles on a noon-to-noon run during her maiden outward-bound voyage. Her average speed for the twenty-four hours was almost 20 knots!

Clippers were the perfect fit for the challenge that came with the tea market out of China, and the need to get cargoes of tea back to America and Europe as quickly as possible. This was a test that became the basis for legendary races between rival ships, races that could today be identified as the first trans-ocean sailing contests the world has known.

For those on board, the greatest adrenalin rush came when a clipper would surf down a large sea then become semi-submerged as the white, foaming bow wave burst onto the foredeck and flooded aft. Yet such occasions were made even more exciting when there was a rival in sight, as was the case in this reflection (probably embellished) from midshipman Frederick Paton. At the time he was well braced on the deck of the charging tea clipper *Flying Spur*:

> One morning *Flying Spur* was snoring through the NE trades under all sail to royal staysails, with her lower yards just touching the backstays. At 11.20am a sail was sighted on the horizon ahead. This proved to be the Glasgow clipper, *Lochleven Castle*, 80 days out from Rangoon to Liverpool. At 1pm the *Flying Spur* was up with her, and as we went foaming by, the *Lochleven Castle*'s main topgallant sail went to ribbons with a clap of thunder, and her mainsail split from top to bottom; at the same moment our cook with all his pots and pans was washed from the galley to the break of the poop. An hour and a half later the *Lochleven Castle* was out of sight astern.

After three spectacular decades – from 1845 to 1875 – the era of the clipper ships began to wane. Their presence on the high seas began to be overtaken by that of the smoke-belching, coal-consuming, soot-covered steamships. Worse still, for so many of the men and women who had been part of this most majestic period in maritime history, the transition from one form of ocean transport to another was difficult to witness – like seeing the ever-so-graceful albatross, which glided effortlessly across the undulating surface of a seemingly boundless blue ocean, replaced by an ungainly mechanical contraption.

However, in those thirty or so years when the clippers were in their prime, they played a key role in the transformation of much of the world.

Commercially, the timing of the clippers' emergence proved more providential than anyone could have imagined to the tea trade and other businesses. Yet almost simultaneously, much broader opportunities transpired: to carry millions of passengers along maritime highways to the scenes of the two major 1850s gold rushes, and to transfer migrants from their home countries to emerging lands of hope and opportunity. The impact of clipper ships was such that it has been asserted *Marco Polo* alone carried 15,000 passengers to Australia, and as a result more than 1 million Australians can now lay claim to being descendants of those same travellers.

While the presence of the clippers in commercial enterprise spanned only three decades, their record-breaking achievements would stand unmatched in the history of sail. And on rare occasions, the commanders and navigators who helped achieve these feats were actually women.

The true spirit of these clippers was embodied in their names. Many ships built in the first half of the nineteenth century were registered with uninspiring names like *Agnes*, *Maggie Lauder*, *Euphemia*, *Ellen* and *Wallace*. But not the clippers. They sailed proudly under names such as *Champion of the Seas*, *Romance of the Seas*, *Cutty Sark*, *Dreadnought*, *Flying Cloud*, *Great Australia*, *Lightning*, *Great Republic*, *Neptune's Car* and *Sea Witch*.

These ships were so magnificent to see under sail that some observers drew on the words of Lord Byron's poem *The Corsair* to best describe them:

She walks the waters like a thing of life
And seems to dare the elements to strife

The clippers were ground-breaking, record-breaking and history-making. There was nothing else like them, nor will there ever be.

CHAPTER 1

The Golden Clippers

The Californian gold rush, the American clipper industry
and the first female sailors

In the mid-nineteenth century, the finding of two gold nuggets in the shallow and crystal-clear water of an American mountain stream, and the discovery of more nuggets in the Australian bush, would dramatically enrich the history and growth of both countries in an almost identical way.

The great gold rushes that both these events triggered – the first in California in 1848 and the second in Australia three years later – were fuelled by a belief among prospectors that unimaginable wealth could be unearthed with ease. But there were as many benefits for the State as there were for successful diggers.

In both circumstances, the discovery of gold could not have come at a more expedient time for national development. Life for the majority in both countries was tough, migration to many areas – particularly to rural regions – had stagnated, and consequently the economic future of both nations was cloaked in uncertainty.

Then, almost overnight, in both America and Australia, gold fever brought the masses to the diggings from across the nation and the world. And linking both historic events were the mighty clipper ships, the fastest form of maritime transport for prospectors heading from both distant and foreign ports to the fields of gold.

But such a phenomenon was not unprecedented: gold had been pivotal in bringing wealth and benefits to society for millennia. It was the first precious metal known to mankind. Its brilliant lustre, its resistance to tarnishing and corrosion, its ability to be easily smelted and moulded, its scarcity and the fact that it could be found in a near-pure state made it highly prized. It became a visible sign of wealth, and a symbol of immortality and kingship.

Gold was first used within ancient communities for ornamental purposes. Priam's Treasure, named after the mythical King of Troy, was unearthed in what is now Turkey in 1870. This large and spectacular hoard, dating back to between 2600 and 2450 BC, comprised a wide variety of gold artefacts including jewellery, dazzling ornamental items and dining pieces. Still more splendid were the Mask of Agamemnon, uncovered at Mycenae in Greece, and the golden treasures of King Tutankhamun of Egypt. The Incas referred to gold as 'the tears of the sun', and it inspired the Colombian legend of El Dorado.

In Greek mythology, Jason and the Argonauts' quest for the Golden Fleece takes on new meaning when it is realised that miners in ancient times used a sheep's fleece to recover alluvial gold. They would filter a mixture of gold-bearing sand or soil and water through the wool of a sheep's hide. The flakes of gold would become trapped in the wool, which, when fully saturated, was dried in the sun then gently beaten so the flakes of gold would fall out and be recovered.

Historians suggest that gold became a form of currency around 700 BC, and as the skill of metallurgists increased, the variety of applications grew. Across centuries and cultures, its value has never diminished.

Conversely, gold has always been recognised as a cause of evil, greed and heartbreak. In his great epic the *Aeneid*, the Roman poet Virgil makes reference to '*auri sacra fames*', 'the infernal thirst for gold'. Likewise, the thousands of hopefuls who came to dig it from the ground of California in the 1850s would come to see its power as both a blessing and a curse.

*

As historic as it became, the Californian gold rush of 1848 was not the first in America. That occurred fifty years earlier, more than 2000 miles away to the east, in Cabarrus County, North Carolina. It started with the discovery of a 17-pound nugget and led more than 30,000 fortune-hunters to descend on the region.

However, history recognises 24 January 1848 as the day 'the big one' started. That was the day when James Wilson Marshall, a carpenter working on the construction of a timber mill for local pioneer farmer John Sutter, was standing at the edge of the South Fork of the American River, in Coloma, California, when a golden glint coming from among the smooth river stones caught his eye. He bent down, put his hand into the water and picked up two shiny objects. They would prove to be gold nuggets!

Marshall was euphoric at his discovery, but ironically, his excitement was countered by Sutter's dismay: the landholder knew immediately that if news of the find went public, his plans for establishing a large farming venture in Coloma, high and remote in the Sierra Nevada mountains, would be wrecked.

Inevitably, his worst fears were soon realised: it was impossible to suppress general awareness of such a discovery, especially after the extent of the deposit became apparent. Initially the news spread quite slowly by word of mouth, but that changed dramatically in March when Samuel Brannan – a Mormon newspaper publisher in the small seaport town of San Francisco, 100 miles to the south-west of Coloma – made it headline news. Opportunist that he was, Brannan is said to have then set up a store in the middle of Sutter's Fort (modern Sacramento), near the site of the find, where he sold everything a prospector might need. He promoted this business by striding along the streets of San Francisco holding aloft a small glass vial containing gold, shouting as he went: 'Gold! Gold! Gold from the American River!'

Within a few weeks of the discovery, the first participants in what was perhaps the largest human migration associated with a single purpose since the Crusades were already heading for the Sierra Nevadas. Much of the initial wave of fortune seekers came from within California and neighbouring Oregon, the Sandwich Islands (Hawaii), South America and Asia.

The cause of this early onslaught from beyond American shores was geographical: news of the Coloma gold discovery reached nearby Pacific ports far earlier than it did towns on the east coast, so it was from there that much of the rush's first wave originated.

With a transcontinental railroad still two decades away, there were only two viable options for travelling from California to the more populous east coast: by painfully slow and physically demanding wagon trains, or by ship via Cape Horn. So it took about five months – the minimum time it took to sail from San Francisco to New York – before the east was afire with the golden gossip. On 19 August 1848 the *New York Herald* published the story of the discovery, and from there, the news spread across America and the rest of the world like the surge of a massive flood.

Crews of every ship departing New York for coastal and foreign ports, and folk on wagon trains crisscrossing the land, all told of the remarkable discovery. In some cases it circulated like Chinese whispers, and fanciful declarations further fuelled the excitement: it was suggested that one need only stand on the bank of the shallow American River to see the sun-soaked glint of nuggets that were there for the taking. Payable gold had apparently never been so easy to find. The year after the discovery, government officials added to the excitement by gazetting that the region around Coloma would be officially identified as El Dorado.

Ironically, it was only a few weeks after Marshall made his discovery that Mexico and the United States signed the treaty to end the American–Mexican War, which ceded California and a considerable portion of the North American south-west to the United States. On 9 September 1850, after all the necessary formalities were completed, the United States, under President James K. Polk, would purchase from the Mexican Government, for little more than $18 million, land that would eventually be divided among seven separate States.

Edward Gould Buffum, a New York journalist and author, had fought in the Mexican–American War and decided to stay on in California and head for Coloma. He described in his book *Six Months in the Gold Mine* what he saw as the consequences of the gold rush:

> ... never in the world's history was there a better opportunity for a great, free, and republican nation like ours to offer to the oppressed and downtrodden of the whole world an asylum and a place where ... they can build themselves happy homes and live like free men ...

On 5 December 1848, President Polk announced to Congress details of Marshall's discovery, and the fact that considerably more gold had been either unearthed or removed from the riverbed since then. He told the Congress: 'the accounts of the abundance of gold in that territory are of such an extraordinary character as would scarcely command belief were they not corroborated by authentic reports'. The promise of easy wealth was further boosted by a display in Washington, DC, of gold nuggets and flakes that had come from Coloma.

For Polk and the Congress, this event was their own gold strike: they recognised that the associated stampede to the west would help hasten the achievement of the government's desire for the territory of Alta California to become a State of the Union sooner rather than later. (On 9 September 1850, the western part of that territory would become California, the thirty-first American State.)

By the end of 1848, Australians, New Zealanders and Europeans were following the path to the goldfields. Rivalry amongst the shipping companies was intense: they did everything they could to entice fortune hunters to their ships destined for San Francisco.

It is believed that around 6200 Australians ventured to California to join the onslaught of 'Argonauts': a significant figure considering that the country's population at the time was around 400,000, with many of them living away from the main cities. Fittingly, the gold-seeking foreigners who arrived early in the new year of 1849, along with their American counterparts, became known as 'forty-niners'. It is a tag that has survived in San Francisco to this day: the city's famous football team is known as the 49ers.

Estimates suggest that at the time of Marshall's discovery, there were only 157,000 people in what was referred to as California: 150,000 Native Americans, 6500 people of Spanish or Mexican origin, and fewer than 800 other foreigners. In under two years, this foreign population climbed at a staggering rate to more than 100,000. By the mid-1850s the number had increased to more than 300,000 (of whom only about 8 per cent were women). Over all, it was estimated by American authorities that one in every ninety people in the land was living in California.

Yet there was a terrible downside to this massive population influx: it had a devastating effect on the Native population. California's first governor, Peter Hardeman Burnett, an avowed racist with no consideration for Native Americans, African Americans or the Chinese, was the driving force behind a major genocide against the Natives. During his Second Annual Message to the Legislature, delivered on 7 January 1851, he declared: 'That a war of extermination will continue to be waged between the two races until the Indian race becomes extinct, must be expected.' Bounties were set on the scalps of Native men, women and children, and this led many miners, along with timber-getters and settlers, to form vigilante groups and mount killing raids on Native villages. It is estimated that by 1890, the already decimated Native population of California was reduced to less than 20,000.

While the gold hunters worked almost shoulder to shoulder in their relentless search for a fortune, the State, the nation and many entrepreneurial individuals were reaping considerable financial benefits through licence fees, taxes and commercial enterprises. In 1850, a foreign miner's tax of $20 a month was levied by the Californian State Legislature on all gold diggers who had come from overseas. These foreigners saw the fee – which equates to over AU$700 a month today – as being grossly unfair. Not surprisingly, then, this financial imposition led to ugly scenes between American and non-American miners. The situation became so bad that the authorities were forced to rescind the tax, which they did within two years of its introduction. But the Chinese diggers, who were the most disliked of all nationalities on the fields because of their relentless work ethic and unsociable attitudes, were singled out for a tax of $2 per month (more than AU$70 today).

Beyond the taxes, the financial and social effects of the gold rush were far-reaching. The need for food was such that the immediate area around Coloma became a food bowl for the masses. Similarly, there were widespread gains for industry: roads had to be built and ports developed. The rush also made it apparent that a transcontinental railway linking California to the east was essential, so survey work soon began to determine a potential route.

Like the gold rush's first millionaire, newspaperman Samuel Brannan, many astute individuals looked beyond the goldfields for their fortune and succeeded in grand style. One, Levi Strauss, saw a unique business opportunity when he moved from New York to San Francisco in 1853. He had with him some canvas which he intended to use for the manufacture of tents and wagon covers, but he quickly realised the heavy-duty fabric was ideal for making hard-wearing trousers for the miners. Within twelve months, Levi Strauss was the largest manufacturer of trousers in California. Eventually, his 'blue jeans' became a fashion statement around the world.

Similar success came to Johnnie Studebaker, who took a job in California making wheelbarrows for miners. This soon led him to establish his own business designing and making similar products. Having amassed a considerable fortune, in 1858 he decided to return to his home town, South Bend, Indiana, with a new idea. He and his brother soon formed a company to make wagons for westward-bound settlers. It went on to become the famous Studebaker motor vehicle company.

But it was the tiny waterfront port of San Francisco that benefited most, as the feeder port for the gold rush. A large number of its shrewder inhabitants, along with many from across America and beyond, were quick to realise that there was probably a greater opportunity to make a true fortune in the town than there was on the goldfields.

East-coast lawyer and politician Richard Dana, who sailed into San Francisco Bay fifteen years prior to the gold rush, offers us an early picture of the town. He arrived aboard a hide-trading vessel, *Pilgrim*, which had completed an arduous voyage from Boston via Cape Horn.

San Francisco's expansive bay, which measures around 45 miles from north to south, was discovered by Sir Francis Drake in 1579. At the time of Dana's visit, however, there was still little evidence of any European influence. He noted in his famous book *Two Years Before the Mast* that only one ship was riding at anchor when *Pilgrim* sailed through the bay's narrow entrance to the tiny town of San Francisco, located on the southern side. Dana described it as 'a magnificent bay, containing several good harbours, great depth of water, and surrounded by a fertile and finely wooded country'. Of particular note was that there were few houses to be seen.

If ever clear evidence was needed of the impact a major gold discovery might have on a small settlement, then San Francisco provided it abundantly. At the time when the *New York Herald* headlined the news of Marshall's exciting find, there were fewer than eighty buildings of any note in the town. Then, within a year, the local population had grown from less than 1000 to more than 100,000, and a shanty town comprising tents and hovel-like mud-brick huts stretched as far as the eye could see. At the same time, the bay was filled with countless ships at anchor, often gunwale to gunwale – the majority of them having been abandoned by their crews, who had left for the goldfields.

Every conceivable business sprang up in San Francisco to cater to the demands of the hopeful hordes heading for the Sierra Nevadas – businesses that were making their owners very rich, like food and clothing stores, mining equipment suppliers, hotels, hostels, bars, brothels and banks. Many of the mark-ups on essential items were exorbitant: a barrel of flour costing $5 anywhere else was selling for $50, and a single egg could cost as much as $1.

The owners of the clipper ships were among those eager to capitalise on this opportunity to the full. For example, in 1850 the clipper *Samuel Russell* returned her owners an astounding profit after she arrived in San Francisco crowded with passengers and carrying 1200 tons of merchandise, primarily flour. That same year the record-setting *Sea Witch* departed New York with a cargo of essential supplies costing $84,600. The lot was sold for $275,000 on arrival in San Francisco: enough money to build *four* clipper ships.

In the twelve months to April 1848, only thirteen commercial vessels from Atlantic ports had called at San Francisco; for the twelve months of 1849, that figure exploded to no fewer than 775 vessels from the east coast.

This number included the first ever clipper ship to arrive there, *Memnon*. Her voyage set a precedent: she amazed local residents and seafarers alike by taking just 122 days to cover the 16,000 nautical miles from New York, some eighty days less than the vast majority of ships before her.

Ironically, her time would have been considerably better had it not been for a mutiny en route. Donald Gunn Ross III, in his book *The Era of the Clipper Ships*, writes that the captain, J.R. Gordon, was confronted by his crew halfway down the east coast of South America. They were refusing to do their duties because they felt he was demanding far too much of them in the tough conditions. Fortunately, some remained loyal to the captain, so he was able to sail into Montevideo in Uruguay, where he discharged the troublemakers and signed on additional men for the remainder of the passage.

The human invasion that descended on San Francisco placed overwhelming pressure on the supply of materials needed for the construction of buildings. It took only one individual to look out across the bay and apply some logic, and the problem was solved. In no time the abandoned ships were being hauled in close to the shore and dismantled.

They proved to be the source of many types of timber, canvas, metal items, rope and cordage. And any ship that wasn't worth pulling apart wasn't wasted. She was scuttled on the waterfront so she could form part of the foundations for the port's much-needed docks.

With all this activity, it is not surprising that it took only two years for San Francisco to establish itself as the most important settlement on the west coast – a burgeoning town that was already a vital and vibrant commercial, naval and financial centre. By 1870 it was the tenth-largest community in the United States.

*

The demands of the New York-to-San Francisco run and the enormous profits that accompanied each east-to-west voyage caused almost every ship owner in America to abandon the tea trade from Asia and concentrate on the gold-rush bonanza. While the clippers' cargo-carrying capacity was nowhere near that of the full-bodied and sluggish merchant vessels, they were ideal as passenger ships for those wanting to reach the west coast. The influence of events in California on this transformation of maritime voyaging was stated succinctly at the time by a newspaper reporter in San Francisco:

> ... the discovery of our golden sands has done more in
> four years towards improvement in the style of ship
> building, than would have occurred from other general
> causes in half a century ...

The 224-foot extreme clipper *Challenge*, built in New York at a cost of $150,000 and launched in 1851, was the largest and potentially fastest commercial vessel ever to have been constructed to that point, and the first triple-decker. Her one purpose was to transport the maximum number of passengers in the shortest possible time from New York to the goldfields. Fittingly, her sail area, spread across three masts, was then the largest ever seen.

Such a ship demanded the best master for her maiden voyage, and Bully Waterman, a captain who (like Bully Forbes) had become as infamous as he was famous, was deemed by *Challenge*'s owners, N.L. & G. Griswold shipping company, to be the only man for the job. Unfortunately, though, he had taken early retirement, so it wasn't until there was an offer of a $10,000 bonus for reaching San Francisco within ninety days of departure that he decided to accept the appointment.

Over the years, the legend of Bully Waterman had spread way beyond distant horizons, and it had become increasingly apparent how he had gotten the 'Bully' tag. It was founded as much on his often tyrannical behaviour and brutal confrontations with crew as it was on his status as a master who drove his ship beyond the usual limits. And some of the worst incidents of his career would occur on this voyage aboard *Challenge*.

The odds were stacked against Waterman even before the ship set sail from New York: there were few qualified crewmen available, as the majority of good men, having already sailed to San Francisco, had jumped ship there and rushed to the goldfields, most never to return. This meant that of the sixty men who signed on for the voyage, all but two were foreigners and inexperienced seafarers, and a mere six had the ability to take a trick at the helm. Waterman was unperturbed by this; he was no doubt confident he could mould the motley crew of men into a solid working unit as the ship progressed on what would be a passage of more than 16,000 nautical miles.

However, that wasn't to be the case. There was dissension among the crew on their very first day at sea, and this led the captain to dismiss the first mate and replace him with James Douglass, whom he hired from the crew of a packet that was sailing off Sandy Hook, near the entrance to New York Harbour. Douglass would prove to be as brutal as his boss.

By the time *Challenge* was off the coast of Brazil – well into the voyage – she had become a hell ship. Waterman, frustrated by the inabilities of his crew, returned to his wicked ways, at one stage almost scalping the ship's cook with a carving knife, and beating two ailing sailors for malingering while on watch.

But the crew's greatest distaste was for Douglass, whom many of them conspired to kill. They attacked him, stabbing and beating him repeatedly, before Waterman, who had been standing at the poop taking navigation sights, was alerted to the drama by a passenger. He rushed forward and burst into the fray, saving Douglass from death. Within minutes, the eight would-be mutineers were lined up and flogged severely, even though Waterman knew that Congress had outlawed such punishment aboard merchant ships the previous year. Douglass recovered, then continued to unleash vehement physical and mental abuse on the crew for the remainder of the voyage, often with the master's consent.

In a few words in his log, Waterman also noted another incident that occurred when *Challenge* was rounding the southern tip of South America: 'Off Cape Horn three men fell from the mizzen topsail yard and were killed'. It would later be revealed that at the time the ship had been in the teeth of a monstrous winter storm, and was being pitched and hurled about by huge waves while the wind howled through the rigging. The three men had been sent aloft to furl a wildly flogging sail, but as they gingerly ventured out along the yard while standing on the constantly swaying footropes, crew on the deck mistakenly eased the braces, causing the yards to sway so violently that the men were catapulted into the icy sea.

Challenge's progress was continually hamstrung by unfavourable weather and rough seas, so that any chance Waterman had of collecting his $10,000 bonus was gone well before San Francisco was reached. In the end, it took the ship 108 days to get there.

Waterman's woes continued once in port. Word of his treatment of the crew reached a local newspaper, causing uproar across the town. The newspaper suggested the captain should be 'burned alive', while some residents wanted to lynch him.

Both Waterman and Douglass were eventually arrested and tried, Waterman for beating a sick crewman, and Douglass for murder. Both were found guilty but no sentence was imposed.

*

As the gold rush went on, orders for new clippers saw shipyards on the east coast enjoying boom times – times that presented an opportunity for some exceptional individuals to come to the fore. Of the colourful tales to emerge from this era, none was more remarkable than that of shipbuilder Donald McKay.

McKay was born in 1810 on the family farm at Jordan Falls, on the banks of Jordan Bay in Nova Scotia, Canada, one of fifteen children. As a young teenager, his temptation to explore the waters of the bay and the Jordan River was such that he built a small sailing dinghy. The adventures he enjoyed on board this tiny craft set his life on a course that would bring him great fame and fortune.

At age sixteen he boarded a coastal schooner in Halifax and sailed to New York, where it was his intention to find a job as an apprentice shipbuilder. He was soon indentured to the man the industry knew as 'the Father of Shipbuilders', Isaac Webb, who operated a successful yard on the banks of the East River. Young McKay's employment agreement, which entitled him 'to learn the art, trade and mystery of a ship-carpenter', reflected the morality of the times. It read in part:

> From the date of the date hereof, for and during and
> until the full end and term of four years, six months and
> eleven days next ensuing; during all of which time the
> said apprentice his master faithfully shall serve, his secrets
> keep, and his lawful commands everywhere readily
> obey: ... he shall not contract matrimony within the said
> term: at cards, dice, or any other unlawful game he shall
> not play ... nor haunt ale-houses, taverns, dance-houses

or playhouses; but in all things behave himself as a
faithful apprentice ought to do during the said term.

These terms would have been onerous for many, but McKay's work ethic and talent were such that he was released from his apprenticeship after just four years, aged twenty, and allowed to take up a position with another nearby shipbuilder, Jacob Bell. This opportunity led him to befriend John Willis Griffiths – already a noted designer, though his development of *Rainbow* was still some fifteen years away. The pair spent a considerable amount of time discussing ships' design and ways to improve their speed.

McKay's ability and talent saw him outclass nearly 1000 other men to become a foreman at the Brooklyn Navy Yard. His reputation continued to grow over the ensuing years, and in 1844, at the age of thirty-four, he was financed into his own shipbuilding yard in Boston by a wealthy local merchant, Enoch Train. This gave him the first chance to apply his own thinking, and many of the theories he had developed with Griffiths, to his own designs – and from that point there was no holding him back. Over the next twenty-five years, he would set new standards in ship design and production.

His first ship, designed specifically for the California trade, was the extreme clipper *Stag Hound*, launched in 1850 – a sharp-bowed, powerfully proportioned and stunningly swift sailing ship that was like no other. This vessel alone confirmed that McKay had already perfected the clipper concept.

When launched, *Stag Hound* was the largest commercial vessel in America. Much to the delight of her owners, she returned every cent of her construction cost ($45,000) from the profit achieved on her maiden voyage, a passage that took her to California and Asia. Most importantly for McKay, her success immediately elevated him to the status of pre-eminent shipbuilder of the era. This mantle was enhanced by the efficiency of his shipyard: he was able to significantly reduce the build time through his own ingenuity. Among other innovations, he created a steam-operated derrick, and a steam saw that proved to be far more efficient than the two-man pit saw that had been the standard until then.

The second clipper ship McKay built, *Flying Cloud*, was the most famous ever to come from his yard, and one of the most impressive ships of her type to cross the world's oceans. She is seen by many as unsurpassed in the history of American sailing ships, clocking some amazing times for passages between the world's great seaports. Later in her career she would play an important role in early Australian history, completing seven voyages carrying migrants from England on what was referred to as 'the Queensland Run'.

Launched on 15 April 1851, she measured 235 feet over all, with a beam of 41 feet and draft of 19 feet. Her cargo capacity of 1783 tons was almost twice that of Griffiths's *Sea Witch*, the tallest and most innovative ship afloat when launched just five years earlier.

There were more than a thousand spectators who crowded around McKay's yard or stood aboard small boats on the river to watch the launching of this mighty and majestic ship. Such was the celebration within the small community that church bells rang out across Boston from the moment the man standing on the deck – probably McKay – commenced proceedings.

Recognising that the tide was at its peak, he signalled the yard hands, positioned beneath the hull carrying large sledgehammers, to begin smashing the wooden support chocks out from under the long, straight keel. Within a few minutes the ship slowly began to move down the slipway towards the water: the signal for the admiring and excited crowd to fill the air with cheers. As they did so, *Flying Cloud* accelerated down the heavily greased wooden ways and into the water, all the time remaining perfectly upright.

In his poem 'The Launching', Longfellow wrote of the moment:

> She starts – she moves – she seems to feel
> The thrill of life along her keel,
> And, spurning with her foot the ground,
> With one exulting, joyous bound,
> She leaps into the ocean's arms!

A reporter from the *Boston Daily Atlas* recorded for his readers: 'If great length, sharpness of ends, with proportionate breadth and depth, conduce to speed the *Flying Cloud* must be uncommonly swift, for in all these she is great.'

However, it was not just her record-breaking achievements under sail that earned *Flying Cloud* her formidable reputation. Her fame was greatly enhanced by the pair who held the roles (respectively) of captain and navigator. Her commander was Josiah Perkins Creesy (better known as Perkins) – and her navigator was his much-loved wife, Eleanor.

While it was not unusual for a master to have his wife accompany him on voyages, for her to be actively involved in the operation of the ship – particularly in the senior position of navigator – certainly was.

Born Eleanor Prentiss in the east-coast seaport of Marblehead, Massachusetts, in 1814, she was fascinated from an early age by the fundamentals of navigation thanks to her father, who was a master mariner. Her enthusiasm was fuelled by her experiences when sailing with her father aboard his coastal trading schooner. His ability to navigate using the sun and the stars for guidance generated considerable intrigue in her fertile young mind – so much so that she did everything possible to expand her field of knowledge by studying mathematics, astronomy and weather patterns, and learning from her father how to use a sextant. Her studies inevitably caused her to become a disciple of Matthew Maury, and an avid reader of his influential publications.

It was Eleanor's task to plot every part of the course that would take *Flying Cloud* safely from port to port, which meant that she needed to calculate the ship's position around the clock.

*

Within seven weeks of her launch, *Flying Cloud* had been fully rigged and fitted out and had sailed to New York under the captaincy of Perkins and Eleanor. Once there, the ship was loaded with $50,000 worth of cargo, including 190 dozen brandied peaches, 100 dozen jars of tomato and pepper sauce, sixty-eight boxes of candles, 500 kegs of white lead, 100 cases of imperial black paint, lamp black, and 100 cans of turpentine. Additionally, there were twelve passengers, most of whom were travelling to San Francisco on business.

This maiden voyage, using developing navigation techniques, would be one of ocean sailing's great tests. The Creesys weren't expecting it to be easy – and it wasn't.

On the afternoon of 2 June 1851, the anchor was hauled up and some sails set to suit a course towards Sandy Hook, 10 nautical miles away to the east. Once there, at 7pm the pilot guiding *Flying Cloud* away from the entrance to New York's Hudson River was transferred to a small boat so he could return to shore. Then, as *Flying Cloud* was steered towards the open sea, Eleanor would have confirmed with her captain husband that the desired course was to the south-east, a course that would take them close to Bermuda and on towards the easternmost point of South America, around 3500 nautical miles away.

Within days, as the wind increased in strength and the seas rose in stature, *Flying Cloud* showed she was indeed a maritime charger: she appeared to be registering unprecedented speeds, speeds that caused Eleanor to double-check her calculations, thinking she must have made an error. But she hadn't.

However, the rapid progress was not without its dramas: problems were emerging with the rig, something not unexpected on such a radical and untried ship, but still a development that caused considerable concern. Three days out from New York she went close to losing her mainmast because of rigging failure, then the main topgallant and mizzen topgallant yards exploded into splinters.

Captain Creesy opted to reduce speed until the broken spars were replaced and additional checks were made of the tension on all rigging. Consequently, it was discovered that there was a problem with the mainmast: it could come crashing down across the deck if the usual amount of sail were set. So the call was for the giant timber section not to be overloaded for the reminder of the voyage. Yet even under reduced sail, *Flying Cloud* was achieving speeds never before seen by any sailing ship.

The captain's log soon noted that they had crossed the Equator two days faster than any other ship that had headed south from New York. The thought then was that a record time to Cape Horn was in the offing, but that became doubtful when a powerful mid-ocean storm – one capped by heavy cloud and delivering strong winds and rough seas – crossed their path, haunting them for days.

This storm's dense, lead-coloured cloud stretched from horizon to horizon, meaning that Eleanor Creesy was unable to get the sun or star sights she needed to accurately plot the ship's position. Instead, she had to apply her real skills as a navigator and go by 'dead-reckoning'. This method of navigation saw her plot the ship's position on a chart by applying estimates of the average speed through the water and the course steered over a nominated period.

It was a challenging and intense around-the-clock effort for Eleanor, lasting more than ten days and extending over 1000 nautical miles. When she completed each plot, Eleanor would discuss the situation with her husband, then decide whether it was safe to continue on the current course or if it would be preferable to call for a change of course. It was like flying blind.

Yet when the weather finally cleared, the captain and navigator were more than pleased with what they had achieved. There, only a few miles to the west of the ship, the snow-capped highlands just north of Cape Horn were visible: *Flying Cloud* was almost exactly where her navigator had expected her to be.

Despite the ship's teething problems, Cape Horn was rounded in record time, and fortunately for all on board it proved to be a fair-weather experience. Once 'around the corner' and sailing north, with guidance from Maury's sailing directions, the Creesys were able to hold a surprisingly speedy course towards San Francisco. No one on the ship had ever travelled so fast – not even on land.

With at least twenty-seven sails set at the best of times, *Flying Cloud* was romping along, her long, lean bow knifing effortlessly through the waves while tossing a mane of white water high into the air. No doubt everyone on board was impressed by both her sea-kindliness and her amazing speed. A record run seemed inevitable.

Sure enough, *Flying Cloud* sailed a world-record speed of 374 nautical miles in twenty-four hours. Her average speed was 15.5 knots, and at one stage her mechanical log confirmed her top speed as better than 18 knots. Not even the unpredictable conditions of the horse latitudes (between 30 and 38 degrees south) could stop the ship from maintaining a remarkable speed; in fact, it wasn't until she was three days out from San Francisco that she struck fickle winds.

Still, *Flying Cloud* continued to glide towards her goal until, on 31 August, she emerged from a misty horizon and entered San Francisco Bay. Her time from New York was an astounding eighty-nine days and twenty-one hours: a record that was under half the time it had taken some ships to sail the same passage at the start of the gold rush less than three years earlier, and a full week faster than the previous record-holder, another clipper ship, *Surprise*.

Once their ship was safely anchored, Eleanor and Perkins Creesy became instant celebrities. Masses of people clamoured to meet them, while others rushed to North Beach to see the wonder ship.

The day after *Flying Cloud* reached port, the town's *Daily Alta California* newspaper described her as a 'skimmer of the seas', adding that she would 'stand, as long as she lasts, a monument of Yankee talent in the way of ship building'. The east-coast media were similarly jubilant at the news, especially in New York, and the record even made headlines in the London *Times* on 22 October 1851. Consequently, after only one voyage, *Flying Cloud* had become the most famous sailing ship in the world.

Two years later, Eleanor and Perkins Creesy did it again with *Flying Cloud*: they broke their own record by thirteen hours – a mark that stands to this day for a square-rigged sailing ship.

*

Another woman gained national and international prominence as the wife of a ship's captain just three years after *Flying Cloud* logged her second record-breaking passage, and it came on the same run.

On 1 July 1856, the clipper ship *Neptune's Car* cleared Sandy Hook at the entrance to New York Harbour, turned to starboard and began the long voyage to San Francisco. Her captain was twenty-nine year old Joshua Adams Patten, and he was accompanied by his nineteen year old wife Mary, then four months pregnant with their first child. Captain Patten had been master of the ship for two years, and during that time Mary had accompanied him on a long and very interesting passage from New York to San Francisco, then China, London and finally back to New York.

To pass the time on that previous voyage, Mary had worked with great interest alongside her husband whenever he was navigating the ship and calculating her position. Mary was intrigued by how, by taking sun sights with the sextant, the angles could be plotted with near-pinpoint accuracy onto the chart. This led her to spend many hours on deck each day, learning how to use the sextant then convert the data and confirm the position of the ship via both latitude and longitude. She also learned how to calculate dead-reckoning as an alternative method of navigation. As an additional form of self-education, Mary studied medical procedures – a fortunate exercise, since several crew members were injured when *Neptune's Car* was struck by lightning on this current passage to San Francisco. Mary's newfound abilities caused her husband to note: 'Mrs Patten is uncommon handy about the ship, even in weather, and would doubtless be of service if a man.'

Yet Joshua was unaware that he was suffering from an advanced stage of tuberculosis (then known as 'brain fever'), and collapsed through exhaustion while *Neptune's Car* was battling her way around Cape Horn in extremely rough seas and high winds. The ship's problems were exacerbated by the fact that he had been forced to confine the first officer to his cabin for the duration of the voyage: he had become a troublemaker among the crew, and been found asleep while standing a watch. Patten had then been without an immediate assistant, and been forced to rely on his second officer – illiterate and thus unable to navigate – for support.

Mary immediately adopted the role of nurse for her seriously ill husband, whom she had to tie to his bunk so that he would not be thrown out in rough weather. But her most urgent dilemma when her husband took ill was that the ship now had no navigator – until she realised there was still one person on board with that expertise: herself.

The troublesome first officer pleaded with Mary to be released from his cabin so he could assist with the running of *Neptune's Car*, but, fearing he might instigate a mutiny among the crew and take control of the ship, she stood her ground. She would become the navigator and he would remain confined to his cabin.

For the next fifty-two days, during which time her husband slipped into a coma, Mary commanded the 1600-ton ship and navigated her north from Cape Horn to San Francisco. It was an achievement that sees her recognised today as the first female commander of an American merchant vessel.

Within days of arriving in San Francisco, Mary and her gravely ill husband boarded a steamship bound for New York, and on arrival there she took him home to Boston. Sadly, he remained unconscious, so was unaware that Mary gave birth to a son on 10 March 1857.

On hearing of Mary's remarkable effort in guiding *Neptune's Car* safely to San Francisco, the ship's insurers awarded her $1000 in recognition of saving the ship and the valuable cargo. Responding to this unexpected reward, Mary said, 'I have endeavoured to perform that which seemed to me, under the circumstances, only the plain duty of a wife towards a good husband, stricken down by what we now fear to be a hopeless disease.'

Joshua died in July 1857, while Mary, tragically, contracted his tuberculosis and passed away in 1861 at the age of twenty-four.

*

By the year of Joshua's death, the brief but glorious era of the American clippers was already in decline.

The facts are in the figures. While not precise, they are accurate enough to show the impact the clippers had on maritime transport.

The vast majority of the estimated total of 455 clippers came from some 100 shipyards in America's north-east, and north of the border in Canada. It is thought that twenty-four clippers were launched in 1850, all from the north-east coast of America. The majority of these were extreme clippers – the largest, sleekest, fastest and most powerful vessels.

The number of launchings rose rapidly over the next two years, until 1853 – the year of *Marco Polo*'s great achievements on the Australian run — saw the construction and launching of these ocean greyhounds at its zenith. That year, no fewer than 120 extreme clippers slid down the ways and into the water after a bottle of either red wine or Champagne was smashed on the bow and the ship's name revealed to the world.

But as gold supplies dried up in California, the number of launchings dropped dramatically over the next few years. By 1858, the boom time for clipper building had come to an abrupt end, due mainly to what became known as the Panic of 1857, which spread from America to Britain and is regarded by many as the first worldwide economic crisis.

With land values declining and migration rates falling on the west coast as the flood of gold dwindled to a trickle, speculators could no longer finance the railroads intended to connect the goldfields with the east. Then in August 1857 the Ohio Life Insurance and Trust Company's New York branch shut its doors amid rumours that the bank's entire assets had been embezzled by its cashier. With no central banking system to provide security, the panic that ensued saw other banks shut down within hours and stock values on Wall Street go into a rapid decline.

The chaos was exacerbated by the sinking of a ship. The steamship *Central America* — which sailed out of San Francisco in September, bound for New York with a cargo of California gold worth $2 million — was meant to be the economy's saviour. The $2 million cache was designed to bolster the rapidly dwindling gold reserves of banks on the east coast. But

Central America sank in a hurricane off North Carolina, taking the lifeline with it.

The Panic of 1857 would have far-reaching effects beyond the decline of the shipping industry. The crisis also heightened the simmering tensions between the north and south over the issue of slavery, which would boil over into civil war just four years later.

But the heyday of the clippers didn't end there: more great maritime achievements and historic moments were already occurring on the other side of the world. The focus of fortune hunters had turned away from California towards immense fields of gold in Australia.

While the tentacles of the 1857 financial crisis did reach Australia, the impact on the economy was minimal, due in no small way to the gold rush and its associated mass migration. Instead of being a financial storm for Australia, it was a mere gale.

News of discoveries in New South Wales and then the new colony of Victoria brought the desired — and some not-so-desired — results. Many men's dreams would end in ruin, but the hoped-for benefits were there for all to appreciate: the gold rush helped fill the colonies' coffers while generating great wealth for many individuals. It also delivered tens of thousands of migrants who might otherwise never have considered venturing to Australia. Moreover, it proved to be the birthplace of a national identity for an emerging nation.

CHAPTER 2

'The El Dorado of the World'

The gold rush comes to Australia

In 1849, the spontaneous departure of thousands of men, certain that instant wealth awaited them in the Sierra Nevadas, presented wide-ranging problems for colonial officials in Australia. The reversal of the shift in migration to Australia, small as it was at that stage, had the potential to cause long-term damage to the program that had seen the arrival of a steady stream of migrants, particularly from Britain. With the colony of New South Wales barely six decades old, any significant loss in population could easily jeopardise its future.

For much of the first half of the nineteenth century the colonial government, with the full support of the British Colonial Office, did everything it could to deter the search for gold. It was believed that this was in the best interests of the nation's fragile economy. Should payable gold be discovered in any quantity, there would be massive upheavals: they were certain that farm workers would abandon their income-producing livestock and crops and rush to the goldfields, and, worse still, convicts would be tempted to escape at any opportunity and head in the same direction.

However, by the time gold was discovered in California, the members of the legislature were changing their thinking. It was nearly a decade since legislation had been introduced to abolish transportation to New South Wales: a move that had been welcomed by the ever-increasing number of free settlers, who had a distinct distaste for the 'convict stain' the country had borne since the First Fleet arrived in 1788.

It was now believed that gold discoveries could be a *good* thing for the fledgling colony. As early as 1845, the *Journal of the Royal Geographical Society of London* printed an article that read, in part:

> Our colonies in Australia are now in a condition which
> would render the discovery of valuable minerals of the
> very highest importance. The amount of agricultural
> produce raised in these colonies is considerably above
> that required for the consumption of the inhabitants,
> who are now anxiously looking about the world for a
> market for their surplus produce, and such a market
> would be afforded by a population employed in mining
> operations.

After closely monitoring the favourable consequences of the Californian gold rush, in 1849 the powers that be decided that there was just one way to turn the tide back in Australia's favour: a similar gold discovery. It was already known that gold deposits did exist in New South Wales, so there was little doubt that should they be unearthed in similar quantities to the finds in California, the prosperity of the colony would be guaranteed.

Governor Charles FitzRoy applied to the Colonial Office for a change of policy on mineral exploration; a geologist, Samuel Stutchbury, was appointed to survey the colony, and permission was granted to develop any valuable mineral resources he might find. Such finds, FitzRoy concluded, would bring a double benefit to the fledgling colony: the lure of gold would deliver not just untold wealth, but also countless thousands of emigrants from across the world, just as it had done in California – and hopefully the majority would stay.

*

Much debate still surrounds the question of who was the first person to discover payable gold in Australia. For decades, students were taught that Englishman Edward Hammond Hargraves held that honour. This is now strongly questioned – even though the New South Wales Government awarded him a rich prize.

Today it is agreed by historians that no individual can be identified beyond doubt as the first to find gold in Australia.

However, the most likely candidate is James McBrien, who, while surveying an area along the banks of the Fish River between Bathurst and Rydal, 80 miles west-north-west of Sydney, noted in his survey book on 15 February 1823: 'At E. [end of survey line] 1 chain 50 links to river and marked a gum tree. At this place I found numerous particles of gold convenient to river.'

Subsequently there were many other claimed discoveries, but none of them was of commercial importance. For instance, in 1846, a small amount of gold was found at Castambul in South Australia and a mine was immediately established there. But it failed to produce gold in significant quantities.

No doubt the most controversial individual who held a desire to discover gold was Paul Edmund de Strzelecki. Born in Prussia in 1797, after spending his early years educating himself in geology, he sailed on commercial ships throughout the Pacific. He visited New Zealand, then arrived in Sydney in April 1839, and soon undertook a geological survey that led him to the Bathurst region of New South Wales. On his return to Sydney he described the mineralogy of the area as being 'very tame': an assessment that would later prove to be far from correct.

In a subsequent geological survey – during which he climbed to the top of Australia's highest peak and named it Mount Kosciuszko in honour of noted Polish military leader Tadeusz Kosciuszko – it is thought that he found some gold-bearing rocks near Hartley, about 37 miles east of Bathurst. In a letter written to an associate on 26 October 1839, he claimed he had uncovered 'a specimen of native silver in horneblende rock and gold specks in silicate, both serving as strong indications of the existence of these precious metals in New South Wales'.

However, Strzelecki made no mention of such a discovery in an account he wrote of his travels, published in 1845. Eventually, though, he would declare that his silence was due to a threat from the Governor of New South Wales, Major Sir George Gipps. Strzelecki wrote:

> I was warned of the responsibility I should incur if I
> gave publicity to the discovery, since, as the Governor
> argued, by proclaiming the colonies to be gold regions,
> the maintenance of discipline among forty-five
> thousand convicts ... would become almost impossible
> ... These reasons of state policy had great weight with
> me, and I willingly deferred to the representations of
> the Governor-General, notwithstanding that they were
> opposed to my private interests.

Strezlecki's note certainly confirms what would eventually become common knowledge: the news of these early discoveries of gold was deliberately suppressed. As mentioned, it would not be until 1849, after word of the Californian gold rush had spread, that this attitude changed. Much to the delight of FitzRoy's government, the new policy brought immediate results, and the long-term benefits were immense.

It was at this point that Edward Hammond Hargraves – the man who eventually claimed the prize – entered the picture. Born in Gosport, Hampshire, in 1816, Hargraves arrived in Sydney in 1832. He worked initially as a farmer beyond the Blue Mountains west of Sydney, and later as an itinerant collector of tortoiseshell and sea cucumber in Torres Strait. He married in 1836 and became a hotelier in East Gosford, north of Sydney. Both the marriage and the business venture failed, so he moved further north and returned to farming then ran a store while he contemplated his future.

When news of the Californian gold rush filtered across Australia, Hargraves immediately knew where he was headed. He quickly sold up and set sail for San Francisco, determined, like everyone with him, to become a wealthy man.

Once at the diggings, Hargraves met with little success in finding gold. In his book *Australia and Its Gold Fields*, published in 1855, he would write:

> My attention was naturally drawn to the form and geological structure of the surrounding country, and it soon struck me that I had, some eighteen years before, travelled through a country very similar to the one I was now in, in New South Wales. I said to myself, there are the same class of rocks, slates, quartz, granite, red soil, and everything else that appears necessary to constitute a gold field.

In the book he went on to quote a letter he had written on 5 March 1850 to a friend in Sydney:

> I am very forcibly impressed that I have been in a gold region in New South Wales, within 300 miles of Sydney; and unless you knew how to find it you might live a century in the region and know nothing of its existence.

According to his account, this idea came to obsess him more and more. Come November, 'I set sail for Port Jackson ... bent on making that discovery which had so long occupied my thoughts'.

Hargraves joined the first wave of miners to sail from San Francisco to Sydney, a voyage that took more than two months to complete. When the barque *Emma* arrived back in Sydney in January 1851, Hargraves had been absent for just eighteen months. He, and the gold diggers of numerous nationalities who had travelled with him, brought the latest knowledge in practical mining methods, in particular sluicing-box and panning techniques. But for Hargraves, there was much more to this endeavour than having acquired the knowledge of how to unearth gold: it was a race in which being the first to find it in New South Wales was all that mattered.

It is now widely believed that when Hargraves was living as a small-time squatter near Bathurst not long after he first arrived in Australia, he became aware of the discovery of small amounts of gold nearby, especially by a geologist from Sydney, Rev. William Branwhite Clarke, in 1841. On 9 May 1844, Clarke had displayed a sample of this gold to Governor Gipps, who had exclaimed: 'Put it away, Mr Clarke, or we shall all have our throats cut!' Besides, there was no evidence that the gold existed in any substantial quantity.

Here the question must be asked: was Hargraves planning a fraud from the time in California when he first became aware of the colonial government's decision to promote the discovery of payable gold in Australia – hoping to pass off Rev. Clarke's discovery as his own and negotiate a rich reward?

This appears distinctly possible, and Rev. Clarke himself would later state he believed Hargraves was helped by 'a series of fortunate accidents' and a liberal dose of fiction. Clarke would reject Hargraves's explanation for his 'discovery' and declare emphatically that there was no similarity at all between the land forms of the Californian goldfields and the region near Bathurst where Hargraves went on to 'discover' gold.

On 5 February 1851, not long after he had arrived back in Sydney, the heavily bearded Hargraves threw his 114-kilogram bulk onto the back of a horse and commenced a three-day ride to Bathurst, then continued for another two days over 30 miles west along rough bush tracks to Guyong. His book states that there he enlisted an eighteen-year-old local lad named John Lister as a guide and assistant – a disputed fact. He said the pair then rode some 11 miles north to Lewis Ponds

Creek, where Hargraves announced to a supposedly stunned Lister 'that we were now in the gold fields, and that the gold was under his feet'. Hargraves would write:

> He stared with incredulous amazement, and, on my telling him that I would now find some gold, watched my movements with the most intense interest. My own excitement, probably, was far more intense than his. I took the pick and scratched the gravel off a schistose dyke, which ran across the creek at right angles with its side; and, with the trowel, I dug a panful of earth, which I washed in the water-hole. The first trial produced a little piece of gold. 'Here it is!' I exclaimed; and then I washed five panfuls in succession, obtaining gold from all but one. No further proof was necessary.

Yet Hargraves's recollection of events is in direct contrast to those of Lister and also of William, James and (to a lesser extent) Henry Tom, locals who later claimed they agreed to work with Hargraves in an effort to find gold in the area of Lewis Ponds Creek. They said that after a week of unsuccessful searching using the pans and sluicing-cradle techniques that he had brought back to Australia, Hargraves gave up on the search and returned to Sydney to visit family and friends.

The Tom brothers and Lister then moved their search for gold to the banks of Summer Hill Creek, near the junction with the Macquarie River, just 11 miles from the Tom family home. Within a very short time, William Tom had found a nugget weighing half an ounce, and soon afterwards Lister found another weighing 2 ounces.

Within a matter of days they had panned and sluiced more than 4 ounces of gold from the riverbank, sufficient to confirm that there was payable gold in the region. They then returned home carrying the gold and full of excitement, which was shared with the Toms' father, 'Parson' William Tom Senior, a lay preacher. On seeing the gold, Parson Tom, who was forever quoting passages from the Bible, exclaimed, 'And they came to Ophir and fetched from thence gold.' This reference from the first book of Kings in the Old Testament led the Toms and Lister to decide that the area around where the gold had been found should become known as 'Ophir'.

Trusting individuals that they were, the Tom brothers and Lister agreed that Parson Tom should take the 4 ounces of gold to Sydney to show Hargraves. On seeing the gold, Hargraves asked that it be left with him, and the trusting 'parson' obliged.

Neither the Tom family nor Lister heard from Hargraves again – and it soon became apparent why. Hargraves took the gold straight to the Colonial Secretary, Edward Deas Thompson, claiming the discovery was his own and that he was entitled to a reward for being the first person to find payable gold in the colony.

Little more than four weeks after the Tom brothers and Lister had made their discovery, the news was made public in the *Sydney Morning Herald*. But instead of stating that there had been *five* men involved, the story read that Hargraves alone had found the gold, while the others had been merely associates and not his partners in the search.

Hargraves went on to live a lavish life thanks to the £10,000 reward he received after the government agreed he was entitled to it. Today this offer would be roughly equal to $1.4 million. His lot improved even more when, in 1877, he was granted an annuity of £250 per annum for the rest of his life. Soon after receiving the initial payment, he was also employed by the government as the Commissioner of Gold Fields, his task being to locate new gold deposits across the country. However, he proved to be so inept in this position that his services were dispensed with after a very short time.

For two decades after Hargraves received the £10,000, the Toms and Lister tried desperately to right the wrong via political channels, but were unsuccessful. Still, they persisted until 1884, when William Tom decided to use the power of the press over political persuasion to present their case to the nation. In a letter dated 22 July 1884, written at Sunrise, Guyong, and titled 'First Gold Discovery', he wrote:

> The following evidence touching the first gold
> discovery in Australia was prepared by us in 1876 and
> will read accordingly. It was prepared to read to a
> Committee of the New South Wales Parliament, but

having tried by all legitimate means for 20 years to obtain a hearing by that August body without success we now adopt the Pres[s] (the only alternative left to us) in order that the public mind may be disabused of its error in supposing Mr. Hargraves to be the sole discoverer of the first payable gold, or in supposing that he ever did more to the discovery than introducing the tin-dish system and finding some less than a farthing's worth of gold to which he was taken by John Lester [*sic*] and James Tom. We can assign no reason whatever for why the public mind should not receive the truth and be undeceived … If this letter under the circumstances it was written does not show most clearly to the reader the unfair, wily, and deep-designing character of Mr. Hargraves whom we have had to contend with we have no idea of anything that will show him … It will show most clearly how he wished to hoodwink the Government; to deceive the public, and bamboozle us and Mr. James Tom, – in all of which he has tolerably well succeeded.

William Tom then persisted with presenting his case against Hargraves, but it was another seven years before due recognition was confirmed. On 2 September 1891, a Select Committee of the New South Wales Legislative Assembly presented its report to the assembly regarding the matter. The first few lines said it all:

Your Committee having carefully considered the
Report referred to them, find as follows:–
(1) That although Mr. E.H. Hargraves is entitled to the
credit of having taught the claimants, Messrs. W. and J.
Tom and Lister, the use of the dish and cradle, and
otherwise the proper methods of searching for gold, which
his then recent visit to the Californian gold-fields enabled
him to do, your Committee are satisfied that Messrs. Tom
and Lister were undoubtedly the first discoverers of gold
obtained in Australia in payable quantity.

Ironically, the proclamation from the government came just
eight weeks before Hargraves's death in Sydney. Unfortunately
for the Tom brothers and Lister, the mighty gold rush that
followed their find was, by this time, well and truly over, and
there was no reward available to them.

*

As a consequence of the discovery by Lister and the Toms, a
simple article on page four of the local newspaper – the
Bathurst Free Press – on 10 May 1851 brought Australia's first
gold rush to life in spectacular fashion. The article declared:

The suddenness with which the announcement of a
discovery of such magnitude has come upon us – a
discovery which must, if true, be productive of such

gigantic results not only to the inhabitants of these
districts but to the whole colony, affects the mind with
astonishment, and wonder in such a manner as almost
to unfit it for the deductions of plain truth, sober
reason, and common sense …

This story actually jumped the gun: it came before colonial geologist Stutchbury had confirmed that payable gold had been found in the region. Those few words, however, were sufficient to change the face of Australian society almost overnight. Everyday life as it was known became paralysed as would-be gold diggers abandoned their families and livelihoods and made haste towards the diggings. The news was sufficient for seventeen seafarers to immediately desert their ships in Sydney Harbour and join the rush – the first of many.

Within days, the same newspaper was fuelling the frenzy: 'A complete mental madness appears to have seized almost every member of the community, and as a natural consequence, there has been an universal rush to the diggin[g]s.' On 15 May, the *Sydney Morning Herald* painted a word picture describing the impact Sydney was experiencing: 'go where you will, talk with whomsoever you may, diverge into any other subject you like, you will begin and finish with the diggings'.

In the inevitable stampede that followed, the route west from Sydney across the Blue Mountains to Bathurst and beyond to Ophir, over nearly 200 miles of winding, rocky, undulating and rugged dirt road, was soon clogged with one-way traffic. Hundreds of men on horseback, driving horse-drawn carts or travelling in stagecoaches were all bound by a common thread: they had abandoned their senses, believing that gold would be easily found, and in considerable amounts. Even the *Sydney Morning Herald* propagated the notion in verse in late May 1851:

> The Bathurst way is steep and long,
> The mountain airs are keen and strong;
> The winter rains are heavy, too,
> And food is scarce, and dwellings few.
> These things are disagreeable, no doubt,
> But virgin gold is lying all about.

The gold seekers soon extended their search well beyond the area around Ophir. Many moved their focus to areas some distance away from where the Tom brothers and Lister had made their initial find. All were toiling away in the expectation of discovering their own bonanza, but this was, of course, a delusion in the majority of cases. Rarely was a nugget weighing more than 1 ounce recovered from the pans and cradles, and what was recovered was usually in the form of small grains.

However, there was no cure for gold fever, no stopping the massive migration to Ophir and its surrounds. It is believed that within a few days of the announcement of the discovery there were more than 1000 prospectors working their way along the banks of Ophir's creek. By late May, 100 more were arriving each day, and by early June it was estimated by the *Sydney Morning Herald* that there were 1700 men searching for their fortune in the area. All that in less than three weeks.

Inevitably, local businesses benefited to an enormous degree, as did a large number of opportunistic individuals making haste towards Bathurst, Guyong and Ophir with the plan of profiting from the rapid growth of these communities. In Bathurst the *Free Press* noted: 'The blacksmiths of the town could not turn out the picks fast enough, and the manufacture of cradles was the second briskest business of the place.' Not surprisingly, the price of everything, from food to footwear, tools to tents and liquor to laces, rose at an astronomical rate, just as had been the case in California.

In a matter of months, word of the discovery of gold had reached every populated point of the continent, resulting in a mass exodus of men headed for the Bathurst region. More importantly, just as the colonial government had hoped, every ship departing Sydney bound for England, America or continental Europe was transporting the news of Australia as the new land of golden opportunity.

The growing city of Melbourne didn't escape the associated upheaval, as a merchant there, William Hall, noted:

I cannot describe the effect it had upon the sober,
plodding and industrious people of Melbourne. Our
labourers left us by ship-loads for the fields of Ophir and

Sophala [Sofala], and it became difficult to carry on
trade, labour became so scarce and valuable.

Realising the detrimental impact the discovery at Ophir was
having on Melbourne's population and commercial activities,
on 9 June the local superintendent, Charles LaTrobe,
established a Gold Discovery Committee. This authority's first
task was to find a way to counter the negative influence of the
gold finds further north. In a matter of days, it was decided
that a reward of £200 would be offered to the first person to
find payable gold within 200 miles of Melbourne. The hope
was that a gold rush would then head Melbourne's way.

*

When Edward Hargraves returned to Sydney from California
in 1851, there was another prospector aboard the same ship,
James William Esmond, who was harbouring similar ambitions.
The men apparently did not meet during the voyage, but they
were equally determined to be the first to find payable gold on
home turf. The one difference was that while Hargraves
headed inland from Sydney towards Bathurst, Esmond boarded
a coastal steamer and sailed south for Melbourne.

Unbeknown to the new Gold Discovery Committee when
it announced the offer of a reward, gold had already been
discovered by pastoralist William Campbell in March 1850 on
a grazing property at Clunes, 75 miles north-west of

Melbourne. However, the landowner, Campbell's brother-in-law Donald Cameron, had decided to stay mum on the find for fear that his property would be overrun by hundreds, if not thousands, of inconsiderate diggers. Still, that didn't stop the rumours from circulating.

Meanwhile, Esmond headed to Buninyong (now an outer suburb of Ballarat), where he had been working prior to his unsuccessful stint in the Californian goldfields. There he encountered a German physician, Dr George Hermann Bruhn, who had earlier departed Melbourne to research 'the mineral resources of this colony'. He had recently been in Clunes and spoken to Donald Cameron, and he told Esmond of a quartz reef he had seen in the area. Esmond headed there with his workmate James Pugh, hiring two sawyers to help, and announced a finding of marketable gold in July 1851 – the same month as what had been known as the Port Phillip District became an independent colony and was named Victoria.

Within days, another discovery had been made near Warrandyte, in the Yarra Ranges north-east of Melbourne. A month later, more gold was found in the Buninyong area, and it was quickly realised that nearby Ballarat was also located atop a gold mass of grand proportions. In September, a further find at Forest Creek (renamed Castlemaine in 1854) was quickly followed by a rush to nearby Bendigo, which would prove to be the richest goldfield of them all. By the end of 1851, Victoria could boast one of the world's largest gold-bearing regions, encompassing hundreds of square miles between Ballarat, Bendigo, Clunes and beyond. The gold-finding frenzy had led to nineteen significant confirmed discoveries since the first find at Ophir. The most notable individual find in that time was Kerr's Hundredweight, a mass of gold and quartz weighing 136 kilograms, of which 50.8 kilograms were gold. It was found in July 1851 by an Aboriginal stockman on a property near the village of Hargraves, 135 miles west, as the crow flies, of the New South Wales coastal town of Newcastle.

The combined returns from the Victorian and New South Wales goldfields were nothing short of astonishing. Within eighteen months an estimated £16 million sterling worth of gold had been unearthed.

But the value of the gold rush went well beyond that. Equally important was the bonus of mass migration to Australia that it delivered. In little more than twelve months, Australia's migrant intake had exploded from around 100,000 individuals annually to some 340,000. It was an increase aided in no small way by the grossly exaggerated stories that accompanied the euphoria of the rush, like the rumour that miners 'were picking up golden nuggets like potatoes being gathered from a field'. Regardless, the fact was that the colonial governments of New South Wales and Victoria could not have wished for a better result from their carefully controlled policies relating to the discovery of gold.

By February 1852 newspapers across Great Britain were making their readerships aware of the arrival of the first shipment of gold from Australia on board the clipper *Phoenician*, and confirming the vast extent of the gold discoveries. A report in the *Liverpool Mercury* on 7 February, concerning the discoveries in Ballarat, told readers: 'This is the El Dorado of the world ... the whole country for hundreds of miles around is one immense goldfield.'

While this sounds like an outlandish statement, time would prove that there was a great deal of truth in it. In the decade following the discovery of Kerr's Hundredweight, Australia was responsible for one-third of the world's gold production, and by the end of the century was the world's largest producer of the precious metal. Until then wool had been the principal income earner for the colonies – but not any more.

Suddenly the world viewed Australia as the new land of opportunity – especially ship owners and builders in England and America. For them, the run there and back would soon become more lucrative than any other: carrying hundreds of would-be prospectors on each outbound voyage, and returning home with valuable cargoes of wool and gold. Shipping lines were experiencing their second boom time in less than three years.

Colonial censuses in the early 1850s suggested that there were approximately 440,000 settlers in Australia at the time, and that the figure was escalating rapidly. This was certainly evident by 1861, when official figures revealed the country's population had more than doubled to 1.2 million.

Certainly, not everyone sailed to the Antipodes with the intention of finding gold, but those not searching for it would, more than likely, have benefited indirectly through the associated boom time. Many migrants – families and single women in particular – were travelling to the major centres of Perth, Adelaide, Melbourne, Sydney and Brisbane on assisted passages, while the remainder paid their own way – and all were seeking a new lifestyle, one way or another. Some planned to set up a business, and others who held no desire to go to the goldfields were seeking any form of employment they could find in the towns, outlying villages or remote rural areas. Many, but not all, would succeed. Of all employment opportunities, most were associated with farming, since an alarming number of farm workers had abandoned their jobs overnight and disappeared across the countryside in the general direction of the goldfields.

Of the many hundreds of new businesses established in Australia in the era of the gold rush, the Cobb & Co coach company was among the most famous. It was the entrepreneurial mind of twenty-three year old Freeman Cobb from Massachusetts, allied with the commercial expertise of three of his countrymen – John Murray Peck, James Swanton and John Lambert – that saw an opportunity ripe for exploitation. When their company was formed in 1853, travel from Melbourne to outlying centres was slow, arduous and extremely uncomfortable. All the coach companies operating at the time were using heavy, rigid-bodied, English-built vehicles which, while perfectly suited to the well-made roads of the Mother Country, were totally inappropriate for the rough Australian terrain.

Cobb and his associates seized on the opportunity to provide a faster and far more comfortable mode of travel using Concord coaches, which they imported from America. These carriages had been designed for the rugged trails of the American 'Wild West', and had proved so successful that they had become the mainstay of passenger transport for the famous Wells Fargo company. Even today, one of the enduring images of America in the mid–1800s is that of a Wells Fargo six-horse Concord stagecoach thundering across the arid west loaded with gold. In 1870 author Mark Twain referred to the Wells Fargo Concord coach as 'an imposing cradle on wheels'. Little wonder, then, that the Concords completely outclassed their English counterparts in Australia.

Being lighter, the Cobb & Co coaches were considerably faster than their rivals: on the company's first journey from Collins Street in the heart of Melbourne to the Forest Creek diggings, the travel time was halved. This success was due in part to the decision of the company founders to establish 'changing stations' every 10 or 20 miles, while their opposition travelled far greater distances between stops. The Cobb & Co drivers were able to bring fresh horses into harness each time they stopped, and thus were able to maintain a greater average speed for the duration of a trip.

The company was a success from the outset, and in 1856 Cobb and his partners decided to sell the business for a figure reputed to be £16,000 (more than $2.1 million today). The purchasers, a consortium of nine men led by James Rutherford, took Cobb & Co to the pinnacle of its success over the next five decades. An extensive web of travel routes was established across Victoria, New South Wales and Queensland, where, as well as carrying travellers, the coaches provided a lifeline to isolated communities through the delivery of mail and packages.

*

Success stories like that of Cobb & Co greatly enhanced the appeal of Australia in the eyes of potential migrants, but it was still the gold rush that drove the insatiable demand for travel to the Antipodes.

When travellers arrived in Sydney, they were welcomed into a bustling and rapidly changing community of almost 40,000 that was emerging from the shadow of its convict past. The precinct had been declared a city in 1842 and its community, like that of Melbourne, was benefiting considerably from the gold rush ... but not to the same degree.

In Victoria, the impact of the gold discoveries was far greater than anyone could have anticipated. In just one year the new colony's populace more than doubled from 77,345 to 171,989. By 1861, the gold rush would result in a sevenfold population increase to more than half a million. By then the colony would be home to 47 per cent of Australia's entire population.

Because of its proximity to the largest goldfields, and the fact that it was an easy port to achieve, Melbourne was the most popular destination for pioneers travelling from England and Europe. The arrival of hundreds of adults and children on Melbourne's doorstep at the start of the gold rush heralded the beginning of what would become an overwhelming problem for the town and its 20,000 residents. There was virtually no accommodation, or facilities in general, to cope with such an influx. What public lodgings were available were few and small, while the majority of residences, many roughly hewn from timber, were so tiny they could not take in any visitors.

The colony's authorities did what they could to assist the homeless horde, but it was nowhere near enough. As a result, most of the migrants were left to fend for themselves. Some of them decided to cross the Princes Bridge leading out of the city to vacant land on the river's south bank and establish a camp there. Many more followed and became occupants of what would become known as 'Canvas Town'. Some of the residents were fortunate enough to have tents, while others used what they could find to provide shelter for their families and themselves.

In the rush to get to Melbourne, the majority of migrants had not considered the finer details, such as how far the goldfields were from Melbourne, how they were going to get there, and what equipment would be needed. Because of this, many were forced to remain in Melbourne much longer than anticipated, and having no income, what little money they had quickly evaporated. A significant number were then compelled to 'set up shop' in Flinders Street, in the heart of the town, and sell what they could of the possessions they had brought with them.

The population of Canvas Town exploded with the arrival of each ship bringing more migrants, and in little more than six months it was home to nearly 8000 people. Inevitably, the camp established its own identity and became a mini-village, where some of the residents set up stores selling the necessities of life. Eventually, though, the crush of humanity at the site was overwhelming and it degenerated into little more than a slum.

The situation would only get worse. As more ships reached Port Phillip Bay, Melbourne was confronted by its serious lack of facilities and preparedness. While an increase in migration was just what the new colony had hoped for, it was a case of too many people too soon. Over a four-month period in 1852, 619 ships carrying 55,057 passengers came to anchor in Port Phillip. The following year more than 2500 ships arrived!

There was, however, a bright spot for the migrants in these difficult times, and it was evident to them in the streets of Melbourne every day. If they wanted any confirmation that wealth was to be had from the colony's goldfields, they needed only to stand on one of the main thoroughfares and observe the antics of diggers who had come to town flaunting their newfound wealth. The majority frequented the bars, where plenty of booze was readily available, while others followed a tradition known to have sprung up during the Californian gold rush by hiring a horse-drawn carriage, filling it with as many women as wanted to ride, then parading around town – often at a fair clip – sipping Champagne and making as much attention-grabbing noise as possible.

For most, this flashy, raucous and often illegal behaviour remained beyond the reach of the law, simply because the police force in Melbourne was a grossly undermanned assembly comprising mainly migrants, whose sole symbol of authority was the helmet they wore. They were an inexperienced and ineffective lot who were nothing more than off-the-street replacements for the large number of police officers who had abandoned their duties and beaten a hasty trail to the goldfields.

If anything, the lawlessness on the goldfields themselves was even worse. The emerging settlements of Ballarat and Bendigo, the locations of the two biggest finds, were already under siege from a population explosion.

Almost every form of entertainment in such settlements was well patronised – like the 'gallant and determined mill [fist fight] between Jim Kelly and Jonathan Smith, for £400', which was staged on 3 December 1855 at Fiery Creek near Beaufort, 100 miles north-west of Melbourne. Billed as the 'knights of the knuckle', Kelly and Smith made history with their bare-knuckle stoush, recognised to this day as the longest fight ever – an astounding six hours and fifteen minutes.

But most popular of all among the diggers was Irish-born dancer and courtesan Lola Montez, whose reputation had preceded her by the time she arrived on the goldfields. She had already achieved international notoriety for her erotic 'Spider Dance', in which she either shocked or teased her audience by lifting her skirts so high that it was obvious she was naked underneath.

Such was her fame during her short life – she died in New York aged forty-two – that she was recognised across America, Europe and Australia for her 'social activities' as much as her dancing ability. Lola could possibly lay claim to having more husbands and lovers during her life than any other woman of her time. Her paramours included mere military lieutenants, owner of the *San Francisco Whig* newspaper Patrick Purdy Hull, and King Ludwig I of Bavaria.

She and a young actor, Noel Follin, sailed for Sydney from San Francisco in May 1855, and immediately after their arrival she performed at the Royal Victoria Theatre. However, within two weeks of being in Sydney, she and Follin found themselves on the wrong side of the law, accused of committing fraud. The pair decided to escape to Melbourne aboard the coastal steamer *Waratah* – a plan that looked set to go awry when the sheriff boarded the ship prior to departure with a warrant for Lola's arrest. On being confronted in her cabin, Lola simply removed all her clothes and dared the officer to arrest her. It was a successful manoeuvre: the sheriff was last seen being rowed away from *Waratah* without his quarry.

Lola was greeted by packed houses when she performed her show for the first time in Ballarat on 16 February 1856. Her reception was such that miners are said to have tossed nuggets at her feet in recognition of her dancing prowess. However, she did not impress the editor of the *Ballarat Times*, Henry Seekamp, who published an article questioning her fame. But this only helped her achieve even greater notoriety: she publicly horsewhipped him after having him restrained at the United States Hotel.

There was, however, at least one time when she was on the receiving end of a 'flogging' while in the goldfields: the wife of her manager at the time took a distinct dislike to her, and assaulted her to the degree that it took her a month to recover. Undeterred, Lola went on to tour Bendigo, Castlemaine and other diggings.

*

The gold rush also spawned a colloquialism that we still recognise: the digger. The commonly used reference to Australian and New Zealand soldiers as 'diggers' during World War I originated from the mateship and shoulder-to-shoulder toil of the miners on the goldfields. It is easy to understand how the ANZACs who dug trenches during the bloody confrontations at Gallipoli and on the Western Front became identified by the same name.

And on the goldfields of Ballarat towards the end of 1854, a group of miners would fight their own battle: the only occasion when men have taken up arms on Australian soil to protest against unfair laws.

As had happened in California, the Colony of Victoria sought to profit from the gold rush through hefty miners' licences, which many were unable to pay. The system was enforced by regular 'licence hunts' in which any man who could not produce his licence was arrested on the spot. Miners could not vote in elections and could not own their own land, and the Gold Commission police who administered law and order on the goldfields were frequently brutal and corrupt.

The miners' discontent with these restrictions escalated to the point where they decided to take matters into their own hands. On 11 November, 10,000 diggers met to form the Ballarat Reform League, and on 2 December 1854, a group of them manned an enclosure they named the Eureka Stockade and prepared to take a stand against the oppressive colonial forces. The ensuing battle in the early hours of Sunday 3 December – the Eureka Rebellion – is seen by many as the birth of Australian democracy. It lasted less than thirty minutes, but when the bullets stopped flying and the dust settled, twenty-seven men had been killed, the majority being miners.

Although around 120 diggers were arrested and thirteen eventually committed for trial, there was a huge groundswell of public support for them, and in the end just one man – *Ballarat Times* editor Henry Seekamp – was charged in relation to the incident. Eventually, a Royal Commission that had been set up by Governor Charles Hotham before the rebellion recommended almost all of the reforms the diggers had asked for. Their leader, Peter Lalor, was even elected to the Victorian Parliament in 1855 and rose to become Speaker of the House.

*

However, there was a dark side to the 'victory' at the Eureka Stockade. There was one group of miners who did not take part in the fight for better rights at Eureka: the Chinese.

The Victorian gold rush, in particular, spawned the largest pre-Federation Chinese migration to Australia. It was estimated that between 1853 and 1860, some 40,000 made the three-month journey from Canton to what was being recognised in China as 'the New Gold Mountain', a second land of opportunity after 'the Old Gold Mountain' in California.

This large volume of Chinese passengers caused the route from Asia to Melbourne to become one of the most profitable in the world. Ship owners and captains literally jammed as many Chinese fortune-hunters on board as humanly possible, almost always ignoring reasonable standards of hygiene, safety and comfort. Many of these travellers did not have the money needed for the fare, so they offered their wives and children as virtual slaves to business owners in China in return for the funds needed to get them to Australia. Others borrowed money on the understanding that a greater amount would be repaid when the hopefully successful miner returned home. Virtually no women made the journey: for example, in 1861 it was calculated that there were 5367 Chinese men at the goldfields in Bendigo and only one Chinese woman.

Local politicians in Melbourne quickly realised that this great influx of Chinese workers was destined to cause great problems within the community, especially at the diggings, where the Chinese had demonstrated that they were prepared to toil almost around the clock in an effort to find gold. The Royal Commission into the goldfields reported that:

> A most serious social question with reference to the gold-fields, and one that has lately crept on with rapid but almost unobserved steps, is with reference to the great number of the Chinese ... The question of the influx of such large numbers of a pagan and inferior race is a very serious one ... a comparative handful of colonists may be buried in a countless throng of Chinamen ... some step is here necessary, if not to prohibit, at least to check and diminish this influx.

As a consequence of this particular objection, in 1855 the Victorian Parliament introduced the *Chinese Immigration Act*, a direct attempt to limit Chinese immigration to the colony. The Act placed a bounty of £10 – to be paid by shipping lines – on the head of every Chinese migrant who arrived in

Melbourne. Ship owners were also limited to a specified number of Chinese travellers relative to the amount of cargo being carried.

This law was a major blow to the ship owners operating on the China run, but within a very short space of time almost every one of them had adopted a tactic to circumvent the legislation. Instead of sailing into Melbourne, they sailed to either Adelaide or, more often, Robe, near the South Australian–Victorian border. There, the Chinese passengers were put ashore and told that they would have to walk between 200 and 250 miles to the gold diggings at Ballarat.

Robe's population more than doubled overnight, and entrepreneurial locals saw the influx as an outstanding business opportunity: they would become guides and lead the Chinese cross-country to the diggings. However, not all guides were ethical in their approach. After being paid in advance for their services, some were known to lead the unsuspecting visitors into the bush, point in the general direction of Ballarat, then abandon them before returning to Robe, to gather another group wanting to follow the same route.

The exceedingly high number of Chinese continuing to migrate to Australia was marked by controversy and community disquiet for many decades. This sentiment was reflected in a ditty sung by Charles Thatcher, a popular music hall entertainer who provided light relief for the diggers in the Victorian goldfields:

You doubtless read the paper
And, as men of observation,
Of course you watch the progress of
Chinese immigration.
A thousand of these pig-tailed chaps
In Adelaide are landing,
And why they let such numbers come
Exceeds my understanding!

Eventually, the South Australian Government became aware of the extent of the problem, and in 1858 passed legislation almost identical to the Act in Victoria.

The new laws might have stopped the flow of new Chinese miners onto the goldfields, but it did little to stop the other diggers from regarding the Chinese with suspicion and resentment. These strong emotions boiled over into a series of anti-Chinese riots, including an attack by around 120 diggers in the Buckland Valley in July 1857 that led to the deaths of at least three Chinese miners. Far worse were the evictions of Chinese diggers that took place during a later gold rush at what is now Young in New South Wales – culminating in a riot on 30 June 1861, in which up to 2000 men looted and destroyed a Chinese camp at Lambing Flat. The New South Wales *Chinese Immigration Regulation and Restriction Act* was rushed into being.

After Australian Federation in 1901, one of the first pieces of legislation passed was the *Immigration Restriction Act*, which

91

marked the beginning of the so-called White Australia Policy, the last traces of which would remain in place until 1973.

Fortunately, though, that was not the end of the story. The spirit of the gold rush and the massive migration it inspired had an impact that remains with us to this day. During the five years when the gold rush was at its peak, it is estimated that 100,000 English, 60,000 Irish, 50,000 Scots, 25,000 Chinese, 8000 Germans, 4000 Welsh, 3000 Americans and 1500 French arrived seeking their fortune. And as the White Australia Policy was dismantled and Australia began to open its doors once more, the influx of thousands more migrants of widely varying nationalities became the catalyst for the unique multicultural melting pot that Australia is today.

CHAPTER 3

Not a Place for Everyone

Populating Australia

By 1852, the swift-sailing clipper ships were playing a pivotal role in meeting the demands of the gold rushes – so much so that they were riding the crest of a wave as the most popular form of transport for passengers and cargo to and from Australia and across the world. It was estimated that during that year that clippers rounded Cape Horn on near 200 occasions, some voyaging between New York and San Francisco, but the majority sailing from England to Australia and New Zealand then home again. Australia's gold rush was creating a demand for bigger, faster and more comfortable ships.

For the British and Europeans especially, arriving in Australia as a migrant brought an abrupt and often unanticipated change of lifestyle. Those who had come from more established locations would find it impossible to contemplate – despite the newspaper stories of excitement and riches – what they would have to endure. This strange experience caused many migrants to pen their interesting first impressions of the new land. Others went to greater lengths, writing books that told of their unique experiences in an alien environment.

It was when a ship was closing on the Australian coast, after an often harrowing and arduous non-stop passage of more than 100 days from England, that passengers received the first of many lasting impressions. Such was the case for prolific English author and traveller William Howitt, who arrived in Melbourne in September 1852 and spent two years in Victoria:

> Tomorrow, if the wind is favourable, I trust we shall
> cast anchor off Melbourne, after a voyage of 102 days!
> This morning, at ninety miles from land, on opening
> the scuttle in my cabin, I perceived an aromatic odour,
> as of spicy flowers, blown from the land … The wind is
> blowing strong off the shore; and the fragrance
> continues, something like the scent of a hayfield, but
> more spicy. I expect it is the yellow mimosa [wattle],
> which my brother Richard said we should now find in
> flower all over the valleys.

Englishwoman Ellen Clacy, whose diarised writing was as colourful as her character, garnered a very different first impression of Australia when she arrived in Melbourne the same year as Howitt. The twenty-year-old later converted her notes into a book, *A Lady's Visit to the Gold Diggings of Australia in 1852–1853*, a highly readable publication that told of her remarkable experiences in great detail: leaving England, shipboard life, her arrival in Melbourne, her cross-country travels and the time she spent in the goldfields.

Her desire to travel to Australia was spontaneous: it came in April 1852 as a consequence of newspaper reports of the gold rush, which 'induced my brother to fling aside his Homer and Euclid for the various "Guides" printed for the benefit of the intending gold-seeker, or to ponder over the shipping columns of the daily papers. The love of adventure must be contagious, for three weeks after I found myself accompanying him to those auriferous [gold-bearing] regions.'

There was, however, an inauspicious start to the voyage:

> Everything was ready – boxes packed, tinned, and corded; farewells taken, and ourselves whirling down by rail to Gravesend – too much excited – too full of the future to experience that sickening of the heart, that desolation of the feelings, which usually accompanies an expatriation, however voluntary, from the dearly loved shores of one's native land.
>
> The sea was very rough, but as we were anxious to get on board without farther delay, we entrusted our valuable lives in a four-oared boat, despite the dismal prognostications of our worthy host. A pleasant row that was, at one moment covered over with salt-water, the next riding on the top of a wave, ten times the size of

our frail conveyance, then came a sudden concussion, [our boat] smashed into a smaller boat, which immediately filled and sank, and our rowers disheartened at this mishap would go no farther. The return was still rougher – my face smarted dreadfully from the cutting splashes of the salt-water; they contrived, however, to land us safely … though in a most pitiable plight; charging only a sovereign for this delightful trip; very moderate, considering the number of salt-water baths they had given us gratis. In the evening a second trial proved more successful, and we reached our vessel safely.

Ellen told how her first ever night on board while the ship lay at anchor was an unexpected experience: waking in the morning in a tiny cot 'scarce wide enough to turn around in', in a claustrophobic little cabin that was a far cry from her usual four-poster bed in a good-sized room. That morning they bade farewell to London:

The first sound that awoke me was the 'cheerily' song of the sailors, as the anchor was heaved – not again, we trusted, to be lowered till our eyes should rest on the waters of Port Phillip. And then the cry of 'raise tacks and sheets' (which I, in nautical ignorance, interpreted 'hay-stacks and sheep') sent many a sluggard from their berths to bid a last farewell to the banks of the Thames.

Nearly two months after sailing down the English Channel then out into the wide blue waters of the Atlantic, Ellen and her fellow travellers were experiencing the energy-sapping, humidity-laden doldrums of the equatorial region. They were becalmed for more than a week, until Sunday, 6 June, when the faintest of puffs saw them finally 'cross the line', much to everyone's delight:

> We were weary of gazing upon the unruffled waters around us, or watching the sails as they idly flapped to and fro. Chess, backgammon, books and cards, had ceased to beguile the hours away, and the only amusement left was lowering a boat and rowing about within a short distance of the ship, but this (even by those not pulling at the oars) was considered too fatiguing work, for a tropical sun was above us, and the heat was most intense. Our only resource was to give ourselves up to a sort of DOLCE FAR NIENTE [pleasantly idle] existence, and lounge upon the deck, sipping lemonade or lime-juice, beneath a large awning which extended from the fore to the mizzen masts.

Eight weeks later, with the ship powering east, 260 nautical miles south of Adelaide and a similar distance from the entrance to Port Phillip Bay, Ellen – who was the daughter of a clergyman – observed, with great reverence, a burial at sea:

Early this morning one of the sailors died, and before noon the last services of the Church of England were read over his body; this was the first and only death that occurred during our long passage, and the solemnity of committing his last remains to their watery grave cast a saddening influence over the most thoughtless. I shall never forget the moment when the sewn-up hammock, with a gaily coloured flag wrapped round it, was launched into the deep; those who can witness with indifference a funeral on land, would, I think, find it impossible to resist the thrilling awe inspired by such an event at sea.

It was Friday, 20 August when she and all on board excitedly fixed their gaze on the entrance to the bay. The captain had his crew trimming and retrimming the sails, all the time working wind and tide so their ship would be safely guided through 'the Rip', the narrow, reef-riddled entrance to Port Phillip.

Inside the bay, the pilot – a 'smart and active fellow' – boarded the ship after being rowed out from the shore in a longboat. He suggested to the captain that the ship anchor just inside the entrance, as a severe storm was brewing in the north. That was the call from the captain, and it was two days before the weather turned in favour of a passage north to the anchorage off Melbourne.

Soon after the sails were set and the anchor raised, the value of having the pilot on board became apparent to Ellen, and everyone else:

Got under way at half-past seven in the morning, and passed the wrecks of two vessels, whose captains had attempted to come in without a pilot, rather than wait for one – the increased number of vessels arriving, causing the pilots to be frequently all engaged. The bay, which is truly splendid, was crowded with shipping. In a few hours our anchor was lowered for the last time. Boats were put off towards our ship from the Lairdet's Beach [Port Melbourne]. We were lowered into the first that came alongside, and after a twenty minutes' pull to the landing-place we trod the golden shores of Victoria.

However, treading those shores brought an unexpected sensation. Ellen noted that, after four months at sea, everyone's sea legs were not prepared to leave them immediately. This was of no great concern, though, 'for we are in the colonies, walking with undignified, awkward gait, not on a fashionable promenade, but upon a little wooden pier'. She continued:

And now the cry of 'Here's the bus,' brought us quickly outside again, where we found several new arrivals also waiting for it. I had hoped, from the name, or rather misname, of the conveyance, to gladden my eyes with the sight of something civilized. Alas, for my disappointment! There stood a long, tumble-to-pieces-looking wagon, not covered in, with a plank down each side to sit upon, and a miserable narrow plank it was.

Into this vehicle were crammed a dozen people and an innumerable host of portmanteaus, large and small, carpet-bags, baskets, brown-paper parcels, bird-cage and inmate, etc., all of which, as is generally the case, were packed in a manner the most calculated to contribute the largest amount of inconvenience to the live portion of the cargo. And to drag this grand affair into Melbourne were harnessed thereto the most wretched-looking objects in the shape of horses that I had ever beheld.

The journey into Melbourne gave Ellen her first impression of the country she had sailed halfway round the world to experience – and it wasn't what she was expecting:

'And is this the beautiful scenery of Australia?' was my first melancholy reflection. Mud and swamp – swamp and mud – relieved here and there by some few trees which looked as starved and miserable as ourselves. The cattle we passed appeared in a wretched condition, and the human beings on the road seemed all to belong to one family, so truly Vandemonian [like a convict of Van Diemen's Land] was the cast of the countenances.

'The rainy season's not over,' observed the driver, in an apologetic tone. Our eyes and uneasy limbs most FEELINGLY corroborated his statement, for as we moved along at a foot-pace, the rolling of the omnibus, owing to the deep ruts and heavy soil, brought us into most unpleasant contact with the various packages before-mentioned. On we went towards Melbourne – now stopping for the unhappy horses to take breath – then passing our pedestrian messmates, and now arriving at a small specimen of a swamp; and whilst they (with trousers tucked high above the knee and boots well saturated) step, slide and tumble manfully through it, we give a fearful roll to the left, ditto, ditto to the right, then a regular stand-still, or perhaps, by way of variety, are all but jolted over the animals' heads, till at length all minor considerations of bumps and bruises are merged in the anxiety to escape without broken bones.

At one stage during this journey, the new arrivals were advised that the Yarra River could be seen straight ahead, but for them a river it wasn't. Ellen innocently asked, 'Where?', then, when looking in that general direction, she could only see something that to her 'resembled the fens of Lincolnshire, as they were some years ago, before draining was introduced into that county'.

During the voyage out from England, Ellen's brother and four other young men had decided to go to the diggings as a group. They bought a dray for £100 and two 'strong cart horses' for another £190, plus all the sundry digging and camping equipment they thought necessary. After departing Melbourne on 7 September – 'a damp and dismal day' – with

Ellen riding on the dray and all the others walking, they set out for the diggings near Kyneton, more than 50 miles north along an often rugged track. Having spoken to diggers who had gone that way before them, they decided it was best to camp out as often as possible, 'and thus avoid the vicinity of the inns and halting-places on the way, which are frequently the lurking places of thieves and bushrangers'.

As they progressed towards their destination, they became increasingly intrigued by the names given to the many gullies they crossed. All related to the finding of gold or associated incidents: Peg-leg Gully took its name from three men, all of whom had a wooden leg; Golden Gully was where a man had pulled a tuft of grass from the ground and found a nugget below its roots; while Murderer's Flat and Choke'em Gully convinced Ellen and her group to keep moving. The most interesting of all was White Horse Gully, where a raging horse had plunged its hooves into the soft ground and unearthed a nugget that sold for an impressive £5000.

During their goldfields adventure, which also took them to diggings near Bendigo and Ballarat, Ellen, her brother and his friends did find small amounts of gold which they happily converted to cash. Throughout this time Ellen continued to update her highly detailed diary; in fact, the book that it eventually became was so thorough in its depiction of her travels that it proved a respected guide for would-be prospectors and migrants planning to venture from foreign shores to Australia and its goldfields.

*

Apart from Ellen Clacy's book, there were, until the mid–1850s, only a few detailed guides that would adequately prepare new arrivals for the physical and emotional burdens they would encounter in Australia. The most professional of them was titled *The Emigrant's Guide to Australia*, written by John Capper and published in England in 1856. In his opening paragraph the author explained:

> The deep interest taken by almost every class of
> society in all that relates to Australia and the doings,
> or rather 'diggings', of its colonists, renders any
> attempt at diffusing practical information upon such
> matters, at once important and acceptable ... The
> majority of the present generation may easily
> remember the 'great South Land' as containing but
> one or two small penal settlements – as a remote
> region of desert, unfriendly soil, difficult of access,
> offering no inducements to settlers, and tempting none
> but the most wretched to visit its shores. It was, in
> fact, at no further date than thirty years since, a place
> of crime, of chains and stripes; a vast jail in the
> wilderness, a criminal lazarhouse [leper colony] at the
> antipodes, a voyage to which was as much dreaded, as
> would have been a trip to Siberia or Russian Tartary
> [in northern and central Asia].

Capper then sketched an image of the new Australia, based on his own experiences and those of others. The same generation that had held the preceding view of 'a criminal lazarhouse at the antipodes' was now quite justifiably seeing it as a 'land flowing with something better than milk and honey'. He described the continent as rich beyond exaggeration in gold, copper and timber, and similarly wealthy in corn, wool, wine and oil. The forests were so vast they could supply the world with sufficient timber 'for the next dozen centuries', and Australia was 'blessed with a climate so admirably adapted to the human frame that in most parts of the country the profession of a medical man is a poor and unneeded one'.

His portrait of Australia was painted with a broad brush; he touched on every possible aspect of city and country life, and explained what parts of the land had been explored and what remained a mystery. He told of many superb coastal ports and detailed what was known of the inland, but, quite understandably, focused on the largest towns.

He was effusive in his praise of Sydney, declaring that it presented 'an elegant and uniform appearance that could scarcely be excelled by that of any English town of similar size'. Along with an abundance of beautiful buildings, it had an air of European civilisation not expected by the newly arrived: 'the thickly-studded waters swarming with sailing craft and steam vessels, rushing crowds on shore, all tend to impress the stranger most favourably with the beauty and importance of this Australian capital'.

The author's impressions of Melbourne were little different from those of Ellen Clacy. Because of the gold rush, it was one of the world's fastest-growing towns, and accordingly offered many of the comforts and experiences English and other migrants wished to enjoy.

Capper's most important chapter for his readers was titled 'Who Should Emigrate, And How, With a few Words to Those who had Better Remain at Home'. Here he stressed that while Australia could easily be seen as a land proffering employment and significant financial gains, it was not for everyone, in particular the 'struggling classes'. Many small-scale miners would find nothing on the goldfields, and in the towns the Australian population was growing faster than employment opportunities. They would face similar difficulties in Australia to those they had experienced in England.

*

While many immigrants would fail to find either gold or a decent livelihood, in the popular imagination, Australia was a land of golden opportunity for all. But it could so easily have been very different...

Without the gold rush, many of these people would have known little, if anything, about the land down under. Many would never have even heard of Australia, and those who had would have thought of it as nothing more than a dumping ground for loathsome felons. Little wonder, then, that so few people saw any reason to consider migrating there.

It was not until news of the discovery of large amounts of gold in Australia spilled into the northern hemisphere that the country's image and appeal changed, virtually overnight. Before that – ever since the First Fleet's arrival in 1788 – colonial authorities had constantly struggled to attract free settlers to this vast antipodean land.

*

Since the earliest years of the nineteenth century, the British Government had held a firm belief that colonising the entire Australian continent was a high priority. It would be the most positive way to build up the colony's fledgling economy, and deter the enemy, France, from laying claim to any of the country. But to achieve these things they needed people to occupy the land.

Obviously the western side of Australia, where there was no British presence, was the most vulnerable region. In 1826, the British Secretary of State for War and the Colonies, Henry Bathurst, suggested to the colonial government that King George Sound, near the south-western corner of the continent, was an ideal location for a settlement: it was close to the route taken by ships sailing from England to Australian ports to the east, and was well protected.

The Governor of New South Wales, General Sir Ralph Darling, directed Major Edmund Lockyer to command an expedition to the region. Should the French be encountered on the voyage, he was to land troops so that the enemy would be left in no doubt that 'the whole of New Holland [Australia] is subject to His Britannic Majesty's Government', and that 'orders have been given for the Establishment at King George's Sound of a Settlement for the reception of Criminals accordingly'.

Lockyer departed Sydney on 9 November 1826 aboard His Majesty's brig *Amity*, with a party of twenty-three troops and twenty-three convicts – the latter being the project's workforce – and supplies for six months. Less than seven weeks later, *Amity* had sailed west through Bass Strait and across the Great Australian Bight and had anchored in King George Sound.

It was 26 December when the troops, convicts and supplies were put ashore and the first stage of a camp established. A month later, on 21 January, Lockyer decided it was time to enact the formalities expected of him. With the Union Jack wafting proudly in the breeze, the troops fired a *feu de joie* rifle salute as Lockyer declared to all present that he was formally taking possession of the western third of the Australian continent on behalf of the British Crown. The site of the camp would soon be named Frederick Town in recognition of Prince Frederick, Duke of York and Albany (the brother of King George IV).

The following year, Captain James Stirling explored the Swan River region further north, then petitioned the British Government to establish a free colony there. The Swan River Colony was proclaimed on 18 June 1829, but from the start its residents objected to the presence of a penal outpost to the south. So in 1831 Frederick Town was made part of the Swan River Colony and renamed Albany, and its convicts and military personnel were sent back to New South Wales. Meanwhile, two separate sites developed along the Swan River, which soon became the port of Fremantle and the colonial capital of Perth.

*

While this beachhead in the west would hopefully protect the region from occupation by foreigners, much work was still needed to increase the continent's European population. For decades there had been growing disquiet in government ranks about the lack of skilled workers, particularly skilled rural labourers, among the new arrivals.

There was also a disconcerting imbalance of men and women. In 1830 the ratio was four to one in major centres, and an alarming twenty men to every woman in rural areas. Part of this disparity was due to the number of male convicts who had served their time and subsequently been emancipated. Something needed to be done to improve that balance and accelerate migration.

Over the ensuing fifteen years, three programs were introduced in the hope that they would increase the flow of migrants to Australia from Britain. These were assisted passages, a bounty system, and various charitable schemes that sought to relieve overcrowding and other problems in Britain while assisting the struggling colonies. All three did deliver positive results, but none was as effective as had been hoped.

The government recognised that many would-be emigrants from Great Britain and Europe, particularly families, could not afford the cost of relocation, so in 1830 the assisted passage scheme was introduced. This was financed by the sale of government-owned land in New South Wales. It was a concept that was sufficiently successful for it to remain in place for twenty years – a period during which 187,000 new settlers were brought to Australia, most of them under an assisted passage.

The bounty system, introduced in 1835, was structured around an incentive program for shipping agents: they were paid a reward by the New South Wales colonial government for each commercially skilled young couple, or single woman, they secured as emigrants. Unfortunately, though, the scheme was full of loopholes that made it easy for money-hungry agents and ship owners to grossly overload their ships and maximise their profits. In time, few people wanted to emigrate under those circumstances, and this led the program to be abandoned after just six years of operation.

Then there were the schemes set up, often by private groups, to provide relief to specific communities suffering various forms of hardship. The 'Earl Grey Scheme' – named after its creator, the British Secretary of State for War and the Colonies – brought 4000 young women out to Australia from Irish workhouses, in an effort to improve the gender imbalance. However, the new arrivals were frowned upon as being poor workers of low moral character, and the scheme only lasted from 1848 to 1850.

Much better received was a scheme to assist 5000 crofters – poor tenant farmers – affected by the Highland Clearances in the western Scottish Highlands and Hebrides Islands.

The clearances occurred during a dark period in Scottish history in which wealthy landholders evicted their struggling farmer tenants, their wives and children using the most violent of methods. Their aim was to convert their extensive land holdings into sheep-grazing properties, which would be far more financially rewarding than the virtual subsistence farming then being undertaken.

Too often the evictions came at short notice from the aristocratic land owners and were nothing short of inhumane. Perhaps the most ruthless participants in these mass evictions in the first half of the nineteenth century were the First Duke and Duchess of Sutherland. They forcibly removed thousands of crofters from their land so it could become a thriving wool- and meat-producing property. While the callous expulsions were occurring, the duchess took time to write a letter to a friend in England in which she described the starving crofters and their families on the Sutherland estate as follows: 'Scotch people are of happier constitution and do not fatten like the larger breed of animals.'

If the crofters and their families refused to leave the land then the landlords went to any length to remove them, including the use of fire. Local stonemason Donald McLeod detailed the horror of such an event:

> The consternation and confusion were extreme. Little or no time was given for the removal of persons or property; the people striving to remove the sick and the helpless before the fire should reach them; next, struggling to save the most valuable of their effects. The cries of the women and children, the roaring of the affrighted cattle, hunted at the same time by the yelling dogs of the shepherds amid the smoke and fire, altogether presented a scene that completely baffles description – it required to be seen to be believed. A dense cloud of smoke enveloped the whole country by day, and even extended far out to sea. At night an awfully grand but terrific scene presented itself – all the houses in an extensive district in flames at once. I myself ascended a height about eleven o'clock in the evening, and counted two hundred and fifty blazing houses, many of the owners of which I personally knew, but whose present condition – whether in or out of the

flames – I could not tell. The conflagration lasted six days, till the whole of the dwellings were reduced to ashes or smoking ruins.

In the isolated western Highlands and islands, tenants were evicted to coastal towns, where their plight added to the woes of an already overpopulated region, especially with little church and community assistance available. Their miserable existence forced them to rely on potatoes as a large part of their diet, so when the crop was affected by a severe blight in 1846, the impact was devastating.

Grave community concerns led to the formation of a charitable organisation, the Skye Emigration Society (SES), in 1851, which aimed to provide a solution via migration. Yet it soon became very evident to society members that the situation was only destined to deteriorate, as the majority of locals did not want to leave. This left the SES with no option but to take a firm stance. Consequently, it released a statement that spelled out the facts of life for all to contemplate:

> … you are to consider what you are to do hereafter
> without this assistance, for every one of you must know
> that such relief is not to be expected again … But,
> whether you desire it or not, it cannot be looked for.
> Destitution … will be regarded in a different light, and
> those who wilfully neglect any means of escape that are
> offered to them, and choose to remain in circumstances

[from] which destitution is inseparable, will obtain very
little sympathy or assistance.

In short, the society would not accept any further responsibility
for those who did not agree to being resettled via migration.
The government did send some food supplies – mainly
oatmeal – to ports on Scotland's west coast, but that just
prolonged the agony rather than provided a solution.

It wasn't until the Assistant Secretary to Her Majesty's
Treasury in London, Sir Charles Trevelyan, intervened that real
progress was achieved. He saw the emergency food deliveries as
a 'useless palliative', and stated, 'This community is tortured
and preyed upon … and the "patient" and "loyal" Highlander
being tamed by the mistaken kindness of his friends into a
Professional Mendicant.'

He agreed that Scotland's western Highlanders had to be
relocated, a decision that led him to establish, in January 1852,
the Highland and Island Emigration Society (HIES), along
with one of the region's high profile residents, Sir John
McNeill, and the Chairman of the Colonial Land and
Emigration Commissioners, Sir Thomas Murdoch. They based
their operation in Skye, and the former SES became part of this
larger organisation. Prince Albert, husband of Queen Victoria,
was named the society's patron, and the Queen and other
prominent individuals donated large amounts towards this
worthy cause.

The most vexing question facing the three committee members was where to send these poor, homeless and starving people. But the answer soon became apparent. Trevelyan announced 'the necessity of adopting a final measure of relief for the Western Highlands and Islands by transferring the surplus of the population to Australia'.

This was a win–win decision. With many farmers now abandoning the land and flocking to the goldfields, Australia desperately needed migrants with a rural background, and every one of these crofters had just that.

It was May 1852 when the HIES published its rules relating to emigration to Australia:

The Emigration will be conducted, as much as possible, by entire families, and in accordance with the rules of the Colonial Land and Emigration Commissioners.

Passages to Australia are provided by the Commissioners, from Colonial funds, for able-bodied men and women of good character … The emigrants will he required to repay to the Society the whole of the sums advanced to them, which will again be applied in the same manner as the original fund. The owners or trustees of the properties from which the emigrants depart will be expected to pay one-third of the sum disbursed on account of the emigrants by the Society.

The program was so successful that today in one particular area – the Moidart region, 25 miles west of Fort William – there are fewer actual residents than there are descendants in Australia of the people who emigrated with the support of the HIES.

*

By the late 1840s, the various immigration schemes were beginning to make a difference to Australia's population growth. Then in 1849, as we have seen, this growth hit a snag with the seemingly unstoppable exodus of thousands of fortune hunters headed to the Californian goldfields – but the decline was more than reversed when Australia's own gold rush commenced just two years later. With new discoveries being declared almost every week and immigrants flooding to Australian shores, the colonial authorities could not have been happier with the decision to no longer suppress news of gold discoveries.

However, woollen goods producers in England were soon expressing their concern about the consequences of the gold rush on their industry, and the probable interruption to the supply of wool from Australia. They feared that many sheep farmers and shearers would join the gold rush in preference to remaining on the land. The government in London immediately initiated a scheme designed to encourage rural workers in England to migrate to Australia and take up the slack. Yet it proved to be unsuccessful: almost every rural worker who travelled to Australia did so with the sole intent of looking for gold.

By the late 1850s, though, the number of migrant ships coming to Australia was declining. The decrease was due mainly to a waning of the gold-rush euphoria. Some migrants were still arriving in Australia with the goldfields as their ultimate destination, but in nowhere near the numbers that had come when the news of the first gold finds had been trumpeted to the world.

Fortunately, when the gold could no longer be found, a vast proportion of the foreign visitors elected to stay. Consequently, millions of Australians today can trace their family heritage back to those intoxicating days of gold fever and the clipper ships.

It would be a similar scenario in New Zealand a decade later: a significant number of today's New Zealanders have the roots of their family trees firmly embedded in the Otago gold rush of the early 1860s.

*

The western side of the continent would also receive its share of gold-rush frenzy, but not until 1885, when prospector Charles Hall discovered alluvial gold in the Kimberleys. The big discoveries – the finds that caused men to abandon their lifestyles in the east and head west as quickly as possible – did not come until gold was uncovered in large quantities in Coolgardie in 1892 and Kalgoorlie the following year. Like all the large discoveries that preceded them, these two finds transformed the colony and the lot of its people.

This reversal of the colony's fortunes was badly needed. Though the Swan River Colony – renamed Western Australia in 1832 – had been founded as a free settlement, over the following two decades its economy had stagnated so badly that the only solution lay in converting it to a penal settlement. Convict labour was free, and this asset would prove invaluable to the colony's growth.

Between 1850 and 1868, forty-three ships – some of them clippers – landed nearly 10,000 convicts in Fremantle. The last ship to bring England's unwanted to Australia, the 875-ton *Hougoumont*, arrived off Fremantle on 9 January 1868, with 280 convicts and 108 passengers on her manifest.

The final prisoner to be hustled onto the dock from *Hougoumont* that day was the last of more than 165,000 convicts transported to Australian between 1788 and 1868. In recent times it has been calculated that 2 million Britons and 4 million Australians can today lay claim to convict ancestry.

*

Incredibly, some 70,000 of those 165,000-plus male and female convicts found themselves in Van Diemen's Land (renamed Tasmania in 1856), which never had the benefit of a gold rush to attract new settlers. Some of the felons were used as free labour in the colony's coal mines, which began operation in 1805, and as timber-getters.

After a large number of the island colony's much-needed free settlers, particularly rural workers, responded to the news of the 1851 gold discoveries by quitting their jobs and heading to the mainland, the government took quick action. To counter the exodus, Van Diemen's Land offered assisted passages and small parcels of farmland in the colony's north and north-west.

The majority who accepted this proposition first sailed to Melbourne aboard one of the Black Ball Line clippers that plied this route – like *Lightning* and *James Baines* – then transferred to a small steamer or sailing vessel that was heading across Bass Strait to Launceston, on Tasmania's northern coast. Some clippers, like *Commodore Perry*, did sail directly to Launceston – as was reported on page two of the *Launceston Examiner* on 10 April 1855:

> This splendid ship, belonging to Messrs Baines and Co.,
> commanded by Captain Mundle, arrived from
> Liverpool on Saturday last, after a passage of 85 days.
> She sailed from Liverpool on 11th January, with about
> 800 passengers for this port and Sydney.

It was also reported that 350 of the 800 passengers were migrating to Van Diemen's Land.

That same year, a total of 5000 assisted immigrants arrived in Van Diemen's Land, 858 of whom were Germans, but from that time on, the island colony became the poor cousin of the mainland colonies when it came to attracting migrants. In 1866, only 53 migrants arrived, while a mere 700 were welcomed between 1866 and 1882.

*

Of all the Australian colonies, it was Queensland – founded in 1859 – that best demonstrated how to attract desperately needed migrants without the benefit of a gold rush or the opportunity to draw on a convict labour force. It did so via a scheme implemented in the mid–1860s – one so successful that, apart from attracting immigrants on a large scale, it brought new life to the then waning migrant and passenger ship business out of England. Between 1861 and 1900, Queensland received more immigrants than any other Australian colony.

Surprisingly, during the entire period of convict transportation to Australia, only two convict ships were directed to Moreton Bay, where Brisbane lies today. In November 1849 *Mount Stewart Elphinstone* arrived there carrying 225 male convicts, and five months later, *Bangalore* sailed into the Brisbane River and landed 292 male convicts.

However, between 1824 and when these ships arrived, records reveal that 2240 convicts – both men and women –

were 're-transported' from New South Wales to Moreton Bay. The first convict settlement was established there in 1824 at Redcliffe, in the north-western sector of the bay, only to be relocated a few years later to a more secure site on the banks of the Brisbane River (now the centre of Brisbane). Those prisoners had been transferred north from Sydney for one reason: they were among the most dangerous offenders sent to Australia from England – so bad that they could not be trusted as workers outside the compound walls.

In 1846, more than two decades after those first convicts were sent north from Sydney to Moreton Bay, a proposal was put forward by the New South Wales Government to establish a vast new colony, North Australia, encompassing all Australian territory north of 26 degrees latitude. The Letters of Patent were issued by Queen Victoria in May 1846 and the new colony was born.

The *Moreton Bay Courier*, which began publication as a weekly newspaper that same year, told its readers where North Australia's inhabitants would come from:

> All the liberated convicts in Van Diemen's Land who may throw themselves for support on the Government of that Colony, and, in future, all the exiles from the mother country, are to be sent to this settlement on their arrival … land will be assigned to them to be cultivated, and it is expected that with little comparative aid from the Government, they will be able to maintain themselves.

To obviate the objection that North Australia will be composed of males only, a portion, if not the whole, of the female convicts will be sent there direct from England, and also all the female convicts from Van Diemen's Land, who may be unable to obtain employment. Married men, who have regained their freedom, will have their wives and children sent out to them.

The story went on to warn that the proposal for the creation of North Australia was 'avowedly an experiment and one which must end in complete failure unless the plan be greatly modified'.

This was an astute observation on the part of the editor, because on 6 March the following year *Courier* readers were being informed, 'all is not well with North Australia'. The radical and costly plan was abandoned two months later. (The British Government had decided to revoke the Letters Patent in December 1846 but the news did not reach North Australia until May 1847.) The local parliamentary representative, Rev. Dunmore Lang, suggested the new colony be called Cooksland and extend further south into modern New South Wales, but at last the borders were agreed upon in their current form. It is thought that when Queen Victoria signed fresh Letters of Patent in 1859 to finally form the new colony in the north, the name Queensland was her suggestion.

From the outset the dilemma for Queensland's government was that the colony lacked inhabitants, especially those needed for the development of its extensive areas of farmland, in order to produce the one valuable export commodity of the time: wool. In short, Queensland had little to recommend it as a destination for migrants, and consequently was virtually unknown in the British Isles and Europe.

This lack of awareness became the greatest challenge facing Queensland's first governor, Sir George Bowen, and his administration; they had to find a way to change the colony's profile so that it could emerge from obscurity and appeal to would-be emigrants looking for a new start in life. Eventually, after much debate and consideration, it was decided that the only way to succeed was simply to hand the problem to the colony's first agent-general for immigration, Henry Jordan, and have him come up with a solution.

This was a brave call by the government, as their chosen man appeared to have only one qualification that would make him suitable for the momentous task: he was a migrant!

Jordan commenced his professional career as a dentist, in Derby, England. He migrated as a missionary to South Australia in the early 1850s, but his health failed and he reapplied himself to the dentistry profession in Sydney. A few years later he moved to Brisbane and was soon elected a member of Queensland's first parliament. At that time the colony's white population stood at 28,000: one person for every 25 square miles.

Jordan's immediate plan was to find a unique way to break into the very competitive migration market in England. To counter offers to migrants being made by other Australian colonies and by America, he would have to present a more appealing incentive. America alone was attracting 100,000 new settlers annually from around the world.

Jordan's task was made doubly difficult by the fact that he would be starting from scratch. This meant he must take a completely different approach. So, with the endorsement of the Queensland Parliament, he sailed to London with a plan in place and a strong determination to succeed.

He had realised that Queensland had one major asset: land – and plenty of it. Therefore, migrants who were willing to pay for their own passage to Queensland would receive a land grant. Simultaneously, those too poor to pay their fare would be guaranteed employment as much-needed labourers.

To cover the costs of the fares of this latter group and their families, Jordan very cleverly negotiated a deal with the Black Ball Line, owners of the famous *Marco Polo*: they would transport them free on their giant clippers, in return for government-guaranteed land parcels in Queensland – land parcels that the shipping company could sell at a later date.

The key to Jordan's success, however, was his marketing approach: instead of sitting in London or Liverpool and waiting for the people to come to him, *he* went to *them* to sell his Queensland message at town meetings. In 1866, he made a highly successful foray into Wales, staging nine meetings, the majority in rural areas. In Cardiff 1300 people attended his event, and in Caernarfon 700. His 'sell' obviously worked: in addition to signing up as migrants, many of those who attended the meetings went out and spread the word about Queensland.

Jordan's success was such that in the years 1865 and 1866 alone, nearly 20,000 immigrants headed to the emerging colony. They became known as 'Jordan's Lambs', simply because the long lines they formed on the docks conjured images of lambs heading to an unknown destiny, be it a shearing shed or a slaughterhouse. Not surprisingly then, Jordan was often referred to as 'the shepherd'.

Jordan's efforts also contributed greatly to the reinvigoration of the Black Ball Line's passenger market. In 1863, sixty-eight ships set sail on the Australia run under the company flag – the highest annual figure in its history – and the impressive numbers continued for some time. In 1864 the figure was sixty-seven, and in 1865 sixty-two.

There was one other history-making event associated with Jordan's program for getting migrants to Queensland. Until this time the longest non-stop voyage for a sailing ship anywhere in the world had been the 14,000-nautical-mile passage from New York to San Francisco via Cape Horn, or vice versa. However, some of the clippers delivering Jordan's Lambs to Queensland put an end to that claim.

Not all migrants were bound for Brisbane; some were headed for Rockhampton, 370 nautical miles further north, where their farming land grants were located. This region was first settled in 1854 and gained a short-term benefit from a gold rush at nearby Canoona in 1858 – a gold rush that became a non-event, as there was very little of the precious metal to be found. The non-stop voyage from England that ended at Keppel Bay – where the ships were anchored and the Rockhampton migrants rowed ashore – was 500 nautical miles longer than the coast-to-coast course between New York and San Francisco.

*

In 1866 the British answered the on-going demand for passages to Australia with what was considered to be one of the two greatest clipper ships built on that side of the Atlantic. Named *Sobraon* and with a hull length of 317 feet overall, she, along with the ill-fated *Schomberg*, were the only two clippers that were comparable in size to the giants coming out of Donald McKay's yard in Boston. Built by Alexander Hall & Company in Aberdeen, *Sabraon* was the largest composite clipper ship ever built: she featured iron beams and frames and Malabar teak planking, and was copper fastened. Her sail area was enormous: a spread of canvas that would cover two acres.

The one significant difference between the design of these two British ships and the largest of the Yankee clippers was that the British ships had greater overall length and their rivals greater beam.

From day one, she went onto the run to the Antipodes: from 1866–71 to Sydney, then from 1872–91 to Melbourne. The unique feature of her voyages was that she never returned home via Cape Horn; it was always back around the Cape of Good Hope.

Sobraon quickly became the most popular ship sailing to Australia, mainly because of her size, high standard of accommodation and quality of service. Equally satisfying was the expertise and attention of her captain, Lieutenant J.A. Elmslie, R.N.R., who held that position for 24 years.

Her crew totalled 69 including the captain. There were four officers, eight apprentices, a carpenter, a sailmaker, a bosun, an engineer, two bosun's mates, 26 able seamen, four ordinary seamen, two boys, sixteen stewards and two stewardesses.

Sobraon made only one trip per year downunder, but because of the premium service and conditions onboard and the timing of the voyage – departing London in September and arriving in Australia in February – there was always great demand from passengers eager to travel. She accommodated 90 in first class and 40 in the second saloon. Guests wanted for nothing, especially when it came to food and beverage selections. On each voyage, she carried three bullocks, 90 sheep, 50 pigs, three cows for milking and more than 300 geese, chickens and ducks. There was also an ice chamber containing several tons of ice.

Not surprisingly, this was the vessel of choice for the most discerning of travellers. In 1867, Lord Belmore and his wife sailed to Sydney aboard *Sobraon* so he could take up the position of Governor of New South Wales. Then, while at anchor in Sydney Harbour following that passage, Captain Elmslie entertained the Duke of Edinburgh on board while the ship acted as flagship for the Sydney Regatta.

Sobraon was no slouch under sail, especially when running down her easting in the southern seas. On many occasions, she topped 300 nautical miles in a day; her best ever run was 340.

Maritime historian Basil Lubbock described magnificently what it was like to sail a giant ship like this downwind in a howling gale – a 'real snorter'. Two of Captain Elmslie's sons sailed with him for many years, and Lubbock quoted the captain's eldest son, 'C.T. Elmslie', who told of a major storm the ship endured in 1889. At the time *Sobraon* was just north of Iles Crozets, a sub-Antarctic archipelago 1500 nautical miles east-south-east of the Cape of Good Hope:

> … by 4 p.m. *Sobraon* had been shortened down to
> foresail, lower fore topsail, upper fore topsail reefed,
> main lower topsail and fore topmast staysail … the yards
> were hardly round before the foresail went and in a few
> moments there was nothing left of it. The sea was
> running in mountainous ridges, and with the foresail
> gone threatened every moment to poop her badly. It
> was too late to heave to and the ship was kept away
> before it. After four hours' battling and over 30 men

aloft a brand new foresail was bent and set reefed.
This was hardly done before the fore upper topsail blew
away. However, with the foresail reefed and two lower
topsails *Sobraon* fled before the blast like a startled deer.
The squalls every few minutes were terrific and in spite
of such short canvas *Sobraon* was making over 14 knots
an hour.

The sea was all the time running higher and higher
and breaking aboard in the most alarming fashion.
During the night the greater portion of the bulwarks
on the port side was carried away; a boat in davits,
hanging 22 feet above the water, was filled by a sea and
disappeared, the davits breaking short off: the main
skylight over the saloon was washed away and tons of
water found its way below before the open space could
be covered over. The amount of water in the saloon at
this time can be imagined when passengers were
actually being washed off their feet. On deck there
were many narrow escapes of men being washed
overboard, the broken bulwarks being a great source of
danger. The mate and three of the men were washed
from the main[mast] fiferail to the break of the poop,
and, after being dashed up against the heavy boarding
which had been put up to protect the fore end of the
poop, managed to save themselves by the life-lines
which had been stretched across. The forward deck
house which held the galley and engine room was

almost demolished and everything moveable in it was washed over the side.

The storm continued at its height from the Sunday afternoon until Wednesday morning. The passengers, who had been battened down for three days, were in a sorry plight owing to the quantities of water that had got below and the catering for them under such conditions proved very difficult. As is usually the case after such a storm, the wind subsided very much quicker than the sea, and for a few hours on the Wednesday night, the wind having dropped completely and the ship losing way, the rolling was terrific.

Sobraon's stellar career over a quarter of a century left no doubt that British clipper ship designers and builders were on a par with the best to be found in America and Canada. One can only wonder how great *Schomberg* would have been had her career not been curtailed by a headstrong Bully Forbes.

By the time of Federation in 1901, the non-indigenous population of Australia stood at 3,773,801, and it was the mighty clipper ships that had contributed significantly to this story of growth. The rate of migration would increase exponentially over the coming century – particularly as the White Australia Policy (which existed from Federation until it began to be dismantled in 1949) came to an end. This then led to a surge of migrants of many nationalities arriving in the country and setting the foundation for its now-multicultural character.

Though the earliest clippers plying the Britain-to-Australia route had been designed and built in America, by the time the famous Black Ball Line was conveying passengers to the new colony of Queensland in the 1860s, Britain had a thriving clipper-building industry of its own. London and the northern port city of Liverpool became the home ports for ships plying the lucrative Australia run, and fierce rivalries developed between the shipping companies. As this competition gathered pace, the British-built clippers would go on to compete on a par with their American-built rivals.

CHAPTER 4

Black Ball and White Star

The British shipping industry fights back

When the first extreme clippers like *Rainbow* and *Sea Witch* were being launched in America in the mid–1840s, the majority of British seafarers were still lumbering around the world in the more traditional and considerably slower 'Blackwall frigates', which were based on a design concept that had originated in the 1830s.

The reason for this was simple: British maritime laws, some of which had been in place for two centuries, ensured that British vessels were a 'protected species'. The laws prohibited foreign-flagged vessels from competing with British ships on all trade routes to and from British colonies. They gave Britain and its colonies a monopoly on all trade with each other and between them and foreign countries.

Soon after the clipper boom began, the British Government realised that their archaic maritime laws no longer served the purposes for which they had been designed.

131

Neither the British shipbuilding industry nor British shipping companies were benefiting as originally intended. Meanwhile, on the opposite side of the Atlantic, the American shipbuilding industry was booming, as a result of the intense rivalry ship owners were experiencing between themselves and with other nations competing for cargoes. Competitiveness was the name of the game, so the American clippers were becoming bigger, faster and more efficient than any ship that had ever been built in Britain.

In May 1849, when the liberal-thinking Whig Party was elected to government, the reasons for repealing the Navigation Acts were unmistakable. At the time, the largest commercial ship built in Britain had a burthen of less than 1000 tons, while the Americans were already designing ships twice that size, and capable of nearly double the speed of the Blackwallers.

British shipbuilders recognised that clippers were now dominating maritime trade, but because their industry was protected, they did little about challenging the concept. It was as if their industry had run aground on the world scene, and they weren't overly enthusiastic about salvaging it. Yes, they continued to build ships, but they didn't seem interested in supplying what most of the market wanted. They seemed content with plodding along in the tried and proved Blackwallers.

The first Blackwall frigate, launched in 1837, had been designed and built in a yard owned by George Green and brothers Money and Henry Wigram, located on the northern bank of the Thames at Blackwall, seven miles from London. When other yards started building similar ships, they were all recognised by the colloquial name of Blackwall frigates.

Compared with the later clippers, many English whips were impressive in size but not in style. In design terms they were impressive in size but not in style. In design terms they resembled bluff-bowed barges, while their rigs were inefficient, their sails ill-fitting and, as maritime historian Basil Lubbock has noted, they had 'a promenade deck no longer than the traditional two steps and overboard'. He added: 'These Colonial wagons were navigated by rum-soaked, illiterate, bear-like officers, who could not work out the ordinary meridian observation with any degree of accuracy, and either trusted to dead-reckoning or a blackboard held up by a passing ship for their longitude.'

The voyage to Australia from Liverpool or London on board one of these vessels was often painfully slow, and a horrific experience for many, particularly those who had paid the minimum fare and were travelling in 'steerage class'. Their quarters were usually overcrowded, with ventilation almost non-existent and privacy unknown.

The horrors that steerage-class passengers had to endure on the passage to Australia were revealed in a first-hand report delivered to a Parliamentary Committee in London in 1844. It certainly confirmed that the experience they endured was little better than that of convicts, who were still being transported to the colonies at this time:

It was scarcely possible to induce the passengers to sweep the decks after their meals or to be decent in respect to the common wants of nature; in many cases, in bad weather, they would not go on deck, their health suffered so much that their strength was gone, and they had not the power to help themselves. Hence the between decks were like a loathsome dungeon.

When hatchways were opened, under which the people were stowed, the steam rose and the stench was like that from a pen of pigs. The few beds they had were in a dreadful state, for the straw, once wet with sea water, soon rotted, besides which they used the between decks for all sorts of filthy purposes. Whenever vessels put back from distress, all these miseries and sufferings were exhibited in the most aggravated form.

In one case it appeared that, the vessel having experienced rough weather, the people were unable to go on deck and cook their provision: the strongest maintained the upper hand over the weakest, and it was even said that there were women who died of starvation. At that time the passengers were expected to cook for themselves and from their being unable to do this the greatest suffering arose.

It was naturally at the commencement of the voyage that this system produced its worst effects, for the first days were those in which the people suffered most from sea-sickness and under the prostration of body thereby induced were wholly incapacitated from cooking. Thus though provisions might be abundant enough, the passengers would be half-starved.

*

When the old Navigation Acts were repealed and the government announced that British trade would no longer be the exclusive domain of British ships, protests erupted in shipping centres across the country. The government, however, remained steadfast.

Sure enough, the barriers came down, allowing American clippers access to a huge new passenger and cargo market, by sailing the prosperous tea route from China to England (previously foreign goods could only arrive in England on English vessels or vessels from their country of origin). More importantly, they now had unimpeded entrée to the burgeoning routes to the Australian gold rush, and beyond to New Zealand.

Additionally, British ship owners were no longer forced to support the local shipbuilding industry. They were now free to buy or charter clipper ships from America – and *Marco Polo* was among the first of the clippers to become part of a British fleet.

However, one British ship designer and builder had already sent out a clear challenge to the supremacy enjoyed by the American clippers on the high seas. His name was Walter

Hood, and his shipyard was in Aberdeen. In 1847, his first clipper, the 146-foot *Phoenician*, slipped down the ways at the Walter Hood & Co Shipyard at Pocra Quay. She was destined to join the White Star fleet of ships sailing the round-the-world route to Australia – and when she did, she certainly impressed.

On her maiden London-to-Sydney passage, *Phoenician* became the first clipper ever to enter Port Jackson, on 21 July 1849. On her third voyage on that route she put her name into the history books for two additional reasons: she set a record time from Sydney to London of eighty-three days – seven days less than she had taken on her outward voyage – and she carried the first Australian gold to be landed in the British Isles: over 80,000 ounces' worth. An article in Melbourne's *Argus* proclaimed:

> An Aberdeen correspondent of the [London] *Times* …
> expresses a hope that when facts are duly considered, it
> would no longer be contended that the American
> clippers have any just claim to be considered the fastest
> sailers, or as worthy of a preference over British ships
> like the *Phoenician*, and others of the same build.

As more and more ships arrived in England from Australia, carrying an ever-increasing amount of gold, the urgency of eager throngs of gold-seekers to get to the Antipodes grew proportionately. Shipping companies in Liverpool and London commenced negotiations to buy or charter Yankee clippers, while diverting their Blackwallers, which had been sailing to and from India, onto the routes to Sydney, and Melbourne in particular. Still, there were insufficient ships to meet the demand.

With all migrants reaching Australia the only way possible – by sea – the England-based shipping lines were running virtual shuttle services, and turnarounds were being completed as quickly as possible. Port Phillip Bay pilots reported that, at their busiest times, it was not unusual to have twelve or more ships waiting at the entrance to the bay for guidance to their anchorage in Hobson's Bay.

The timing of the gold rush could not have been better for the Black Ball Line, newly launched by local shipping identity James Baines, Scotsman Thomas M. MacKay and two junior partners, Joseph Greaves and John Taylor. The company poached its name and flag from a rival American line sailing packets between New York and Liverpool – much to the latter's displeasure.

Baines and MacKay immediately saw golden opportunities sailing the route between Liverpool and Australia. By putting the recently purchased *Marco Polo* under the command of their most talented captain, James (Bully) Forbes, they would have a head start on their business rivals. She would be recognised as the largest clipper on the run, becoming the pioneering ship for the company and the country.

Marco Polo was built by James Smith at his yard in St John, in the Canadian province of New Brunswick, and launched in 1851. Locals obviously didn't see her hull shape as being like that of a fish, as many others had: instead, she was described as being 'as square as a brick fore and aft, with a bow like a savage bulldog ... a big thick lump of a black ship with tremendous beam, a vessel you could carry on to glory in, even to sporting lower and topmast stunsails in a strong gale'.

The ship's origin was somewhat unusual in that she was not built to order. Aware the old navigation laws had been lifted, Smith was smart enough to realise there would be a market for her in England, so not long after the launch, he sailed *Marco Polo* across the Atlantic with a cargo of cotton, and offered her for sale there. A journalist from the *Illustrated London News* had a different view of the ship's design from the people of St John, writing in early 1852:

> The distinguishing feature of the *Marco Polo* is the peculiarity of her hull. Her lines fore and aft are beautifully fine, her bearings are brought well down to the bilge ... she has an entrance as sharp as a steamboat and a run as clean as can be conceived ... in fact, with a bottom like a yacht, she has above water all the appearance of a frigate.

Baines was similarly impressed, because soon after *Marco Polo* arrived in England he negotiated to buy her as the initial flagship for the newly formed Black Ball Line fleet. As a three-decker with the most modern appointments and 8 feet of head room throughout, she was ideal for the emigration trade. Even so, he commissioned her to be refitted so she could carry the maximum number of passengers. It was a competitive market, and if the Black Ball Line wanted to command high prices from its passengers, comfort for all – whether travelling first-class or steerage – was paramount.

A newspaper report in Liverpool provided an insight into the standard of accommodation that passengers might expect:

> On deck forward of the poop, which is used as a ladies'
> cabin, is a 'home on deck' to be used as a dining saloon.
> It is ceiled with maple and the pilasters are panelled
> with richly ornamented and silvered glass.

The new layout was standard for the day: married couples were berthed amidships, single women aft, and single men forward.

When the refit was completed, *Marco Polo* was recognised as being considerably more comfortable than any other emigrant ship. She pioneered the standard for which Black Ball Line ships became renowned: well ventilated below deck, offering state rooms, smoking rooms and tastefully decorated saloons for 'cabin' passengers. Even the accommodation for steerage class travellers was superior to what had previously been experienced. The ship also acquired a reputation for being well rigged and maintained.

Baines even insisted that large lead-lined tubs be positioned on deck so the women passengers could do their laundry.

*

The passengers on the ship's manifest would be seen as one of the first ripples in what would later become a tidal wave of mass migration to Australia. News that gold had been discovered in significant quantities near Melbourne reached England only five months before *Marco Polo* set sail, and from that moment the big gold rush to Australia had begun.

An advertisement that appeared in a Liverpool newspaper at the time read:

> Under agreement to sail on 21 June 1852 for Melbourne and Port Phillip the splendid new frigate built-ship *Marco Polo*, James Nicol Forbes, Commander (who has much experience in the trade). A1 at Lloyd's, 2,500 tons burthen; coppered and copper-fastened; now only on her second voyage; is the largest vessel ever despatched from Liverpool to Australia; and expected to sail as fast as any ship afloat: has splendid accommodation and carries two surgeons – Apply to James Baines & Co.

This was just the first of the boasts about the new ship's speed. A later newspaper report detailing what was referred to as a customary 'dejeuner' held on the main deck prior to the start of the voyage stated that during the celebrations Bully Forbes had made a remarkable statement. The captain 'judged from the appearance of her sticks and timbers that his ship would be obliged to [be fast]; and that they must not be surprised if they found the *Marco Polo* in [Liverpool's] River Mersey [within] six months'.

The majority of local seafarers treated the statement as mere folly – a wine-laced brag. While *Marco Polo* was then the largest ship to undertake the return run to Australia, none before her had ever come close to achieving that time.

But Forbes was as confident as they were not. He was certain that the North American clipper was very much capable of completing the circumnavigation within that time. Besides, what most didn't realise was that Forbes had an added incentive. Baines and MacKay had lured him into the role of captain by offering him a small shareholding in their company, should he return in under six months. Simply put, a record run to Melbourne and back would secure his position within the company, and as a ship's master, for many, many years to come.

Forbes was born in 1821 more than 250 miles north of Liverpool, in the shipping port of Aberdeen, on Scotland's east coast. From his teenage years in the mid-1830s, his passion was the sea, even if the financial reward he gained as a deckhand from around age fourteen would best be described as a pittance.

By eighteen he had not a shilling in his pocket, but he did have one valuable asset: he showed great skill and courage as a seafarer, so much so that he ascended rapidly through the ranks to become captain, aged just twenty-five, of the ship *Prince of Waterloo* on her return voyage from New Orleans to

Liverpool. Sadly, on her next voyage, to Quebec, *Prince of Waterloo* ran aground on Anticosti Island in the Gulf of St Lawrence, but Forbes was able to return to Liverpool as master of the Canadian vessel *Wilson Kennedy*. This was followed by a short stint captaining the White Star Line ship *Wakefield*.

Inevitably, word on the waterfront regarding Forbes's talents filtered through to Baines, another young prodigy – two years younger than Forbes – who had chosen to make his fortune on the other side of the shipping business, perhaps aided by funds from a confectionery business owned by his mother. In 1849, he and his partners had established James Baines & Co, and were on the lookout for reliable, tough, talented, up-and-coming captains.

Before long Forbes had accepted an offer to join the company, and he and Baines would develop a close working relationship. His first position with the company was as the master of *Maria*, then *Cleopatra*, both on the Australian run. He obviously impressed his employer while commanding these ships, as Baines had no hesitation in appointing him captain of the magnificent *Marco Polo* when he set up the Black Ball fleet.

Marco Polo's departure on 4 July was celebrated in grand style. While flags around the port and on the ship fluttered lazily in the gentle breeze, the air was filled with rousing music coming from the ship's band, which was stationed amidships and surrounded by excited passengers.

It was the top of the tide: the right time to be towed out of the River Mersey by small paddle-wheeler tugboats onto the

Irish Sea. The call by the captain for the tugs to take the strain on their tow lines and for the dock lines to be cast off was the signal for high emotion among those on board, and the families and friends farewelling them from the dock.

By the time the tugs had the 2500-ton ship heading downriver, slowly but surely, towards the open sea, Forbes's mind would have been locked onto the passage ahead and the opportunities it might present him and his ship. He was most definitely out to stamp his name and that of *Marco Polo* into maritime history books, and prove that his pre-departure prophecy was actually a promise.

Once clear of the land, the crew members who had been sent aloft and those on deck began unfurling and setting the sails. Soon afterwards, the tow lines from the tugboats were let go and *Marco Polo* was literally 'off the leash', heading away on a circuitous course to a destination some 13,000 nautical miles away.

It was a passage on which only Mother Nature could decide whether there would be fame or failure.

Baines and Forbes were both satisfied with the crew they had assembled. They had signed on many of the best officers they knew to be sailing out of Liverpool, the most important being Charles McDonald, Forbes's second-in-command. There were thirty regular crew aboard, as well as thirty seamen who were working their passage to Australia. Additionally, many of the passengers were keen to help with the sailing of the ship. Their endeavours were often referred to as 'pully-hauly', as they found that hauling on a halyard or a brace alongside the regular crew was a satisfying form of exercise.

The first few days passed without incident, but *Marco Polo* wasn't far into the Atlantic before it became apparent to most that the conditions on board promised by Baines and his company were a far cry from reality. Forbes's impatience to put to sea caused the first problem: much of the cargo and equipment, including the many trunks the passengers had brought with them, had not been stowed correctly.

But the main issue was that the ship was grossly overcrowded, which created difficulties from the outset that could not be overcome. *Marco Polo* was licensed to carry 701 adults, but through an artful manipulation of the law – structured on the number of children accompanying their parents – the manifest documented nearly 150 additional passengers. A significant proportion of them were heading to the goldfields, but an emigration society had also placed on board an overwhelming number of everyday citizens who were being sent to Australia to live, some willingly, others not.

The captain cared little about this overcrowding, or the fact that food supplies would be stretched to unacceptable levels. Forbes's greatest concern was the speed of his ship – and he was certainly satisfied by the swift passage that was achieved down the Atlantic. In little time *Marco Polo* had crossed the Equator, relatively close to the coast of South America, and was on a course towards the southern seas and the Roaring Forties, heading for iceberg territory.

Forbes was determined to maintain this track because it was as close as he dared to go to John Thomas Towson's recently proposed great circle route: the shortest possible distance to his destination, and a saving of around 1000 nautical miles. This course was, in fact, what many referred to as a composite great circle route, a far safer course where, instead of sailing the complete arc that would take them to the edge of the Antarctic Circle – 66 degrees 33 minutes south – they would level off at about 50 degrees south (around 150 nautical miles south of the remote Kerguelen Islands). From there they would sail west along that latitude until they intersected the great circle route's arc where it swept up from the southern seas towards Bass Strait. At that point they would turn north-east and follow the great circle route to Bass Strait. This composite route would save them around 800 nautical miles.

For the passengers, it meant that in a matter of two weeks they would have travelled from the sauna-like climate of the tropics to the depths of a frigid and storm-lashed southern-hemisphere winter.

Even so, they didn't realise it would be far worse than they could have imagined – on two fronts.

Forced to endure appalling weather extremes, many passengers would suffer greatly because they did not have clothing warm enough to cope with the blizzard-like conditions they would encounter in the southern seas – conditions that they had not been warned to expect, nor could ever have contemplated.

Worse still, children were soon beginning to die after being struck down by the plague of the day, measles. The cause was simple: one couple had boarded the ship in Liverpool not knowing that their young child had already contracted the disease. From the moment it began spreading, there was nothing the ship's two doctors could do to slow its progress. Adding to the doctors' woes was the fact that many of the medicines they ordered had not been put aboard prior to departure — possibly because the ship had left before they could be delivered.

Hard as it was to believe, there was even worse to come. As *Marco Polo* headed into the Roaring Forties and continued on her dangerous course, passengers and crew alike were utterly unprepared for the savage storm that hit with sudden force, threatening to engulf the ship and send her to the bottom.

Yet all that Bully Forbes saw was the perfect opportunity to sail his way into the record books. He remained entirely unconcerned about the fears held by his passengers and some crew. He was interested only in harnessing every ounce of energy coming from what he saw right then as the perfect maelstrom. Here was his first chance to show the world what one of the very latest clipper ships could achieve under sail, and become famous while doing so.

*

Convinced for weeks that they might never see land again, the passengers and crew aboard *Marco Polo* felt blessed when they sighted Cape Otway, at the western entrance to Bass Strait. From that point it was only 60 nautical miles to the eagerly anticipated narrow entrance to Port Phillip Bay.

A few hours later, as *Marco Polo* hove into the view of the men of the Port Phillip Pilot Service, stationed on land at the bay's entrance, they were amazed by her great size, and the sleek lines of her black hull. They had never seen a larger or more impressive ship enter the port. She was a thing of beauty, from her stem – where a full-length figurehead of the famous explorer whose name she bore was mounted proudly under the bowsprit – to her stern.

With the pilots aboard and most of the sails hauled up and furled, *Marco Polo* made her way slowly up the bay towards Melbourne, and as she did so, Captain Forbes had every reason to feel proud of the way his ship had performed in all conditions.

However, there had also been a dark side to the voyage. In the ten weeks it had taken to reach Melbourne there had been at least fifty-two burials at sea: two adult women and around fifty children aged under ten. In this era it was not unusual for between 50 and 100 deaths to be recorded on the older and slower vessels that sailed this route, and they carried only half the number of passengers that were aboard *Marco Polo*. Still, there could be no denying that – in addition to overcrowding – Bully Forbes's stubborn determination to sail his ship without mercy through the frigid southern latitudes had contributed to this tragically high toll.

It was Sunday, 19 September 1852 when *Marco Polo* reached her designated anchorage in Hobson's Bay, west of the entrance to the Yarra Yarra River. Within a few hours of her arrival she was the talk of the waterfront. Word spread rapidly that this amazingly large vessel of revolutionary design had completed the passage from Liverpool to the entrance of the bay in an almost incomprehensible sixty-eight days!

For Forbes, however, the job was only half done. Yes, he had proved that his original claim had been no idle boast. But more importantly, he still had to deliver on the second part of his pronouncement: he had to complete the circumnavigation and be back in Liverpool in less than six months.

All thoughts of the storms they had faced and the suffering they had endured faded fast for *Marco Polo*'s passengers from the moment the anchor was set firmly in the sandy bottom of the bay. Instead, there was a mild air of hysteria prevailing: all the majority could think about was getting ashore as quickly as possible and rushing to the goldfields. Some even tried to bribe the pilots to take them ashore in their boat, but the only way to reach shore quickly was to hire one of the watermen who brought small rowboats out from nearby Williamstown.

The town of Melbourne was about six miles upstream along the Yarra Yarra River, and there were only two ways of getting there: travelling by steamboat up the river, which in some places was just 25 feet wide, or walking along rough bush trails. Little did the weary passengers know that their arrival in Melbourne would be just the start of a long, and costly, trek to one of Victoria's many goldfields.

*

Back aboard *Marco Polo*, Forbes had already turned his attention to the return voyage to Liverpool. Being home inside six months was an exciting prospect for him – but before long he realised that his self-imposed challenge could well be destroyed within a matter of days.

As *Marco Polo* was approaching the Hobson's Bay anchorage he was surprised to see as many as fifty large ships lying idle. He would have expected their crews to be busy loading or unloading cargo, but there was no activity to be seen on the decks.

Forbes quickly sought answers from some of their captains, and each response was nearly the same: the majority of the crews, and in some cases even the captains, had deserted their ships and rushed to the goldfields, with no intention of returning. Not even the threat of being shot or bludgeoned with a baton for abandoning ship could stop them, nor could the enticement of huge financial rewards – between £40 and £50 – get them back. Some captains took the extreme measure of visiting the local prisons to try to secure crew, but couldn't find anyone willing to leave town, even if their fines were paid.

Even the steamer *Australian*, a coastal mail carrier, was affected by a crew exodus: in Sydney she had to be assisted away from the dock and down the harbour by men from the English brig *Fantome*, while in Melbourne and Adelaide police were stationed at the bottom of the gangway to ensure her crew stayed on board. A few weeks later, when in Albany, she was delayed for a week, because the men whose job it was to load the coal needed to keep her boilers operating had been locked up in jail to stop them from fleeing to the goldfields.

Forbes was at his wits' end: should his crew jump ship he would be forced to stay in Melbourne for weeks, if not months. He had to move swiftly to counter any such eventuality – and he did. Either through bribing local police officers, or by concocting an enormous lie, he made sure that none of his crew could stray from the ship: he had them arrested, charged with insubordination and promptly locked up! His actions were reported in London in the 1 January 1853 edition of the *Australian and New Zealand Gazette* – a report that he probably embellished in a bid to justify his seemingly harsh measures:

> On arrival of the *Marco Polo* at Melbourne, such was the excitement on account of her rapid passage, that the people threw small nuggets of gold aboard among the crew. The crew having become unruly, Captain Forbes had the whole of them imprisoned until his departure,

and was thus able to get off again without loss of time. Many ships are laid up in Melbourne, for want of hands, which cannot be obtained at any price. One ship had advertised for men at the rate of 30 shillings per month, but no application was made.

Forbes's carefully conceived plot to keep his crew had worked. Just three weeks after *Marco Polo* had arrived in Melbourne, the cargo had been loaded and the crew were back aboard, after he went to the police and paid their fines.

His intention now was no different from when he had set sail from Liverpool on the outward-bound voyage: drive his ship as hard as possible. However, there was one additional challenge: this voyage involved rounding a sailor's most feared graveyard, the craggy and inhospitable Hornos Island, and Cape Horn, its southernmost point.

*

In this era, seafaring and superstition went hand in hand. Belief in such things as a lucky day of the week had a considerable influence on many sailors' lives.

However, for Forbes, who by now had been at sea for half his life, it wasn't until his time in Melbourne that he decided Sunday was *his* day. He was looking at the navigation plots logged during the just-completed voyage when he noted that *Marco Polo* had departed Liverpool on a Sunday, crossed the

Equator on a Sunday, sighted the Cape of Good Hope on a Sunday and arrived in Melbourne on a Sunday.

Consequently, he insisted that his ship weigh anchor and depart Melbourne, on a non-stop passage to Liverpool, on Sunday, 11 October 1852.

Once clear of the entrance to Port Phillip Bay, and after the pilots had been put aboard their small boat so they could return to shore, Forbes set a course south-east, across the Tasman Sea to the Auckland Islands – off the southern tip of New Zealand's south island, 1100 nautical miles away. At that point they would be at a latitude of more than 47 degrees south – well into the Roaring Forties and close to the Furious Fifties.

In this region he was destined to find strong westerly winds: ideal conditions for propelling his ship as fast as possible towards South America. At times astonishing speeds were being achieved hour after hour. *Marco Polo* averaged more than 13 knots over one three-day period, and over the twenty-four hour period up to when she rounded the cape on 3 November, she averaged 15 knots. At times the 2500-ton vessel was careering down massive swells at nearly 20 knots.

In a surprisingly short time Cape Horn was in *Marco Polo*'s wake, and she was headed north towards the Equator. Fortunately, the weather gods continued to look favourably on her progress, so the miles and the latitudes were being ticked off in impressive fashion until, much to the captain's surprise and delight, they crossed the Equator ... on a Sunday! From there, a quick calculation by Forbes on the distance to be sailed to Liverpool confirmed that he was well within range of delivering on his promise to return within six months of departure.

There was an eerie and mysterious encounter for all aboard *Marco Polo* towards the end of her voyage. When she was some 600 nautical miles from Land's End, the south-western point of England, the outline of a barque appeared on the horizon ahead, but it did not appear to be moving. As *Marco Polo* neared this vessel, Forbes and his crew realised it seemed abandoned: there was an empty longboat in the water attached to the ship by a painter, there was no sign of activity on the deck, and the rig was in a dishevelled state. Forbes called for blue lights (the signal flares of the era) to be ignited so they could be seen from the mystery vessel, and for rockets to be fired overhead, but there was no response, so *Marco Polo* resumed her course.

As we have seen, *Marco Polo* had lived up to – indeed, exceeded – all expectations by the time she docked in Liverpool. She had completed the entire circumnavigation in a record-breaking time of just five months and twenty-one days: well inside the six-month limit that would allow Forbes to take a share in the company. Forbes went on to be recognised by many as the greatest ever captain on the lucrative Australian run during the gold-rush era. Inevitably, he also became the centrepiece of incredible maritime legends – stories in which it was difficult to separate fact from fantasy.

He was, no doubt, a man who truly believed in himself – an attribute that was very evident when *Marco Polo* was departing Liverpool for her second voyage to Melbourne. While addressing the passengers on deck in his usual blustering voice, he is said to have bellowed: 'Last trip I astonished the world. This trip I intend to astonish God almighty!'

Forbes had placed wagers on sailing the fastest time of the season, and it is certain that many *earthly* souls were impressed when *Marco Polo* trounced all opposition – including the giant *Antelope*, one of the upstart new steamers.

Having completed two exceptionally fast passages to the Antipodes and back, and only enhancing his reputation for being among the greatest captains of all time, Forbes stepped down as captain of *Marco Polo* at the completion of this second voyage. He was replaced by Charles McDonald, previously his second-in-command.

Forbes spent some months relaxing onshore, but his mind was never far from the sea. Inevitably, James Baines lured him back to the Black Ball Line in 1854 with the offer of an exciting command: as captain of the magnificent new clipper ship *Lightning* on her maiden run to Melbourne. Her race against a ship of the rival White Star Line would become known as one of the most captivating contests of the clipper era.

*

Liverpool's White Star Line, established in 1844, was James Baines's arch-competitor. With *Marco Polo* having proved so successful on the gold-rush route to Melbourne, the White Star Line set about searching for a ship of a similar size and style, with a view to capturing a large share of the highly valuable human exodus to Australia.

They found their solution only a matter of miles upstream along the Mersey, at the Bank Quay Foundry in Warrington, owned by Charles Tayleur. The three-masted clipper chosen as their pioneer on the Australian run was named *Tayleur* as a tribute to the owner of the yard.

Tragically, though, *Tayleur* ran aground and sank on her maiden voyage on 21 January 1854, just two days out from Liverpool.

It was a huge setback for the White Star Line: the company's capacity to carry thousands of passengers to Melbourne and Sydney had been greatly reduced, and the disaster was the first black mark on the company's perfect safety record.

White Star Line's owners, young and commercially savvy shipbrokers John Pilkington and Henry Threlfall Wilson, had no option but to defend their company and its reputation in the only way they knew: replace *Tayleur* with another ship as soon as possible and get back to business.

Bringing added urgency to their situation was the knowledge that their arch-rival the Black Ball Line was about to introduce to the Australian passenger market one of the most spectacular clippers afloat: the recently launched 244-foot

Lightning, built by Canadian-born Donald McKay, the famed creator of *Stag Hound* and *Flying Cloud*.

In the weeks after the sinking of *Tayleur*, fate dealt Pilkington and Wilson a most favourable hand. The magnificently proportioned 260-foot clipper *Red Jacket* had just sailed into the Mersey from America and was on the market. She had been designed by noted American naval architect Samuel Hartt Pook – who already had numerous proven clippers to his credit – and was considered by many mariners at the time to be the handsomest of the large clippers put afloat by American builders. She had been built by Deacon George Thomas, a professional shipbuilder who had also helped found the Second Baptist Church in Rockland, Maine. He had launched twenty-five large vessels prior to *Red Jacket*.

Making this ship very appealing for potential purchasers was the fact that she had just made a record-breaking run across the Atlantic to England. Her time between New York and Liverpool had been thirteen days, one hour and twenty-five minutes: a mark for a commercial sailing vessel that still stands. In one twenty-four hour period during the voyage, *Red Jacket* had covered a noteworthy 417 nautical miles, and she logged 353 miles for each of the final six days.

Her arrival in Liverpool on 23 January 1854 – just two days after the loss of *Tayleur* – could not have been more spectacular. Under the captaincy of the great American seafarer Asa Eldridge, *Red Jacket* sailed into the Mersey at such a pace that the tugs sent out to get lines aboard then tow her to the dock could not keep pace with her.

Not surprisingly, concern spread rapidly among the thousands of onlookers lining both sides of the river: they expected *Red Jacket* either to run aground or to crash into a dock. But within minutes that concern had turned to awe. As if taking a bow before the admiring throng, Eldridge called on his sixty-man crew to hastily shorten sail. He then executed his *pièce de résistance*: a perfectly planned exercise in which he turned *Red Jacket* head-to-wind, back-winded the few sails that remained aloft, then steered her into her designated berth stern-first. An utterly astonished crowd roared in recognition of this amazing display of seamanship. They had never seen anything like it, and probably never would again.

Red Jacket was an immediate sensation with dockside spectators. They were amazed by her size and sweet, sweeping lines, but her most impressive feature was the large, superbly crafted figurehead at her bow. It was a representation of a Native American chief wearing a feathered war headdress and a red jacket – Chief Red Jacket, or Sagoyewatha (He Who Keeps Them Awake), who had aided the British during the American Revolution, a commitment that earned him the red military jacket and subsequently the name.

Some quick-fire negotiations with the representatives of the ship's owners followed *Red Jacket*'s arrival, and in a very short time a contract was in place: the White Star Line would charter *Red Jacket* for a voyage to Australia and back, and have an option to purchase her after that.

Much to the delight of Pilkington and Wilson, their company was back in the main arena of international sea travel. Their immediate challenge was to have *Red Jacket* ready to sail the 13,000 nautical miles to Melbourne as soon as practicable.

They quickly saw their chance to make even more of a stir by staging a showdown with the Black Ball Line's much-lauded *Lightning*. The 'prize' for the fastest time, while not material, was nonetheless extremely valuable. In a market where all that most travellers wanted was to get to Australia as quickly as possible, bragging rights were the most powerful leverage a shipping company could hold.

Regardless of *Red Jacket*'s performance on her maiden voyage from New York, *Lightning* was certainly the crowd favourite for the face-off. For a start, she had the perfect pedigree, as a Donald McKay designed and built ship. But adding further firepower to that qualification was the confirmation that the Black Ball Line had lured the now-legendary Bully Forbes into the role of captain for *Lightning*'s circumnavigation.

Lightning was just 16 feet shorter in overall length than *Red Jacket*, and of the same beam: 44 feet. Her forward sections were typical of McKay ships, the stem being heavily raked, while the form of the hull made a well-proportioned transition from very concave to convex in shape. Like *Red Jacket*, she had an impressive figurehead, described in the *Boston Daily Atlas* as 'a beautiful full-length figure of a young woman holding a golden thunderbolt in her outstretched hand, the flowing white drapery of her graceful form and her streaming hair completing the fair and noble outline of the bow'. Her rig and sail plan were enormous: the mainmast stood 164 feet above the deck, while the main yard on that mast was more than twice the ship's beam – 95 feet. Supporting the three masts were huge 11½-inch-circumference stays made from Russian hemp. Her total sail area measured nearly two acres.

Lightning had set out from Boston for Liverpool on 18 February, about a month after *Red Jacket*. It was a departure that caused Duncan McLean of the *Boston Daily Atlas* to write a glowing report:

> We have seen many vessels pass through the water, but never saw one which disturbed it less. Not a ripple curled before her cutwater, nor did the water break at a single place along her sides. She left a wake as straight as an arrow and this was the only mark of her progress … The voyage so auspiciously begun proved one of the most remarkable ever made by a ship on the ocean; she had left more miles of salt water astern in twenty-four hours than any vessel that has ever sailed the seas propelled by winds and canvas.

Lightning made the crossing to Liverpool in thirteen days, nineteen and a half hours: eighteen hours slower than *Red*

Jacket's record. But the closeness of that 3000-nautical-mile dash, and the fact that they had sailed from different ports, provided grounds for considerable debate as to which ship was the rightful trans-Atlantic record-holder. The distance from Boston was approximately 175 nautical miles shorter than from *Red Jacket*'s departure port, New York. *Lightning* supporters fuelled the controversy by arguing that *Lightning* had been confronted by adverse easterly winds for a considerable part of her voyage. Bully Forbes himself weighed in, disputing the veracity of his rival's astonishing sailing time in a letter to the editor of Liverpool's *Northern Daily Times*.

What could not be argued against was *Lightning*'s incredible record twenty-four hour run of 436 nautical miles on 1 March: an average speed of 18.16 knots, and 19 nautical miles more than *Red Jacket*'s best. This historic mark is even more impressive when it is realised that a quarter-century would pass before *Arizona* became the first steamship to match that average speed over a day.

*

The upside to the great debate that developed around the trans-Atlantic achievements of both ships was that it fostered even greater interest in the 'race' to Melbourne, which would begin within a matter of weeks. From the time when the two ships were in port, the Liverpool waterfront was alive with speculation as to which one would record the fastest time, and accordingly many a wager was laid, apparently even by the two captains.

Forbes was certainly doing his best to stir up would-be punters by announcing that he hoped to reach Melbourne in just sixty days: a new record. He also continued to use the media to question *Red Jacket*'s true potential, then contemptuously announced that the owners of the White Star Line would not back their ship in a bet of 100 to 500 guineas in which the winner would donate the money to charity.

Interestingly, even the announcement that *Red Jacket* had a new captain made no difference to the odds being offered. Asa Eldridge had been replaced by a highly regarded and capable Liverpudlian, forty year old Samuel Reid. His credentials as a master were strong – twenty-five years on the high seas – and while he had never commanded a ship on the route to Australia, Pilkington and Wilson had no hesitation in assigning him to the task. As a token of his commitment, Reid purchased a small shareholding in the ship.

While the *Lightning* and *Red Jacket* face-off held centre stage, their voyages represented only a small part of the business of getting passengers and cargo to Australia. The Black Ball Line was advertising *Lightning* as one of sixteen passenger ships in its fleet, seven of which were new. The White Star Line, while offering fewer ships, had eight new vessels in its fleet.

*

On 4 May 1854, after prayers had been delivered on deck, *Red Jacket*'s dock lines were cast off so she could be eased away ever so slowly from her berth, under tow by steam tugs. On board were sixteen first-class passengers, 438 adults in second class, an unknown number of children and ninety-eight crew. There were tears and cheers as flags were waved, bands played and canon fire boomed across the Mersey.

While enjoying these celebrations, those on the dock and lining the river were left to wonder: would those departing be safe? Would they reach Australia? What of their future? There was no certainty associated with this or any other voyage, not to mention the challenging, life-changing experience that awaited them in the Antipodes.

*

Ten days later, on a Sunday – Bully Forbes's good-luck day of the week – these scenes were repeated as *Lightning* was towed out to sea for her non-stop passage to Melbourne. She was carrying 452 passengers, including forty-five children, plus a complement of more than ninety crew members. As was the case on the majority of voyages to Australia in the mid–1850s, the average age of the passengers was in the low twenties.

One cause of her delayed departure had been the need for last-minute renovations. As impressive as she was, *Lightning* had arrived in Liverpool not ready for a circumnavigation. Some of her accommodation was still to be completed, but the biggest task to be undertaken was the sheathing of her hull with thin sheets of Muntz metal. This material, comprising 60 per cent copper, 40 per cent zinc and a minute trace of iron, had been developed and patented by a British metal-roller, George Fredrick Muntz, in Birmingham in 1832. It had two important advantages over the more common copper sheathing: it had considerably greater anti-fouling capabilities and cost about one-third less.

Ever confident, Bully Forbes held no concern about departing so many days after his rival. His determination to once again make a mark on maritime history saw him hoping that somewhere in the southern seas he would encounter *Red Jacket* and sail past her, before reaching Melbourne in a record time of just sixty days.

*

Because of the circumstances of the *Tayleur* tragedy, which had occurred so soon after her departure, there was considerable anxiety among many of *Red Jacket*'s passengers about the early stages of the voyage. To calm these fears, the White Star Line had promised that *Red Jacket* would be towed west until she was in safe waters off Holyhead – the most north-westerly point of Wales.

That point was reached at midnight on 4 May, but before the tow lines from the two tugs were released, a small steamer that had travelled in convoy from Liverpool went alongside and took on board company representatives and guests so they could be returned to shore. It so happened that there was one additional and unexpected guest on board the steamer: a woman passenger who could not overcome her fear that the ship would meet an awful fate, so much so she insisted that she be returned to shore.

Comfortable conditions during the crossing of the often gale-ravaged Bay of Biscay eased the anxiety of many passengers. There was a steady westerly breeze blowing, so every possible sail was set – from the skysail down to the maincourse, from the flying jib and the main royal staysail through to the spanker, and even four stunsails. In these conditions, the starboard braces were eased, so that, with the yardarms angled forward of abeam, all sails were billowing superbly. *Red Jacket* was in her element, loping her way across gentle seas and heading south at a pleasant 10 knots.

The passage was further brightened by the birth of a baby boy to an Irish family, an event that provided the opportunity for several female passengers to set about making baby clothes for the newborn. The parents had no trouble selecting a name for their son: Red Jacket!

Breakfast each day was at nine o'clock, dinner at two and tea at six. In daylight hours, passengers either relaxed in their accommodation or spent time on deck, chatting with others and enjoying the shipboard atmosphere. Some stood at the bulwarks looking out for any form of marine life – whales, dolphins, sharks or birds. Occasionally, those on deck were entertained by non-paying passengers: giant albatrosses, which to this day superstitious seafarers believe are the souls of lost sailors. It is therefore considered bad luck to kill one. These magnificent birds – which are capable of covering more than 500 nautical miles in a day when gliding across the wave tops – have been known to land on a ship's deck simply to take a rest.

On 11 May, passengers were treated to the unexpected. Whether due to the influence of alcohol, a dare, boredom or youthful exuberance, a young Irishman took it upon himself to climb the ratlines on the mizzenmast and scamper monkey-like through the rigging. He was brought down to the deck by two crewmen, who then lashed him to the rigging and threatened not to release him until he paid a penalty: two bottles of brandy.

By 15 May, the weather was getting warmer, so each evening after tea, weather permitting, the ship's band – comprising musically talented crew members – would assemble on deck and play, and the passengers would dance well into the night.

The day when *Lightning* departed Liverpool, *Red Jacket* was already south of the Canary Islands, nearly 2000 nautical miles from Holyhead, and making good speed towards the Equator. By now almost all passengers were experiencing temperatures higher than they had ever known, so many took their mattresses on deck at night with the hope that the evening breeze, as gentle as it was, would help them sleep. Then, by day, with conditions stifling below, they would search for whatever shady area they could find within their allotted area on deck − which was defined by the class of fare they had paid − in a bid to stay cool.

Inevitably, on-board gossip − fact or fiction − would help while away the hours. Much of the detail relating to the *Red Jacket* voyage has been transcribed from a journal written by a passenger, Frederick Hoare, who was travelling as part of a group to the goldfields in Victoria. He included as much detail as possible about what he saw and what he heard − including all the tittle-tattle.

At this time, everyone was talking about the fact that the second officer had broken a shipboard rule: he was found being 'too intimate' with some of the young female passengers below deck. Hoare's diary went on to tell another tale that would have consequences when the ship reached Melbourne:

> This evening while some of the Cabin Passengers were
> at cards they disagreed and the officers interfered, which
> made a general disturbance in the cabin, so much so
> that the pistols came out and the Captain placed a guard
> with cutlasses, etc, all night.

Hoare then noted, 'other particulars unknown', but it does appear that there was an outcome, for the following day he wrote: 'Three of the cabin passengers, we read, are still in irons.'

*

Well astern of *Red Jacket*, Bully Forbes was planning a course quite different from that of Captain Reid. Using the well-established theories of Matthew Maury, he was busy plotting routes that would allow *Lightning* to gain maximum benefit from known current and wind patterns.

This would see her sail extremely close to the coast of South America. Meanwhile, Reid had his ship sailing a more direct route south. Only time would tell which course was the faster.

*

Hoare wrote of a melancholy moment soon after *Red Jacket* had crossed the Equator:

> The boatswain died on Friday 9 June. The sailmaker made a canvas coffin from an old sail and a collection was taken up among the passengers for his wife. His mortal remains were consigned to the deep at 5am the next day, and in the afternoon, as was the custom, his effects were auctioned to other members of the crew while the passengers looked on … they realised more than their value.

As *Red Jacket* approached the latitude of Cape Town, the ship was prepared for what might be a testing passage across the southern seas. Already, strong squalls had taken a toll on some of the sails, but in general captain and crew were most satisfied with the way the new ship was handling the conditions.

On Sunday, 18 June, rough weather prevented the usual church service from being held on deck, but the highlight of the day for everyone was a heated argument that erupted among the members of one family. Hoare wrote:

> There is a great row below deck – a courtship has
> sprung up during the passage between a Protestant man
> and a Catholic woman and the woman's family are not
> at all agreeable for her to have a Protestant – this caused
> the row.

The following day he told of the consequences:

> The Protestant man, mentioned yesterday, to protect his
> lady-love, was married to her today in the Cabin, by the
> Captain, who feasted them for the day. The man was
> drunk tonight which is not a good beginning.

But passengers would soon have little inclination for such hijinks upon deck. As *Red Jacket* sailed deeper into the southern seas, her average speed increased dramatically: to anything between 288 and 312 nautical miles a day. The extreme cold kept all but the hardiest souls below deck; icicles were hanging from the rigging and rails, and snow showers regularly swept across the ship.

Red Jacket's course was now taking her to the highest southern latitude she would achieve on the voyage: 52.03 degrees, a position approximately 100 nautical miles south of the barren and uninviting Kerguelen Islands. From that point, Captain Reid would begin plotting a course to take the ship directly to Bass Strait and the entrance to Port Phillip Bay, 3200 nautical miles away to the east-north-east.

The anticipation among passengers as to when they would sight land to some degree lessened the monotony that accompanied this challenging, sometimes dangerous and extremely uncomfortable part of the voyage.

*

Unfortunately for Bully Forbes, the chances that *Lightning* would eclipse the performance of *Red Jacket* and beat her into Melbourne were rapidly slipping away. His decision to sail her on the longer course towards the coast of South America had not delivered the anticipated dividend, and since then, the winds had generally not blown in his favour. There was, however, plenty of drama ahead.

In what could be seen as a desire to take a shortcut, *Lightning* went within an ace of coming to grief. Forbes had decided to pass close to the Kerguelen Islands, instead of taking the usual course deeper into the southern seas, where the winds were generally stronger. At the time, the wind was blowing solidly from the west and the ship was making 15 knots under greatly reduced sail.

At 10pm on 16 July, after lights-out for the passengers, Forbes was pressing on in the belief that the rocky, barren and uninhabited Kerguelen archipelago, which comprises more than 300 islands, was 60 nautical miles – some four hours' sailing – to the east. However, about an hour later, a lookout peering into the murky blackness ahead thought he saw something. After focusing on it a moment longer, he bellowed: 'Land ahead!'

That was all that was needed for Forbes to call for all hands on deck. Every set of eyes peering ahead confirmed the crew's greatest fears: *Lightning* was charging directly towards a lee shore, and it appeared that there was no escape. It was the Kerguelens.

In a frantic bid to slow the ship, many crew were ordered to climb aloft and directed to furl or lower sails as quickly as possible. But the situation became even more serious when it was realised that giant waves could be seen breaking on land on both sides of the bow.

There was no way that *Lightning* could turn back; the only hope was that somehow, miraculously, they might be able to con their ship through a gap between the islands – if that existed. Otherwise, there was little doubt that, once the ship's bow smashed into the rocky fortress that appeared to be directly in their path, all 550 souls on board would perish within minutes.

In an effort to maintain some level of composure, Forbes ordered that the bosun would be the only person advising him of what lay ahead. Within minutes of taking up his post, the bosun was shouting to Forbes that he could see a black gap not far away, only identifiable because there was white water on either side of it. This was their one chance of escape. It was then do or die: Forbes was forced to steer *Lightning* directly towards the black hole, while praying that, if it was indeed a gap, there would be sufficient depth for his ship to surf through.

Incredibly, in what some passengers no doubt believed was a miracle heaven-sent, it proved to be a safe passage between two islands; *Lightning* sailed on.

This was the second time during the voyage when *Lightning* had come to the brink of disaster. Earlier, on 9 June, when in the region of the doldrums and with all sails aloft, she was hammered by a tropical rain squall concealing gale-force gusts of wind. Before the crew could react and reduce sail, a powerful squall struck and the giant ship was knocked down onto her beam ends – so far down, in fact, that the outer end of her main yard was in the water.

She was close to capsizing. At that moment, not even the weight of hundreds of tons of rock and shingle ballast in her bilge, and many tons of cargo in the holds, was enough to bring her upright: the pressure of the wind in her sails was far too great.

Another shipboard diarist, passenger John Fenwick, told of how Forbes rushed on deck and, in a bid to save the ship, called on the crew to 'let go the jibs' – release the ropes controlling them. But before that could be achieved, the heavy timber jib boom attached to the bowsprit broke in two and became tangled around the bow.

Without hesitation, Forbes ran forward, planning either to salvage what he could of the boom or to cut it free. Fenwick added, in the uncomplimentary terms typical of his diary, that Forbes was aided by one of his crew, the 'fat Austrian bully, Peter'. Fenwick went on: 'what a roaring of wind, thundering of flapping sails, dashing of spray, shrieking of orders there were before we were any way snug again'.

The fact that Forbes played such a defining role in the resolution of this incident reflected the strength of his determination to win the race against *Red Jacket*. Indeed, crewmen are said to have gone ashore on reaching Port Phillip with the story that when they tried to reason with their captain and have some sails lowered or reefed during a treacherous storm, he stood on the poop deck and levelled a brace of pistols at them.

Forbes's overwhelming resolve to carry as much sail as possible at all times seems to have matched that of the other 'bully' of the high seas, American Bully Waterman. History suggests that at times, both captains padlocked the sheets attached to the sails so petrified crew could not overrule their captain's authority and take it upon themselves to reduce sail.

Forbes was also known for not stepping away from a challenge: on a number of occasions during *Lightning*'s voyage, he allegedly clambered out to the end of the jib-boom, or a stunsail boom, so he could best admire his ship as she charged across the ocean at a remarkable rate of knots. It was quite possible that, if the attached sail had flogged, or the boom had moved suddenly, Forbes would have plunged into the ocean – his last ever sight being the view of *Lightning* as she bowled away towards the horizon while he floundered in her wake.

According to Fenwick, the captain was forever pushing *Lightning* to the very edge of what he believed to be her design limitations. This led Fenwick to write of his concern about the ship's structural integrity: 'the ship seems to twist like an old basket and her trembling when struck by a sea is anything but pleasant … however quick the *Lightning* may be, she is certainly not a strong ship'. Yet this was something he need not have worried about, given the sturdy nature of the vessel.

While the role of captain was an around-the-clock responsibility, in mid-June Forbes had time to turn his attention to an unexpected family event. On board ship was his unmarried twenty-six year old half-sister, Isabella Nicol, who planned to embark on an exciting new life in Melbourne. However, during the voyage she had met Blakiston Robinson, an Englishman of a similar age who was travelling in saloon class. The ensuing romance was soon considered to be true love – so much so that the pair were betrothed then married before *Lightning* reached Melbourne.

*

Meanwhile, *Red Jacket* continued her charge across the southern seas. On 5 July those on board experienced the strongest wind conditions of the entire voyage. With the 2300-ton ship rolling dramatically from gunwale to gunwale, men went aloft to reef and furl sails, while others at the mast and gunwales aided them by controlling sheets, lines and halyards. When Captain Reid decided his ship was snug, she was carrying only three double-reefed sails: the mizzen topsail, the main topsail and the fore topsail. Still, this was enough sail area for her to cover a respectable 288 nautical miles over the next twenty-four hours.

This achievement paled into insignificance, however, over the following twenty-four hour period, when *Red Jacket* topped 400 nautical miles: an average speed of nearly 17 knots. The ship's run through the Roaring Forties in midwinter, between the latitudes of 48 and 52 degrees south, saw her average 14½ knots for five consecutive days. The top speed recorded on the log, when she was bow-down as a result of the weight of the thick cover of frozen spray on deck all the way back to the mainmast, was 18 knots.

One week later, King Island, at the western edge of Bass Strait, was in sight, and by two o'clock that afternoon, *Red Jacket* was safely at anchor inside Port Phillip Bay. She had reached her destination in sixty-seven days. The captain was pleased to note that few sails had blown out, no seas had been shipped on deck and nothing had broken – though one thing *Red Jacket* did break was *Marco Polo*'s record of seventy-seven days for the passage from Liverpool to Melbourne, set in 1852.

*

It was 21 July – one week after *Red Jacket*'s arrival – when *Lightning* registered her best twenty-four hour run of the voyage: 432 nautical miles. John Fenwick wrote that every time it appeared that mountainous following seas were threatening to overwhelm the vessel, she responded beautifully: 'away flies the good ship on the Billow as lightly and as gracefully as a Seabird'. He also noted that there was so much snow on deck that passengers were enjoying snowball fights. However, there was more excitement to come, as he went on to explain:

> Top gallant sails not taken in although the blocks 18 inches
> above the lee rail are frequently under water – the deck is
> on an angle of 45° to 50°. The second mate, whose watch
> it is says 'Now this is what I call carrying on!'

Once in Bass Strait, almost every passenger aboard *Lightning* was on deck so they could enjoy the first views of Port Phillip Bay as the ship navigated the Rip at its entrance. But the greatest impression came from the climate: as Fenwick noted, all were surprised that midwinter in Melbourne was 'as warm as summer at home'.

Eighteen days after *Red Jacket* had sailed into Port Phillip Bay, *Lightning* loomed large at the bay's entrance, and Fenwick was in awe of what he was observing:

> No account of this Bay that I have seen is exaggerated –
> it is magnificent, both as to its scenery and its
> capability – a fine fleet of large ships – the Elite of all
> nations were lying in it.

A few hours later, he had the opportunity to appreciate the full 40-mile length of the bay's eastern side as the ship sailed north to her anchorage at Hobson's Bay.

Within two days of coming to anchor, *Lightning*'s passengers were ashore and heading into Melbourne. The new Sandridge-to-Melbourne railway line was still under construction, so, like thousands of travellers before them, they had to travel upriver by boat.

Somewhat ironically, George Train, the American entrepreneur who was the driving force behind the company building the railway line, had suffered the same fate when he, with wife Wilhelmina, arrived in Melbourne about one year earlier. He wrote of the experience that each passenger 'steps with a light heart and a quick movement on board the dirty little thirty horse power side wheel steamer, paying five shillings for the privilege, and groans when he learns that the captain and supercargo get off with one [shilling]'. Strangely, Train – who, in 1872, ran for President of the United States as an independent candidate – added that passing convict hulks anchored nearby was one of the visual highlights for all on board.

*

Wanting a head start on *Lightning*, and fearing that some of his men would decamp and join the gold rush, Captain Reid had planned the fastest possible turnaround for *Red Jacket*. While there were not as many passengers on board now as there had been during the outbound voyage, Reid was given the responsibility of delivering back to England some 45,000 ounces of gold, worth at that time about £1 million.

However, upon arriving in Melbourne, the captain had had an unexpected and far more pressing matter to deal with: he found himself embroiled in a legal stoush – one that had the potential to delay his departure from Melbourne for an unknown period. This matter related to the incident on board *Red Jacket* alluded to by Frederick Hoare, when five male passengers had become aggressive over a card game and pistols had been drawn.

Soon after arriving in Melbourne, Captain Reid had the five men charged with 'riotous and insubordinate conduct amounting to assault and mutiny'. The case dragged on, with some of the men apparently laying counter-charges against Reid, who had put them into detention aboard *Red Jacket* for the final forty-seven days of the voyage.

It appears that Reid received legal advice suggesting he go into hiding in Melbourne until it was time for *Red Jacket* to sail, and it is highly likely that he accepted this advice. It does appear that there was some sort of resolution to the matter, though, as Reid was indeed back on board when his ship departed for England on 2 August 1854.

*

The return passage to Liverpool was to become another clash between *Red Jacket* and *Lightning*, and first blood went to *Red Jacket* when she set a new record of twenty-one days for the stage from Melbourne to Cape Horn – approximately 5500 nautical miles. Within days, though, any chance of logging a dock-to-dock record was dashed when *Red Jacket* was confronted by an ice field while sailing east of the cape.

There was a real danger that the ship would become ice-bound – trapped and unable to make any headway. An additional concern was that her hull might be damaged when it struck ice floes, something that was impossible to avoid. Reid made the logical call and had the majority of sails lowered or furled so that *Red Jacket*'s progress was slowed to the point where the helmsman barely had steerage. The captain then spent much of his time perched on the second-highest yard on the foremast so he could call a safe course through the ice field and have the helmsman respond accordingly.

An unidentified passenger aboard *Red Jacket* later provided a London newspaper with a graphic account of this incident:

> On 24th August I was roused out of sleep by the noise of shortening sail. Ice had been seen before, but the solid masses had been supposed in the dark to be land. I found we were in smooth water and large masses of ice were floating about us... The ice appeared to extend on every side in solid fields as far as the eye could reach, without any prospect of getting out, so that we had to follow the channel. All sail was clewed up except the topsails, and as there was a good breeze we proceeded along at about four or five knots. Our situation at this time seemed most appalling, as we appeared to be getting further into the ice, so that at 11 o'clock we were almost making up our minds to remain for weeks in this fearful situation. About noon the captain and second mate, who had been on the foretopsail yard all the morning, discovered a clear sea again, to reach which we had to force a passage through dense masses of ice. It was here she sustained the principal damage to her stem and copper.

Yet the relief passengers and crew enjoyed once *Red Jacket* was freed of the ice turned to dismay a few hours later, at 8pm, when they were once again trapped in a huge field of ice. This time, Captain Reid called for a retreat: he had the ship tacked and set on a course that would take her back to where she would be in ice-free waters.

Unfortunately, though, when that point was reached, the broken-up ice presented an equally serious problem. The floes were again so large that they would damage the hull should *Red Jacket* hit one hard enough. Besides this danger, there were icebergs to be avoided, the largest seen being about 2 miles in circumference and 100 feet high. It was a threat so immense that Reid called for the ship to heave to for the night. Fortunately, within forty-eight hours, *Red Jacket* had woven her way through the dangers and was once again on course to the north.

After being trapped by the ice then confronted by fickle winds for the next three weeks, when her average speed was less than 5 knots, *Red Jacket* began to benefit from strong south-westerlies and a very favourable, fast-flowing Gulf Stream, so she was able to reach Liverpool on 15 October, in seventy-three days and twelve hours.

Lightning's passage was far less eventful, so Forbes was able to guide her into the Mersey on 23 October, sixty-four days and three hours after clearing the heads at Port Phillip – a record. In what was a remarkable indication of the similarity between the two ships, *Lightning*'s time for the circumnavigation was just two days and one hour better than *Red Jacket*'s.

*

These two great ships would go on to play significant roles in the transportation of passengers from Britain to Australia. Between them, over the next fifteen years, *Lightning* and *Red Jacket* are believed to have carried upwards of 20,000 migrants and general travellers to the Australian colonies, along with tens of thousands of tons of cargo – vital supplies for the rapidly growing British outpost. This great rivalry came to an end in October 1869 when *Lightning* caught fire and was scuttled while docked in Geelong, 34 nautical miles south-west of Melbourne.

By that stage, while British ship designers and builders were leaving little doubt that they were on a par with their American counterparts; many orders from British shipping companies for new clippers were still going to Donald McKay in Boston. In 1855, what was hoped to be the equal of the American ships was launched in Aberdeen, but the fame that preceded her would be short-lived.

CHAPTER 5

'Let Her Go to Hell'

The demise of Bully Forbes and other
maritime disasters

When he sailed *Lightning* into Liverpool and set the fastest time ever for the passage from Melbourne, the legend of Bully Forbes was at its zenith: his public acclaim as the greatest British captain of the clipper-ship era continued unabated. His three spectacular voyages out to Melbourne and back – two aboard *Marco Polo*, followed by the *Lightning* passage – had brought him international recognition, and the profile and success of the Black Ball Line had grown proportionately.

However, as maritime history reveals, from that point Forbes's star was on the wane.

While *Lightning* was sailing around Cape Horn then heading home to Liverpool, the Black Ball Line's owners, Baines and MacKay, were preparing to welcome the 248-foot-long *Schomberg* into their fleet. This was the vessel that was expected to become the greatest British-built clipper of all:

considered by British shipbuilders and seafarers to be the only local clipper ship that could match, and hopefully beat, the best of the Yankee clippers.

Such a grand ship demanded the grandest of captains, so, without hesitation, the Black Ball Line announced that its highest ranking commander would be assigned to the task: none other than Bully Forbes. His last ship had gone like lightning, Forbes claimed, but he would make *Schomberg* go like greased lightning.

It was 6 October 1855 when Forbes took up a position on *Schomberg*'s deck, close to the helmsman, so he could best coordinate the ship's departure for Melbourne. There were 430 passengers plus crew aboard for this maiden voyage, and they, along with all on the dock, enjoyed an air of excitement inspired by a belief that, weather permitting, the outward voyage would take a mere sixty days: a new record. As well as having a full complement of passengers, *Schomberg* was heavily laden with cargo, the largest consignment being iron railway lines and associated equipment to be used in the construction of the Melbourne-to-Geelong railway.

However, the weather did not favour a fast passage, and when land was first sighted – Cape Bridgewater, 30 miles south-east of the Victoria–South Australia border – *Schomberg* was already sixty-eight days out of Liverpool ... and Forbes was completely frustrated by the ship's sluggish performance and poor handling.

That afternoon – Christmas Eve – a strong but unfavourable easterly headwind developed, a circumstance that called for a 90-degree change of course, close-hauled offshore to the south. As *Schomberg* headed away from the coast, the wind continued to increase, as did the ship's angle of heel. The immediate need then was for a dramatic reduction in sail area, so with crew either aloft or working hard on deck, the mizzen topsail, plus all topgallants and royals, were taken in. Soon after that, the mainsail split from luff to leech and had to be replaced.

After heading offshore for nearly six hours, Forbes called for the ship to be put about and set on a course back towards the coast. But, much to his frustration, the easterly wind prevailed for another two days, so progress towards the entrance to Port Phillip Bay, about 100 nautical miles to the east, was stalled.

Now more than a week behind in the much-vaunted sixty-day run to Melbourne, the captain, it appears, lost all interest in running his ship. His disappointment in her performance meant that he began to spend more time below than he did on deck. This attitude might also have been influenced by a £1000 wager relating to making a record passage which he was rumoured to have made prior to leaving England – a wager he was destined to lose. At around 10.30pm on 26 December, Forbes was playing cards with passengers in the main saloon when the ship's first mate advised him that the wind had died away and *Schomberg* was being carried towards the shore by a fast-flowing current. The mate suggested the ship should be tacked as soon as possible, but Forbes, who was losing the game, told the mate he would be on deck to assess the situation after he had played another hand.

By then, it was far too late.

When Forbes finally arrived on deck, *Schomberg* was almost aground on a sandbar about 35 miles to the west of Cape Otway. Forbes tried desperately to tack her and head back offshore, but with barely a breath of wind blowing, *Schomberg* did not respond to the helm.

As luck would have it, the sea–state was nearly calm. So when the inevitable news came from the crewman sounding the depths that the ship was aground, an irate Forbes is said to have bellowed: 'Let her go to Hell, and tell me when she is on the beach.'

With that he left the deck and retired below.

Fortunately, conditions remained benign overnight, so next morning all passengers and crew were safely transferred to the steamer *Queen*, which had come to the rescue. However, *Schomberg* herself could not be saved. Before long rising seas claimed her; she was washed onto the beach and became a total loss.

The subsequent official inquiry into her sinking cleared Forbes of all blame, on the premise that the sandbank on which the ship grounded was uncharted. But a meeting of the majority of *Schomberg*'s passengers was held soon afterwards at Melbourne's Mechanics' Institute. It was suggested by some of those present that Forbes had been so annoyed by the ship's lack of performance that he had deliberately let her run aground, while others questioned his morality during the voyage and complained of his tyrannical approach to running the ship.

Finally a criminal trial was held and Forbes was exonerated – but the damage to his reputation was terminal, and his fall from international acclaim rapid. He never captained another Black Ball Line ship.

He remained in Melbourne for some time after the loss of *Schomberg* then returned to Liverpool, sad and silent – according to Basil Lubbock in his 1921 book *The Colonial Clippers*, 'the very opposite of his usual self'. He did secure some work out of Hong Kong in 1864, but even then the once legendary and flamboyant Forbes was, Lubbock wrote, 'a seedy, broken-down looking skipper, with the forced joviality of a broken-hearted man'.

Forbes died in Liverpool in 1874 aged fifty-two. The epitaph on his simple headstone salutes him as 'Master of the famous *Marco Polo*'.

*

By the time of *Schomberg*'s loss, the demand in Britain to get to the Australian goldfields was insatiable. It could only be met by putting every available ship on the route, no matter the size or design. Clippers were the preferred mode of transport, but innumerable smaller and slower vessels, which usually offered cheaper fares, also headed for the Antipodes. The average adult cabin fare was then about £25.

Ships heading for Melbourne, Sydney or Brisbane needed only to ride the Roaring Forties across the southern seas, then sweep up to the western end of Bass Strait. Melbourne-bound ships would then enter Port Phillip Bay, while ships heading to Sydney and Brisbane would 'thread the needle' – safely traverse Bass Strait – then turn north and sail up the east coast. More often than not, this latter stage was tough going, as the winds frequently changed in strength and direction, and an adverse south-flowing coastal current also affected their progress.

Sadly, though, not all ships either made it to Australia or completed the return voyage to their home port. Regardless of the style or size of a ship, the perils faced during a circumnavigation to Australia and back were the same: icebergs, fires, remote and unlit islands, or heinous storms in which one mountainous and breaking wave could suddenly overwhelm a vessel. Added to this dangerous mix were the difficulties of navigation: plotting a ship's position was still an inexact science, so errors were not uncommon. Over the ensuing decades all of these and other factors contributed to the loss of many thousands of lives, English, Scottish, Irish and European, on the well-travelled route to Australia.

But still the migrants came!

Ambition, and dreams of a fresh and exciting new life in a burgeoning, gold-laden land of vast proportions, obviously dimmed the fear of perishing on those voyages.

The insatiable demand for travel to the Antipodes continued unabated despite the regular run of drama-laced newspaper headlines proclaiming heart-wrenching and frightening stories of shipwreck, tragedy, abominably rough passages or inconceivably fetid conditions aboard, and tales of ships that had literally disappeared, taking all with them and leaving no clue as to what might have happened.

And no one was safe until the very end. Since white settlement of Australia began, King Island, at the western end of Bass Strait and only 90 nautical miles from the entrance to Port Phillip, is known to have been the scene of more than 140 shipwrecks that claimed over 700 lives. Little wonder that seafarers of the era have referred to this island as 'the Graveyard of Bass Strait'.

In 1845 – some years before the clipper era began – it became the scene of Australia's worst maritime disaster: the sinking of the 800-ton migrant ship *Cataraqui*, and the loss of 406 lives including seventy-eight children.

Cataraqui was transporting migrants from England to Melbourne when, on 3 August, she was hammered by a severe westerly gale and mountainous seas. During preceding days, because of heavy cloud, the captain, Christopher Finlay, had been unable to get sun sights that would have allowed him to accurately plot the ship's position, so he had been navigating using dead reckoning. On the night of 3 August, the captain elected to slow the ship's progress by heaving to until daylight, as his dead reckoning indicated that *Cataraqui* was then between 60 and 70 nautical miles from Port Phillip and in safe water.

With the storm still raging and the ship drifting sideways, at 4.30am there came a thunderous explosion. *Cataraqui* had been picked up by a giant wave and hurled onto the rocky shore of Fitzmaurice Bay, near the southern tip of King Island.

The force of the impact was so powerful that the vessel's interior was flooded within minutes, making it impossible for the majority of passengers and crew below deck to escape. *Cataraqui* began breaking up from the moment she hit the rocks, and as each wave pounded over her, an ever-increasing number of survivors, who were clinging to whatever they could on deck, were washed into the boiling sea and drowned.

When dawn broke, there was virtually nothing of the ship to be seen by the nine fortunate souls who survived and made it to shore.

But as the following decades would prove, not even a tragedy such as this could temper the urge by so many to reach Australia.

*

The shocking *Dunbar* tragedy of 1857 once again showed that no emigrant was safe until they were standing on the dock of their chosen destination.

Measuring 202 feet over all, *Dunbar* was the largest clipper-style Blackwall frigate ever built in Sunderland, on England's east coast. She was named in honour of her wealthy owner, Duncan Dunbar, the prominent English proprietor of the Dunbar Line, which supplied nearly one-third of the vessels that transported convicts to Australia between 1840 and 1868. *Dunbar* was launched on 30 November 1853, having taken sixteen months to build at a cost of £30,000. The traditional shipbuilding timber, English oak, was used for her hull frames, deck frames and hull planks, while her deck planking was made from teak imported from India. The final touch, which was in keeping with the Dunbar company tradition, was a carved figurehead in the shape of a determined-looking lion.

Soon after being launched, *Dunbar* was chartered by the government in London to transport troops to the Crimean War. So it wasn't until three years later that she ventured to Australia on a passenger and cargo run, with Captain James Green in command. *Dunbar* spent three months in Sydney, being first unloaded, then reloaded with cargo for her return voyage. During that time the *Sydney Morning Herald* informed its readers, 'The *Dunbar* is a splendid vessel.'

Dunbar's 15,000 nautical mile non-stop homeward voyage around Cape Horn and back to England was uneventful. Then, in May 1857, after a relatively quick turnaround, she set sail for Sydney once more, this time with sixty-three passengers and fifty-nine crew aboard. Many of the passengers were migrant families leaving England filled with fervour for their new life, while others were residents returning to Sydney after visiting family and friends or doing business in England. All were comforted by the knowledge that this would be Captain Green's ninth voyage to Sydney.

On 20 August 1857, *Dunbar* was south of Botany Bay and closing on Sydney from a considerable distance offshore. Conditions were appalling – a gale was blowing and the large, rolling swells were powerful and breaking at their crests – so Green had his ship running north at a slow pace with little sail set. Heavy rain squalls accompanied the gale, so for much of the time visibility was limited to less than a nautical mile – a fact that caused Green to maintain a course well offshore: in those conditions, sea room translated to safety.

Many on deck peered through the murk in the hope of sighting land, and around sundown they received their wish: the rain cleared long enough for the coastline surrounding the entrance to Botany Bay – 10 nautical miles to the south of the entrance to Sydney's Port Jackson – to be identified a considerable distance to leeward off the port bow.

The captain was then comfortable with the ship's progress, even though *Dunbar*'s approach to Port Jackson would be made in darkness. However, his experience told him that the loom coming from Macquarie Lighthouse – an 85-foot-high cylindrical tower, 1.3 nautical miles south of the harbour's southern entrance – would provide the bearings needed to navigate a safe passage into the port, if the weather was clear enough.

The lighthouse's giant mirrors and lenses, reflecting the flame of a huge oil lamp, and a mechanism driven by a falling weight combined to send a beam of light sweeping across the ocean every ninety seconds. But in thick cloud and heavy rain, when visibility was reduced to a few hundred yards – as was the case on this night – the exact location of the light often could not be pinpointed. Still, the entrance to the harbour was deep and 1 nautical mile wide, so even an approximation of the location of the light should suffice.

However, Green's greatest problem was that he would get only one chance to enter the harbour safely. This was because once he called for the helmsman to change course hard to port, *Dunbar* would be sailing downwind towards a lee shore. Once committed, there was no turning back ...

*

The following morning – Friday 21 August – the steamer *Grafton* entered Port Jackson, having battled her way south through the gale, on a 300-nautical-mile passage from Yamba at the entrance to the Clarence River. On docking in Sydney Cove, the ship's master, Captain Wiseman, advised authorities that, when entering the harbour, he and his crew had observed a considerable amount of wreckage floating near Sydney Heads and inside the port.

At the same time, the waterfront was abuzz with news from riders who had rushed into town on horseback: many bodies had been found washed onto beaches and rocky headlands in Middle Harbour, immediately adjacent to the port's entrance. Soon afterwards, equally alarming information arrived from Watson's Bay, just inside the port at South Head:

articles consistent with a shipwreck, including beds and bundles of clothing, had been washed up onto the beach there.

Consternation and speculation ran rife: had there been a shipwreck near the harbour entrance? If so, what ship might it be?

The flotsam discovered at Watson's Bay indicated that the wreckage had come from an immigrant ship. So, as soon as practicable, the steamer *Washington* was dispatched from Sydney Cove to investigate.

One mile from the harbour entrance, *Washington* found herself amid a vast field of debris that had obviously been washed into the harbour on the flood tide. But any hope of getting outside the heads to locate the source was thwarted by the conditions, which were still extremely rough. Instead, *Washington* was guided into Watson's Bay, where a party of men was put ashore. They were directed to climb to the clifftop on the ocean side of the narrow, rocky peninsula – the area known as the Gap – to see if there was any sign of a shipwreck.

This was how the *Empire* newspaper reported their shocking find on 22 August:

On reaching the Gap, a horrible scene presented itself: the sea was rolling in, mountains high, dashing on the rocks fragments of wreck, large and small, and bodies of men, women, and children, nearly all in a state of nudity … A considerable portion of the wreck had been washed into crevices in the rocks, much of which remained high

and dry … Upwards of twenty human bodies were
counted under the Gap – the waves dashing them against
the rocks and taking them back in their recoil.

The seas were so powerful and the destruction of the ship so
complete that there was no immediate way of discovering her
identity. She might be any one of six or more vessels due to
arrive in Sydney from England, or from another Australian
port. Those sailing from England were always at the mercy of
the winds – they could drift through the doldrums for up to
two weeks – so there was no way of estimating with any
accuracy when they might arrive at their destination. Such a
'guesstimate' could end up being out by a month or more.

Because of the extreme conditions, the search for clues was
concentrated inside the harbour – particularly in Middle
Harbour, where wind, wave and tidal action had caused the
greatest number of bodies and the majority of the debris to
accumulate. The first clue relating to the ship's identity came
with the recovery of a small piece of hull planking from a
lifeboat: it had the word 'London' painted on it in white
letters. An increasing number of small boats joined the search,
which continued throughout the day.

By evening, Port Jackson's superintendent of pilots, Mr
Pockley, was in a position to make an official announcement: a
mailbag had washed ashore in Middle Harbour carrying the
inscription 'No. 2, per *Dunbar*, Plymouth, May 29', and a cask
of tripe, also recovered, was marked 'Ship's stores – *Dunbar*'.

Never in its short history had the colony experienced such a tragedy on its own doorstep. It appeared at that stage, according to the *Empire* report, that all 122 'unhappy beings were swept into eternity with scarcely a moment's warning'. With many of the sixty-three passengers being 'old colonists, or relatives of persons residing in the colony', hundreds of residents made the pilgrimage to South Head the following day to pay their respects and see the little that remained of the 202-foot timber ship.

But that afternoon, amid what was a sombre scene, there were shouts of excitement: one of the sightseers at the Gap thought he'd seen movement on a rock near the water's edge more than 200 feet below. He concentrated on the spot for a short time, then bellowed for all to hear that he could see someone waving an object far below. However, that person, be they man or woman, was obviously in a location from which there was no immediate escape: the shoreline was too rugged and the cliff-face too sheer for whoever it was to reach safety.

Frantic action followed in a bid to organise a land-based rescue attempt. Before long, lengths of rope arrived at the clifftop, and soon a brave soul volunteered to be lowered to the spot where the survivor clung to the rock.

Amazingly, thirty hours after *Dunbar* was wrecked, a dazed, cold and hungry twenty year old able seaman, James Johnson, was hauled up the cliff to safety, along with his rescuer. Johnson would be recognised as the sole survivor of the *Dunbar* tragedy.

However, despite the incredible circumstances surrounding his survival and subsequent rescue, he could enjoy no rest. As the only eyewitness, he was required to attend the investigation into the loss of the ship, which was scheduled for the following day. The reason for such haste was that the thirteen men who had been empanelled as the jury for the inquest were required to view all recovered bodies before they could be released for burial.

When it was Johnson's turn to address the panel, he gave a detailed account of what had occurred on board *Dunbar* prior to the disaster, and the harrowing story of what happened after the ship ploughed into the cliff.

Johnson told the inquest that *Dunbar* had been on a starboard tack, between 10 and 12 miles offshore and sailing parallel to the New South Wales coast. A strong wind had been blowing from the north-east. He explained that 'the weather was squally, accompanied by rain', and from the time Botany Bay was sighted, both the captain and the chief officer were on deck.

Once abeam of Botany Bay, Captain Green had called for sail to be considerably shortened:

> There were three reefs in the main topsail, and the fore-topsail was close-reefed; the mizzen topsail was stowed; the spanker was brailed up; we took the second jib in, and also the maintopmast staysail ...

Soon after darkness fell, the 'Sydney lighthouse' had been seen, and at this point, Johnson – who, despite his young age, already had eleven years under sail – had started to become concerned:

> The vessel was then laying her course about north-east and by north; she had not plenty of room for she was making too much lee-way; I know she was making lee-way, and I believe it was because she had not enough of sail upon her ... at the time it was raining hard; the light at the lighthouse was seen only at intervals; but when seen it was distinctly seen; it was a revolving light I am sure.

When yet another rain squall cleared, Macquarie Lighthouse had been sighted just aft of abeam, and at that time the captain had given orders for the ship to be 'squared away' towards the coast, and what he believed to be the entrance to Port Jackson. At the same time, he had called for the foresail to be hauled up. Johnson stated, 'The ship was then kept away before the wind; the light was distinctly visible but only at times. To the best of my belief, when the word was given to square the yards, the light had just previously been seen'.

He described the conditions as 'blowing very fresh', and went on to add that an able seaman and the ship's second and third mates had been sent to a position on top of the forecastle, from which they could keep a lookout ahead. It is obvious that at this stage Captain Green had believed *Dunbar* was holding a course towards North Head, for he had called to the lookouts: 'Can you see anything of the North Head?' to which they had responded, 'No.' Here it can be stated with almost complete certainty that Captain Green had confused the distinct dip he could see in the tops of the cliffs – which was the Gap – with the harbour entrance.

Within minutes, fear had filled the air: the second mate had shouted, 'Breakers ahead', so the captain, believing the ship was being steered towards North Head, had called for *Dunbar* to be turned to port. From there he had expected to continue on a safe course into Port Jackson.

Instead, the ship had been aiming directly for the shoreline.

Still confident in his judgment, Captain Green had called for the yards to be trimmed to suit the change in wind angle. Almost simultaneously, though, as Johnson told the inquiry, there had been a second alert to imminent danger:

> We were hauling in the port braces when the captain
> told us to haul the yards round; when he told us to haul
> on the port braces, we heard the cry of 'Breakers ahead';
> he then called out, 'Brace the yards sharp up'; the order
> was quickly obeyed. There were 13 able seamen in each
> watch; there was no want of hands to work the ship; we
> could see the light at this time; the light was right over
> us; a few minutes after we hauled the yards round;
> when the captain saw the light, he did not give orders
> to alter the position of the yards; and about 2 minutes

afterwards we bumped upon the rocks; the ship went broadside on to the rocks.

The impact was far more than a 'bump'. *Dunbar* had smashed into the base of a towering sandstone cliff on South Head, just a few hundred yards from the southern entrance to Port Jackson.

Within minutes, the ship had been overwhelmed by huge seas, each one pounding *Dunbar* with a force like that of Thor's giant hammer. 'Passengers had come from between decks and were running about the main deck imploring mercy and uttering piercing and heart-rending cries for succour,' Johnson told the jury. 'The captain was standing upon the poop, cool and collected; I could hear no orders given after the ship struck.'

The initial impact had been so powerful that all three topmasts had broken and toppled over the side, and the first wave that burst over the ship had wrecked the lifeboats. The hull had begun breaking up within five minutes of the grounding.

Johnson had no recollection of how he had escaped the wreck and found himself in a relatively safe situation atop a giant boulder. He told the inquiry how he had climbed onto the windward side of the ship at the mizzen chains – the area where the mizzenmast's side stays were attached to the deck – and how he had seen a steward fire a blue distress flare into the night sky (which obviously went unseen).

At that time, *Dunbar*'s stern was being pounded to pieces, so Johnson had fled forward to the main chains, then eventually the fore-chains near the bow, where he had clung on desperately as huge waves continued to wash over him.

He could not remember what followed; he could only assume that he had somehow been washed onto the rocks by a huge wave, and that the subsequent surge of that wave had lifted him to a point where he could safely cling on to the boulder then clamber to the top of it:

> My senses returned but I could hear nothing except the noise of the sea; the first thing I saw in the morning was the dead bodies floating in the sea – I saw that I was the only person there. I was about 10 yards above the level of the sea. The spray washed the rock upon which I was sitting but it was not at all slippery. I was not in danger of being swept away.

The whole of Sydney mourned the terrible loss. The *Sydney Morning Herald* of 25 August proclaimed that 'never was more genuine and heartfelt sympathy evinced and expressed on a public occasion than there was yesterday, as the funeral pageant of the victims of the wreck of the *Dunbar* passed on'.

The disaster did have one positive outcome, however. The following year saw the opening of the Hornby Lighthouse, on the tip of Sydney's South Head, which ensured that no captains would be confused by the location of South Head again.

*

Nine years after Johnson survived the *Dunbar* wreck, a touch of irony came to pass. After deciding to remain in Australia, he was appointed to a position with the Marine Board in Newcastle, 60 nautical miles north of Sydney. Part of this role involved working in the Nobby's Head Light at the entrance to Newcastle Harbour, at the mouth of the Hunter River.

On 12 July 1866, Johnson was stationed at the lighthouse, observing the incredibly wild weather offshore. The wind was gale force and the breaking seas alarmingly large: perilous conditions for many vessels.

The previous night, the coastal steamer *Cawarra* had departed Sydney carrying sixty-three passengers and crew, bound for Brisbane, but by the time she was almost abeam of Newcastle, the captain was becoming concerned for the safety of the vessel and her passengers. The conditions were so dangerous, in fact, that he decided to make a run for Newcastle.

News spread rapidly around the Newcastle waterfront that, despite the raging seas, a ship was attempting to enter the port. Within half an hour, hundreds were gathered on the 90-foot-high Nobby's Head and on the beaches either side of the river entrance to watch the daring attempt. Everyone was amazed that the captain would elect to try to enter the port, but concluded that, despite the obvious dangers, he considered it to be a safer alternative than staying offshore in the extreme conditions.

The waves were so huge that *Cawarra* often disappeared into the troughs. Eventually, when the appropriate position was reached more than a mile offshore, the captain turned his ship to port and steered for the river mouth, and as he did so, some crew were seen to hoist a small jib, obviously to assist steerage and help maintain the highest possible speed. The crowd onshore was spellbound.

Suddenly, gasps, shouts and cries of dread filled the air. *Cawarra* had got out of control and veered across a mighty, near-breaking wave, almost capsizing.

She was doomed from that moment. Wave after wave thundered over her, and as she lay beam-on to their might, those aboard could be seen being washed into the water. Within minutes she was breaking up, and her funnel and mainmast had gone over the side.

In a very short time *Cawarra* was no longer visible, and bodies and wreckage were being washed onto the shore. Conditions were too dangerous for any rescue boat to venture offshore, so the shocked spectators who had watched the drama unfold were certain there would be no survivors.

However, more than an hour later the lighthouse keeper sighted a person clinging to a large plank and being washed into the river mouth from seaward. He responded immediately, directing his son Henry Hannell, a fisherman named James Francis and *Dunbar* survivor James Johnson to rush to a lifeboat and row out into the teeth of the gale to rescue the man.

Fortunately, they were successful. Fate had given James Johnson an opportunity to 'pay it forward'; the beneficiary of a life-saving good deed had repaid it to another.

*

As well as disasters within a hair's breadth of the ship's destination, there were those that occurred agonisingly close to the ship's home port.

Just one month after *Marco Polo* returned from her second trip to Melbourne in September 1853, the Blackwaller *Dalhousie* sank off Beachy Head on England's southern coast, 50 nautical miles to the east of the Isle of Wight. Fifty passengers and crew perished, and as with the *Dunbar* wreck, there was just one survivor: twenty-two year old able seaman Joseph Reed. He later provided a graphic account of what had happened.

Dalhousie had sailed from the Downs – the ship anchorage off Deal in the Straits of Dover – on 18 October 1853, and headed down the English Channel towards Plymouth, where she was to take on board more passengers. At 10pm that same evening, when the ship was about 10 nautical miles to the west of Dungeness in Kent, the wind changed direction to the south-east and increased rapidly to gale force. By midnight, a rough and powerful sea had developed, so Captain Butterworth called all hands on deck to either lower or furl sails.

The gale persisted and conditions further deteriorated, so, with the ship becoming increasingly difficult to control, the captain called for more sails to be taken in. Before this, Reed, who was at the helm, had found *Dalhousie* 'lively and manageable', but two hours later, that circumstance changed dramatically:

> From the morning of the 19th the ship began to lurch deeply into the sea, going a long way over on her broadside, she seemed unable to recover herself when she rolled. I began to suspect there must be a considerable amount of water in her and mentioned it to one of the shipmates, that the vessel seemed water-logged.

By 5.30am, *Dalhousie* would not respond to the helm, and despite carrying virtually no sail, she rolled over onto her starboard beam ends and remained there at the mercy of the gale. In no time, waves were beginning to break over the ship and passengers and crew were being washed overboard. Reed managed to cut a spar free, but while he remained with the ship, the captain, second mate and another seaman jumped overboard and clung to it. Reed's story continues:

> Many of the people had by this time been drowned, but others remained holding on as they best could on the weather side of the wreck. She lay thus for about ten minutes after Captain Butterworth had left her and then sank, going down head first.

As *Dalhousie* was submerged, Reed scrambled aft to the mizzenmast, which he scaled as the water rose towards him. When he reached the mizzentop yard, he discovered the ship's surgeon already there.

With the ship continuing to sink, Reed took his only option for salvation: to leap into the water and grab a large piece of timber that was drifting by. 'My companions gradually perished one after the other, and I was repeatedly washed off my frail support,' he said.

'Towards 4 o'clock [pm] a brig hove in sight to windward, towards where I was floating. I made signals to her with my handkerchief in the best way I could, which were fortunately seen on board the brig and she bore down to me.'

The crew of the brig managed to heave a line to Reed and drag him aboard: 'when I reached her deck, I was nearly senseless'. He was taken to Dover Roads, and it was soon recognised that there were no other survivors from *Dalhousie*. Reed then travelled to London to relate the story of the wreck to the ship's owners.

*

Just a few months later, the sinking of *Tayleur* a mere two days out from Liverpool was an even bigger tragedy for her ambitious charterers.

Being almost four times larger than any ship previously built at the Warrington shipyard near Liverpool, *Tayleur* was the centre of considerable attention from the locals. The 225-foot-long, iron-hulled, clipper carried square sails on all masts, as well as the customary fore and aft sails, including jibs and staysails. Once she was afloat, a comment regularly heard around the waterfront was that her masts appeared to be positioned further apart than the norm, and that this might affect her balance when under sail. Ironically, this would prove the least serious of her many design flaws.

The White Star Line quickly negotiated a contract to charter this vessel, then set a schedule for her to set sail on her maiden voyage in January 1854 – just twelve weeks away. Such a timeframe would have been a tight turnaround for any well-seasoned ship, so to impose a similar schedule on a ship that had just been launched, and had not undergone sea trials, could be considered an unreasonable expectation. Her captain, twenty-nine year old John Noble, was highly experienced, yet because of the tight timeframe his crew was hastily assembled, and many of them had little or no sea time to their credit.

Still, with competition from their rivals at the Black Ball Line being so intense, there was no stepping back for the White Star Line's founders, John Pilkington and Henry Threlfall Wilson. The midwinter departure date of 19 January 1854 would stand.

When the big day arrived, crowds lined the shore to farewell this mighty vessel, the pride of British shipbuilding. At the allotted time, the paddle-wheeler steam tug *Victory* took *Tayleur* under tow, easing her away from the dock then down the River Mersey towards the open waters of the Irish Sea.

Because of the absence of an accurate manifest, the actual number of passengers and crew on board is uncertain, but the figure was somewhere between 600 and 660. *Tayleur* had her hold loaded from stem to stern with a massive quantity of cargo, including ploughs, wine, beer, 15 tons of fencing wire and thirty blank tombstones.

The vast majority of passengers were heading to Australia for the first time in search of a new life, great wealth or both, while others were preparing for a fresh beginning – like emancipated convict Samuel Carby, who had recently married his sweetheart, Sarah.

More than a decade earlier, Carby had been sentenced in England to ten years' transportation to Van Diemen's Land for killing a sheep while drunk. At the time of the offence he had been with a friend, celebrating the fact that he was about to marry Sarah, with whom he had already had a baby son.

Inevitably, the marriage didn't occur. Instead, Carby was shipped out to the penal settlement. After being pardoned early for good behaviour he joined the gold rush and made himself a considerable amount of money. Then, after an absence of twelve years, he returned to England with the intention of marrying the now thirty-seven year old Sarah then taking her and their son Robert, now aged thirteen, back to Australia aboard *Tayleur*. The marriage took place within days of Samuel's return to his home village of Stamford, then he, Sarah and Robert headed for Liverpool to join the ship.

When *Tayleur* reached the entrance to the Mersey, the pilot who had gone aboard to guide her safely downriver is believed to have advised the captain that he considered the compass readings to be inaccurate: they did not relate to the actual course he knew the ship was then holding. Captain Noble would no doubt have acknowledged this information, while at the same time accepting the fact that he was unable to make any corrections: it was not a simple procedure, because the degree of accuracy would have been different on all points through 360 degrees.

It is highly probable that this problem occurred because of the hurried departure: the pressure of time had become paramount, so 'swinging the compass' to check for accuracy was one of numerous things overlooked. *Tayleur* actually carried three compasses, and all gave different headings when checked simultaneously. The fact was that the compasses were operating in the worst possible environment: the compass needles would have been greatly influenced by the magnetic attraction of the iron hull and the three iron masts.

Once *Tayleur* was on the open sea and able to make her own way under sail in a light breeze, the tow was dropped. The tug then went alongside to collect the pilot and 'those parties who had gone out to see their friends off'. Back in Liverpool some days later, after the *Tayleur* tragedy had unfolded, the pilot related a story of 'extraordinary circumstance' that took place when the tug was alongside the ship:

> An Irishman, a passenger, in the confusion and noise that occurred when this steamer went alongside the ship, thought something was radically wrong, and for self-preservation he jumped on board the tug. It was quite dark at the time the tug left the ship, and when the steamer had receded some distance on her course to Liverpool, someone observed a person standing on the paddle box and said to him 'Come down out of that', to which he replied in amazement, 'Where are we going?' and they told him the steamer was going to Liverpool. He appeared to be dreadfully confused and said he wanted to go to Melbourne. The steamer was then put about with a view to putting him on board the ship, but she was going so fast that we could not catch her, and the man was therefore brought to Liverpool as he stood, leaving his clothes and all he had on board – an accident to him, but one which probably saved his life.

Once underway on the Irish Sea, *Tayleur*'s sails were set to suit a course that would have her head west and leave Holyhead on her port side. When well clear of that landmark, it was the captain's intention to turn south-west towards the Atlantic.

However, while the wind was light and conditions most suitable for sailing, additional problems were surfacing. The most alarming of all was the captain's realisation that the ship was not responding to the helm as would be expected. He immediately had crew check the steering system and it was found to be fully operational. This meant there was only one possible cause: the rudder was too small.

Whether it was the pressure that had been exerted on him by his superiors in what was such a highly competitive passenger market, or a belief that the problems could be managed or rectified to some degree as the ship progressed, Noble chose not to turn back, but to press on.

It proved to be a fateful decision.

While the ship sailed into the night, the passengers tried to gain their sea legs and settle into an alien lifestyle in a claustrophobic environment below decks. It was little different for the crew: they were still literally learning the ropes as *Tayleur* continued on.

The first real cause for concern came in the middle of the night: the wind *Tayleur* had been riding so effortlessly and swiftly seaward suddenly faded to the faintest of puffs. This could mean only one thing: a weather change was coming, and it would more than likely be severe.

The frontal system struck like an explosion just minutes later, before the sailors had time to prepare for it by lowering sails or going aloft up the ratlines to reef them. Suddenly sails were either aback or flogging so wildly they sent shudders through the entire ship, while back on the poop deck the helmsman was trying desperately to regain control via a rudder everyone knew by then lacked the size to be effective in such a circumstance. Making matters considerably worse was the inability of the majority of the crew to respond to the orders being shouted by the bosun, simply because they didn't understand what he wanted: of the seventy-one man crew only thirty-seven were trained seamen, and of that number, ten, who came from China and India and were 'working their passage' to Australia, could not comprehend orders at all because they could not speak English.

While men aloft and on deck tried to contain the thrashing sails, the spray blasting over the bulwarks, combined with the driving rain, led to more problems for the untested ship: many of the new halyards, sheets and lines used to raise, lower and trim the sails were swelling so much from the water that they jammed in the pulley blocks. As a result, what should have been an easily executed manoeuvre became a most challenging and dangerous experience. This single problem meant it was taking an hour and a half to furl a sail instead of just fifteen minutes.

Tayleur laboured on through the night while the hundreds of passengers below deck were hanging on and trying not to be thrown out of their bunks each time a large wave caused the already heeling ship to buck and toss.

Daylight the next morning, 20 July, brought no respite. Apart from the fact that it was a bitingly cold winter day, a dense fog had developed on the Irish Sea, and with that came considerably greater challenges for the captain. Because of the heavy cloud, he was unable to use his sextant to take sun sights and accurately calculate the ship's position, so he was forced to use dead-reckoning for navigation. At best, this procedure was a 'guesstimation'. Noble obviously believed the ship was on a safe course in the middle of the Irish Sea, but when making his estimations he had no way of knowing exactly how imprecise his compasses were.

The fog magnified his problems by a considerable margin. It was as if he were sailing blindfold; it would not be possible for the lookout to sight land until the ship was a very short distance from it.

With the storm still delivering testing conditions, *Tayleur* continued on through that day and into the night. At some stage – probably around 9pm – the captain called for a course change to the south in the belief that his ship would then be heading on a safe track towards the Atlantic. But because of the error with the compasses and a dead-reckoning miscalculation, the new course was not to the south; it was still very much towards the coast of Ireland. Also contributing to this mistake was the fact that Noble had not taken into consideration a strong, north-flowing tidal current that was prevailing at the time.

The first source of genuine alarm for the captain and crew came at around 10pm. With the fog having lifted somewhat, land was sighted unexpectedly in the distance off *Tayleur*'s starboard side. A short time later, the lookout let out a shout that was full of fear: 'Breakers on the starboard bow!' The message was rushed back to the captain, who ordered the helmsman to put the helm down hard and change course away from the danger.

But it wasn't enough. Because this was such a hasty manoeuvre, the crew had no time to react, so the sails were not trimmed to suit the new course; instead, *Tayleur* turned broadside to the danger and stopped making headway.

Once he realised that the ship was drifting sideways towards the now very obvious mass of raging white water off to leeward, Noble shouted for both anchors to be released. It was an action that proved to be totally ineffective: the anchor chains snapped like carrots, and *Tayleur's* agonisingly slow drift towards the rocks continued unchecked.

The inevitable followed in the early hours of 21 January. One huge wave lifted the entire ship and dropped her near 4000 tons onto the rocks with such violence that she shuddered from stem to stern.

Minutes later, while women and men screamed in terror, *Tayleur* was destined for destruction. Her iron hull was no match for the force of the huge seas breaking onto the rocks. With the ship already heeling dramatically towards the shore, the hull was breached and icy-cold water burst through the interior. *Tayleur* had struck the eastern end of Lambay Island, just north of Dublin and only 2 nautical miles off the coast of Ireland. She had travelled a mere 100 nautical miles due west from Liverpool.

The respected Irish newspaper *Freeman's Journal* published a dramatic report of what became a terrible maritime tragedy.

The paper told its readers that after the initial impact, *Tayleur* 'rose on the next wave and drove in rather broadside on; and when she struck again, still heavier, the sea made a clean breach over her amidships, setting everything on deck afloat. After three or more shocks, the ship began to sink by the stern, and the passengers rushed up the hatchways screaming and imploring help.'

The three cook's assistants and three other crew members managed to jump ashore from the bow, and soon afterwards 'a rope and a spar were got across and by this means a number of lives were rescued. Those who attempted to escape by the bows of the vessel, all or nearly, met a miserable fate. The moment they fell into the water, the waves caught them and dashed them violently against the rocks, and the survivors on shore could perceive the unfortunate creatures, with their heads bruised and cut open, struggling amidst the waves, and one by one sinking under them.'

The story also recognised the gallant efforts of the ship's surgeon: 'amid the dire confusion and dismay that prevailed, Surgeon Cunningham was everywhere seen trying to restore confidence and courage among the passengers and endeavouring to preserve order and coolness'.

However, tragedy loomed for this brave man:

He was seen crossing the perilous means of escape with his little child on one arm, supporting the infant still more securely by holding its dress in his mouth. The ship heaved on the surge of the sea, the rope swerved, and he was swept from his hold, and his child was torn from him by the force of the sea and perished. He himself sank twice, but at last made good his grip on a projecting point of rock. While in this precarious position, a drowning woman swept by him – he grasped her, and was observed to raise her up, and hold her above the water. He put her hair back from her eyes and seemed to encourage her; but a heavy wave tore her from his grasp, and she perished. Mr Cunningham then seized hold of a rope ladder hanging over the side of the ship, by which he hauled himself on board, hand over hand, and soon after appeared, carrying his wife for the purpose of rescuing her. He nearly succeeded in getting her across the spar by means of the rope, when another heavy wave rushed on and swept off this devoted man and his wife, who were both swept out in the under tow, and drowned in sight of the survivors.

As soon as *Tayleur* was pounded onto the rocks, an attempt was made to launch one of the longboats carried on deck, but the instant it hit the water it was picked up by a massive, surging wave and smashed into splinters. By then, there were hundreds of passengers and crew clinging to the bulwark on the shoreward side of the steeply sloping deck, hanging on for their lives each time an icy wave broke over them.

It was reported later that it appeared the majority of female passengers remained below, in total darkness, in the belief it was safer to be there awaiting rescue than be amid the mayhem on deck. However, when water began surging through the accommodation areas of the now badly holed ship, it was too late for most of the women to make good their escape: *Tayleur* was by now slipping back into deeper water and slowly submerging.

One of the most graphic eyewitness accounts of the tragedy was published in the northern English *Wakefield Journal* on 6 February 1854. It quoted Edward Tew Junior, a banker's son who had been aboard the ship. He said that despite the chaos on deck when *Tayleur* went aground he had no time to be frightened; he knew that if he were to survive he had to retain his senses. Unlike the majority of passengers, he went to the port side of the ship, away from the shore, to plan his escape:

> I sat down for about half a minute and made up my
> mind to swim a rather different direction in order to
> avoid the dead bodies. I then dropped quietly down a
> chain into the water, and had not swum above a couple
> of yards when I saw a boy about ten years old clinging
> to a piece of wood. I immediately made to him; he was
> crying, and told me his mother was drowned. He said it
> was no use my trying to save him, for he should be
> drowned. However, I ... took him by the collar and

placed him on the top of a large spar, and made him take hold of a piece of iron which was standing out. I still had hold of his collar with my right hand, and kept the broken pieces of wood and spars off with my left hand. It was then I experienced difficulties which required almost superhuman efforts to overcome.

A heavy sea was rolling over us every moment, large spars threatening to crush us, and almost perpendicular rocks, as black as death, staring us in the face. Well, I was determined not to have our heads dashed against the rocks, as had been the fate of so many of my fellow passengers. As we neared the rocks, the boy was washed off the spar, but I still had hold of him. I put out my hand to save our heads and received a cut in the hand, but I felt the land and told the boy we were saved. But not so, for we were washed back out again. I made to land a second time and was washed back again. I tried a third time and was treated in the same way. I was making towards the rock a fourth time, determined to save the lad or die with him, when a spar struck him on the right side of his head – the side I had no control over – and entered his skull; it knocked me under at the same time, but I rose again, and a rope was thrown to me, which I twisted around my arm 20 times at least, and with the assistance of a sailor clambered up the rock. I just got there in time to see the whole ship go down.

Tayleur took a countless number of passengers and crew with her when she finally surrendered to the elements and slid stern-first into deep water. Her hull then disappeared beneath the surface of the rough and raging sea, until only the tops of her masts were visible. Bringing added ghastliness to what was already a horrific scene were the hundreds of bodies either floating near the wreck or washed up onto the rocky shoreline, and the continuing plaintive cries that could be heard coming from desperate, drowning people who were still in the water, all beyond help.

In proper maritime tradition, Captain Noble was among the last to leave the ship – or so he thought. After word of the wreck reached nearby Dublin the following day, the steamer *Prince* was promptly sent to search for survivors. When she reached the wreck site, those on board were astounded to see a passenger, William Vivers, still clinging desperately to the top of one of the masts. He was the only survivor found on board that day.

The captain's desperate battle to reach the rocks was also filled with heartbreak. Young Tew later recalled: 'He swam ashore, and two passengers who had assisted him out of the water were both washed back into the sea again and drowned.' Tew also told of another remarkable scene: one Frenchman who was just about to grab hold of a rope attached to the shore 'saw a child sprawling upon the deck. He snatched it up, took hold of its back with his teeth, and carried it safely to shore. The child is unowned.'

After the survivors had either clambered, or been assisted, up an almost sheer 80-foot cliff to the top of Lambay Island, a myriad of miraculous and heart-rending stories began to unfold. Tew would later relate:

> One man had lost six sisters, four brothers, and a
> mother. A German had lost a whole family. Another
> man told me he had lost his brother, his brother's wife,
> her three sisters, and four children; others had lost their
> wives and children.

There were also stories of frustration and an uncaring crew: it was claimed that some had been utterly paralysed by fear and had done nothing to help save the lives of passengers.

Because there were no accurate passenger manifests for *Tayleur*'s voyage, no precise death toll exists. Even so, the nearest estimates are quite horrific. Almost 400 passengers perished, and of the hundred or so women on board only three survived. It was the same terrible count among the seventy children travelling with their parents: only three were saved. One of the few families who did survive were ex-convict Samuel Carby, his wife Sarah and their son Robert. Within days of the tragedy they returned to their home town of Stamford, 75 miles north of London, with only the clothes they were wearing when the ship went down (which, sadly, did not include the underwear into which Sarah had sewn 200 gold sovereigns). The local community rallied to support them and help them re-establish their lives. Incredibly, though, after a short time in Stamford, husband and wife decided they still wanted to travel to Australia – but their teenage son refused to go; understandably, he'd had enough of seafaring. He opted to stay in Stamford with relatives while his parents went to Australia to improve their lot. Many years later, Samuel and Sarah returned to England and their home town; it is not known whether they ever recouped their lost fortune.

Samuel and his wife obviously were not the only survivors of the wreck of *Tayleur* who found the lure of gold still too powerful. Many clearly made a successful second attempt to reach Australia, because it is known that there are several descendants across the country today of survivors of the *Tayleur* tragedy.

Remarkably, just over half a century after the loss of *Tayleur*, there came an extraordinary coincidence in maritime history when the world-famous steamship *Titanic* sank after colliding with an iceberg in the North Atlantic. Both *Tayleur* and *Titanic* were the largest British-built vessels of their type when launched, and both were on their maiden voyages when lost. Moreover, both were sailing under the flag of the White Star Line.

*

Of the hundreds of shipwrecks that occurred on the Australian run during the clipper era, there was one in which many lives could have been lost but weren't. Instead, it became an incident whose circumstances verged on the ridiculous.

Queen of Nations was an 827-ton wooden clipper launched in Aberdeen in 1861. For the next twenty years she sailed the round-the-world passenger and cargo route between London, Sydney and Auckland under the flag of the Aberdeen Line. Tragedy struck in 1879 while the ship was battling a furious storm in the North Atlantic, when her popular and long-serving master, Captain Archibald Donald, was washed overboard and disappeared into a foaming mass of white ocean.

When *Queen of Nations* returned to England, her owners confirmed that Samuel Bache would be her new captain. He was a well-qualified seafarer of French descent who was seen by many as aloof and arrogant. But he was also hiding a major character flaw.

On 23 February 1881, when Bache guided *Queen of Nations* out of the Thames bound for Sydney, as well as carrying passengers she had in her holds a cargo comprising thousands of bottles of fine wines and spirits – products for which Captain Bache held a great liking.

The temptation for a tipple proved too great for both Bache and his first mate even before the ship had cleared the English Channel: they raided the cargo and consequently (according to later reports) remained 'hopelessly drunk' for the entire passage.

In the pre-dawn hours of 31 May 1881, after ninety-seven days at sea, Bache was so intoxicated that he became convinced a slag-heap fire at a coal mine in the hills behind Wollongong was Macquarie Lighthouse at the entrance to Port Jackson, 40 nautical miles to the north. He ordered that *Queen of Nations* be turned to port and hold a course towards the light and enter Sydney Harbour. It wasn't until she was surrounded by a breaking surf that the captain realised he had got it wrong: his ship was sailing straight up Corrimal Beach, just north of Wollongong.

With the ship run aground, passengers and crew, desperate to escape the drunken captain and his equally intoxicated offsider, could not abandon ship quickly enough: they gathered what they could of their possessions and made plans to reach the shore.

Before long, the first mate, realising what was happening, stumbled up the companionway stairs and staggered onto the deck brandishing two pistols. As he wheeled his way around the deck he shouted that anyone who made an attempt to leave the ship would be shot for desertion.

But not even that menacing threat was enough to dissuade those determined to escape. Men, women and children leaped like proverbial lemmings into the sea and waded to the beach as fast as their legs could carry them. The first mate started firing shots at random, but he was so drunk that they all missed their mark.

Salvage operations commenced almost immediately, but within two weeks a savage Tasman Sea storm swept in, bringing waves so powerful that *Queen of Nations* began to break up. The result was that thousands of bottles of alcohol were washed up onto the beach.

The local 'bush telegraph' swung into action, carrying the message that there was booze for the taking on Corrimal Beach. Hundreds of people are said to have rushed there to plunder the 'treasure', setting the scene for a beach party. The local newspaper reported, 'Public drunkenness was common for weeks after the grounding of the clipper ship *Queen of Nations*.' The crowd on the beach became so large and rowdy that the local police could not control the scene, and had to call in reinforcements from Sydney.

But fierce storms and navigational errors – real or ridiculous – were just some of the challenges faced by ships plying the perilous route to the Antipodes.

CHAPTER 6

Fire, Ice and Fever

More peril on the seas

Sea ice and icebergs were a constant threat for ships plying the southern seas in the winter months – a danger that increased considerably when captains decided to sail the shorter and faster composite great circle route, which took them deeper into the higher latitudes.

Just a few weeks after *Lightning* and *Red Jacket* completed their great race to and from Melbourne, the 233-foot, 2000-ton clipper *Guiding Star* – owned by the Golden Line of Liverpool and built at the Wright shipyard in St John, New Brunswick – disappeared when sailing between the Cape of Good Hope and Melbourne.

The American ship *Mercury* reported that she had sighted *Guiding Star* on 12 February 1855 and all had appeared well. Then the captain of the ship *George Marshall* stated on arrival in Melbourne that, when sailing along the same course as *Guiding Star*, his crew had sighted large icebergs and only avoided them by the narrowest of margins. It was calculated that *Guiding Star* – which was carrying 481 passengers, mostly emigrants, plus sixty-two crew – was only thirty-six hours astern of *George Marshall* at the time of these sightings. It is more than likely that either she was trapped by ice or she ploughed into a berg, some of which were known to be more than 20 miles long and over 200 feet high – probably at night.

Of the all-too-numerous ice incidents endured by clipper ships during their reign, probably the most amazing involved the 1000-ton Canadian-built clipper *Indian Queen*, launched in 1853 and likened to *Marco Polo* in design. On Sunday, 13 March 1859, she sailed from Melbourne for Liverpool with Captain Edmond Brewer in charge and forty passengers on board – thirty men, three women and seven children. The ship was described in the Melbourne *Age* and the *Sydney Morning Herald* as 'one of the favourites of the Black Ball Line', while Captain Brewer was said to be 'a gentleman whose ability and conduct have gained him the reputation of being a kind and trustworthy commander'.

On 27 March, while making good speed halfway between Melbourne and Cape Horn at 58 degrees south – the region recognised as the most isolated location on the planet – conditions suddenly changed. A gale swept in from the north-west, accompanied by a dense fog and fast-rising swells. Sails were reefed at a rapid rate but still the ship maintained a good speed over the next four days.

Then, at 2am on 1 April, during a heavy rain squall, *Indian Queen* thundered into a giant iceberg. The violence of the impact hurled sleeping passengers from their bunks, while the shocked crew members on deck could only watch in horror as masts, yards, sails and rigging either came crashing to the deck or went over the side. This included the foremast, which had sheered off at deck level, and the bowsprit, which exploded into pieces and was soon in the water, wrapped around the bow.

The first passengers to rush aft to the poop deck were stunned to discover that *Indian Queen* was lying beam-on against the face of a towering berg. Every person on board, including the crew, was certain that the ship was doomed. Causing added alarm was the fact that there was no one at the helm, neither was there a single on-watch crew member to be seen.

While off-watch crew members and frightened passengers still below deck groped their way through the darkness and scrambled up the companionway ladders, the cool-headed carpenter, Thomas Howard, responded as might be expected of him. He rushed through the ship's interior to the bow to check for hull damage, which, considering the force of the impact, he expected to be extensive. But, much to his amazement, the ship was still sound. He then made his way back to the deck and announced to those assembled there that *Indian Queen* was not taking on water.

However, the second mate, Philip Leyvret, caused some level of alarm when he declared that the captain, the first mate and most of the on-watch crew had taken the port-side lifeboat and abandoned the ship, apparently convinced that she would sink in a matter of minutes. Such had been Captain Brewer's haste to get to the lifeboat that he had even left behind his own son, who was an apprentice on the ship.

On hearing this, the incredulous crowd on deck looked out to the port side and, peering through the darkness, could make out the faint outline of the missing lifeboat a short distance away. On hearing shouts coming from the ship, Captain Brewer and those with him aboard the lifeboat became convinced *Indian Queen* would remain afloat, so they immediately made efforts to return. Leyvret told of what followed:

> When coming alongside, a back sea [a large backwash coming off the iceberg] filled and swamped the boat. Immediately, the life buoys and a number of spars and ropes were thrown to the struggling crew, but to no effect, they were all drowned.

Leyvret, now the senior officer on board, quickly took control of the situation. He ordered the few remaining seamen, with the assistance of capable passengers, to cut away what they could of the mast, spars and rigging draped across *Indian Queen's* deck. As daylight broke, Leyvret implemented a plan to free the ship from the ice by back-winding at least one of the sails. This proved to be an excellent manoeuvre: the ship slowly drifted along the face of the iceberg, before clearing a corner and freeing herself from it.

But fate would rule that *Indian Queen* was still not out of danger. While some men, including passengers, worked to remove the remaining wreckage and others set about establishing a jury rig so the ship could get back under sail, a shrill and panicked cry was heard: 'Ice to leeward!' Another huge iceberg was looming out of the fog, and *Indian Queen* was heading straight for it.

Leyvret immediately called for the few inefficient sails to be trimmed, in the hope that this would see the ship clear the imminent danger. Tension filled the air as *Indian Queen*, with debris still being dragged behind her, continued to drift towards the menacing berg.

Only 100 metres separated her from the towering mountain of ice when she was finally deemed safe. Moments later, the remnants of a jury-rigged mast crashed to the deck unannounced, and ironically destroyed the one remaining lifeboat.

After a repair effort that lasted many hours, Leyvret decided that the best possible rig had been created from the barely adequate remnants of masts, spars and sails. He then assembled the passengers and remaining crew and advised them that their only option, if they were to have any chance of surviving, was to turn the seriously damaged ship to the north-east and sail almost 4000 nautical miles to Válparaiso in Chile.

After averaging a mere 4 knots over forty days, and enduring a raft of savage gales and rough seas, the battered *Indian Queen* – with her bowsprit and much of her rig missing – limped into Valparaiso, to the relief of everyone on board.

Yet *Indian Queen* was far from being alone when it came to life-threatening clipper encounters with icebergs: even the famous *Marco Polo* went close to being claimed by an icy mass mid-ocean. On 4 March 1861, on a passage from Melbourne, when sailing in the same region where *Indian Queen* had come to grief, *Marco Polo* struck an iceberg and was so badly damaged that the captain considered making the call to abandon ship. Her bowsprit was smashed to splinters, her foremast fractured and her bow stove in so badly that the leaks could not be stopped.

After working for many hours, the crew had the situation stabilised, so the captain's decision was to head for Valparaiso. It took *Marco Polo* more than a month to get there, and during that time, the pumps were operated constantly so that she would stay afloat. Following repairs that took four months to complete, *Marco Polo* sailed for Liverpool. She reached there 183 days after departing Melbourne.

*

While icebergs were a constant threat to the clippers during the southern-hemisphere winter months, fire was another great danger. There is no doubt that a number of ships literally disappeared en route because an uncontrollable fire erupted on board. Generally there were two causes: spontaneous combustion in the holds – especially when wool, hay or similar flammable cargoes were being carried – or a naked flame that took hold in an area such as the galley, a passenger's cabin or the bosun's locker forward. The danger of fire was so great that ships' captains would not tolerate any act that might imperil their vessel.

This was illustrated on 12 January 1855, when the great clipper ship *Lightning* could well have been lost to a fire at sea. The incident was reported in the ship's on-board newspaper:

> About 8pm an alarm of fire was given and great
> excitement prevailed throughout the ship. This danger
> was caused by a drunken woman in the second cabin,
> who set fire to her bonnet; it was soon extinguished and
> the woman put in irons and confined in the 'black hole'
> for the night as a warning.

A fire in a cargo hold was the most dangerous and difficult to contain. On most occasions, it would already have smouldered for a considerable time before finally bursting into flames and sending charcoal-coloured smoke belching through hatches to signal its presence.

Unfortunately the fire-fighting techniques used aboard the wooden-hulled ships were basic, so the chances of

Stability calculations: American John Willis Griffiths, the free-thinking designer of the first true clipper ship, created this diagram in 1854 to display a ship's heeling angle in different sea states. *From 'Treatise on marine and naval architecture; or, Theory and practice blended in ship building' by John Willis Griffiths, 1854 via the Internet Archive*

Masterly man of maps: Portrait of Commander Matthew F. Maury, first superintendent of the United States Naval Observatory. Maury is recognised as the father of the science of oceanography. *Library of Congress*

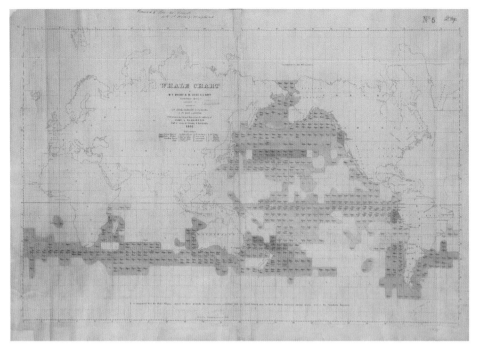

Whale map: The importance of the mid-19th-century American whaling industry is documented in this innovative thematic map by Matthew F. Maury. By collecting data from various sources including logs from whaling ships, Maury compiled this map showing the distribution of several different species of whales, identifying each with a combination of colour and pictorial symbols. *Norman B. Leventhal Map Center at the Boston Public Library*

Proud of their work: The owners of Alexander Hall & Co shipbuilders in Aberdeen, Scotland, along with office staff and shipwrights pose in front of two ships under construction in 1862. The company operated from 1790 to 1957. *Aberdeen Maritime Museum ABDMS018985*

The Way They Go To California: This gold rush cartoon from c1850 shows a New York dock crowded with men with picks and shovels, and men jumping from the dock to reach ships bound for San Francisco. A crowded airship and a man on a rocket fly overhead while a man with a pick and shovel parachutes from the airship. *Library of Congress LC-DIG-pga-05072*

The Way They Come From California: A companion piece to the cartoon above, shows a ship, carrying a full load of successful gold diggers, departing San Francisco for New York while others beg not to be left behind. *Library of Congress LC-DIG-pga-05070*

Rapid transport: An advertisement c1850 promotes the purpose-built new clipper ship, *California*, for the passage from New York to the west coast gold fields. *Wikicommons*

A remarkable seafaring lady: In 1856 Mary Ann Brown Patten took command of the clipper ship, *Neptune's Car*, after her husband fell ill, and navigated it safely from Cape Horn to San Francisco. *National Portrait Gallery, Smithsonian Institution; gift of Dorthy Knouse Koepke*

Canvas Town 1853: Newly arrived immigrants seated with their baggage in front of tents and wooden huts in Melbourne. *Artist Edmund Thomas Newly, State Library of Victoria H15520*

Purchasing a passage: Diggers in a shipping agent's office in Melbourne, probably arranging a return passage to England. The names of the ships on the wall behind include the *Marco Polo*. *Artist T Gill. State Library of Victoria H86.7/39 S.*

Digger on the dock: Newly arrived Chinese men on Sandridge Pier, in Melbourne, seeking directions to the gold fields from a successful digger in a checked shirt and cap. *Artist George Thompson, State Library of Victoria H12631*

Prospecting for a husband: Single ladies preparing to depart Melbourne and head to the goldfields with the hope of finding a husband. *State Library of Victoria H81.35*

Man the yards: Perched precariously on the foot ropes while hanging on for dear life on the windward yard, crew tend a sail on a clipper ship. *State Library of Victoria Acc No: H87.63/2/8 Artist Charles Lyall.*

Riding out a gale: The auxiliary steamer *Queen of the South* rides out a gale in heavy seas – sailors aloft preparing to furl one of the square sails. *Sailors Reefing Topsails* by Charles Lyall c1854. *State Library of Victoria H87.63/6a*

A hammering at The Horn: An artist's impression of a ship rounding Cape Horn in extreme weather. *Library of Congress LC-DIG-pga-05031*

Tough going: A clipper ship in a hurricane. *Library of Congress LC-DIG-pga-04760*

One of the classics: An impression of the record-breaking ship *Marco Polo* painted by marine artist Thomas Robertson in 1859. Robertson spent much of his early life at sea. *SLV H306*

James Nicol 'Bully' Forbes: A graphite on paper drawing of the legendary man himself. *Bridgeman Art Library FIT423998*

Francis Henty: a small clipper ship that was one of the more popular vessels with passengers sailing between England and Australia until 1869. Her cargo on the return run to England usually comprised gold and wool. *Portland showing the ship Francis Henty by Thomas Robertson 1858. State Library of Victoria H13791*

Legend Donald McKay: the pioneering American shipbuilder who led the way with the design and construction of vessels for much of the clipper ship era. *The Metropolitan Museum of Art Acc no:37.14.1*

Finer detail: Passenger contract ticket for Elizabeth Pratt (aged 44) and her son Edward (aged 15) for steerage passage from London to Melbourne on the Black Ball Line clipper ship *Netherby*, departing 25 April 1862. The cost of the ticket was £28 paid in full. *Museum Victoria item 806694*

A haunting night: An impression of the wreck of *Dunbar* by S.T. Gill, c1866, based on information from the sole survivor. *Mitchell Library, State Library of New South Wales a939035 / PXA 1983, f34*

Hard aground: the stranding of the immigrant ship *City of Adelaide*, near Port Adelaide in 1874. *Australasian sketcher. State Library of Victoria A/S03/10/74/108*

A fine vessel: the magnificent *Sobraon* was the largest and most impressive of all clippers built in the UK. *State Library of Queensland Acc No: 2967/11*

Dangerous dining: passengers and crew doing the best they could to dine aboard *Sobraon* in rough weather. *National Library of Australia nla.obj-135546088*

A JOLLY GAME.

IMITATIVE INNOCENT : Here's a lark, Jemmy. This here ship's the Schomberg, and that there gas pipe's a hice berg. Now you see how close I can go without touching.

Schomberg **and the iceberg:** one boy eggs on another to see how close he can get his toy boat to a pipe in a stream without hitting it … their re-enactment of the incident where *Schomberg* reportedly went close to hitting a 'berg. *State Library of Victoria MP00/00/56/197, Melbourne Punch*

CLIPPER SHIP "RED JACKET".

Red Jacket **in ice:** the scene when famous clipper ship *Red Jacket* was trapped by ice near Cape Horn while on her passage from Australia to Liverpool in 1854. *Library of Congress LC-DIG-pga-03627*

BLOWING OUT OF THE SHIP'S STERN.

Tragedy on the high seas: the clipper ship *Cospatrick* explodes and sinks mid-ocean in 1875 with the loss of 473 lives. *The Australasian sketcher, State Library of Victoria A/S20/03/75/201b March 20, 1875*

DEATH OF CAPTAIN ELMSLIE.

To the end: Captain Elmslie carries his wife to the side of *Cospatrick* from where they leapt into the ocean, dying together. *State Library of Victoria A/S20/03/75/201d*

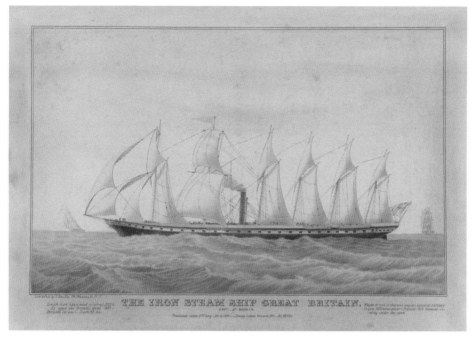

One mighty ship: in 1853 the massive steamship, SS *Great Britain*, became the first commercial vessel of its type to sail between England and Australia. *Library of Congress LC-DIG-pga-05234*

First and foremost: Captain Barnard R. Mathews was the master of SS *Great Britain* on her maiden voyage to the Antipodes. *State Library of Victoria H38678*

Passage denied: Ships at anchor by the Port Said entrance to the Suez Canal, c1860, shortly before the canal was opened. The Suez Canal was unsuited to sailing vessels and thus hastened the end of the age of the clipper ships. *Library of Congress LC-DIG-ppmsca-04472*

The last of the clippers: Launched in 1869, *Cutty Sark* was the fastest, sleekest ship of its time. By 1922, approximately the time this photo was taken, she was the last fully operational clipper ship anywhere in the world. *State Library of Victoria*

extinguishing a large blaze were remote. The likelihood of there being another ship in the region that could come to the rescue was equally slim.

One of the more miraculous escapes from what had seemed certain death for 227 souls – 180 passengers and forty-seven crew – travelling between Liverpool and Melbourne occurred in August 1857, when the Black Ball Line clipper *Eastern City*, under the command of Captain Johnstone, caught fire in an isolated locale – 2500 nautical miles west-north-west of Cape Town, and nearly 1000 nautical miles from the east coast of South America.

At 2pm on 23 August, when *Eastern City* was lumbering her way south-east in a half-gale and heavy seas, great alarm spread rapidly on deck when the shout came that smoke could be seen coming from the forehatch near the bow. Immediately the captain and some of the crew, assisted by able-bodied male passengers, removed the hatch in the hope that they would be able to spot the source of the fire and take appropriate action. But the smoke was so dense and suffocating that they were repelled.

A passenger – Mr J. Fowler – later provided to the *Cape Argus*, a Cape Town newspaper, an accurate account of how the drama unfolded:

> The passengers and crew were ordered on deck, and we then believed they had all obeyed the order; but it was afterwards discovered that one of the steerage

passengers, named Peter Maclean, belonging to the Isle
of Skye, was missing.

Sadly, it was later revealed that Maclean had been ill in his
bunk for many days and had probably suffocated.

Fowler then explained that crew members, aided by
passengers, poured down the forehatch 'vast quantities' of
water, being drawn from the sea using a steam pump.
Meanwhile, Captain Johnstone had hauled up the majority of
sails and turned the ship downwind. All her lifeboats were
provisioned and readied so that they could be lowered over the
side 'at a moment's notice'. Fowler continued:

> The women and children, about 60 in number, were
> removed to the poop, where the captain had placed
> numbers of old sails, carpets, etc., and did everything he
> could to make them as comfortable as possible under
> those terrible circumstances.
>
> All that long and dreadful night both passengers and
> crew continued to work without intermission, pouring
> tons of water down the hatches and forepart of the
> vessel; holes were also cut in the deck, and engine
> pumps and buckets went to work … the captain
> cheering us all the while, and never leaving the deck for
> a moment. I could not but admire his calm courage,
> surrounded as he was on the poop with so many
> weeping women and children, whom he never ceased

to comfort by the assurance that they would all soon be safe in the boats.

The majority of passengers, however, were unaware of the full extent of the danger they faced. The captain and crew knew that with the sea so rough, there was no possible way that any of the ship's boats, which inevitably would be grossly overloaded, would not capsize.

On the morning of 24 August, it was realised that the fire was working its way aft below deck and beginning to burn its way through the foredeck. At midday, the foremast fell to the deck in spectacular fashion, but fortunately no one was injured. Those passengers not directly involved in the efforts to fight the fire spent much of their time standing atop the aftermost cabin, scanning the horizon in the hope that they might sight the sails of another ship. But the odds of that were extremely remote: *Eastern City* was now well wide of the course that ships en route to Australia or Asia would normally take.

Yet fate was about to intervene in an extraordinary way, as Fowler recounted:

At about 2.30pm, when about to say goodbye in case of not meeting again before the final catastrophe, we were startled with the cry of 'a sail'. I do not know how we all tumbled on deck but we were there in an instant. How I looked to windward and how faint and ill I felt when I at first failed to perceive anything but the ocean and a few black clouds just at the edge of the horizon; [then] how we all at last saw the sail just like a distant gull – she was coming down upon us.

Great joy immediately seized the hearts of passengers and crew; some thanked the Lord, while others laughed, hugged and cheered. As Fowler put it, 'men who had probably never prayed before muttered sincere thanksgivings, and ... those who had preserved the greatest indifference when death seemed so near, were now completely overcome'.

The vessel, the British ship *Merchantman*, was sailing from England to Calcutta with a full complement of troops on board. It was later revealed that, earlier in the day, someone on board that ship had sighted a pall of smoke on the horizon and alerted the captain, who had immediately changed course towards it.

It took only a matter of hours for boats from both ships to safely transfer all the passengers to *Merchantman*, which then changed course towards Cape Town, where they would be put ashore.

As *Merchantman* progressed in that direction, it soon became obvious to Fowler and the other survivors how pivotal a role fate, or some other power, had played in their rescue:

We were all truly thankful for our preservation from a terrible and inevitable death, and we all feel that the finger of Providence was in it, for, had *Merchantman* not been obliged to put into Rio de Janeiro in consequence of the illness of the medical officer then in charge of the troops, then [she] could not have been so far out of her course and in a position to rescue us.

*

The 235-foot Yankee clipper *Blue Jacket* met a similar fate. Launched in Boston in 1854 and considered one of the fastest vessels of the day, she plied the Australian and New Zealand run out of England for the next fifteen years. On 13 February 1869, she departed Lyttelton in New Zealand for Liverpool with seventy-one people aboard and a cargo comprising mainly flax. Also locked safely away in a security compartment was more than £63,000 worth of Kiwi gold destined for English banks.

In late February, after riding the summer westerly weather systems across the southern seas without incident, *Blue Jacket* rounded Cape Horn and changed course towards the Falkland Islands, 330 nautical miles to the north-east.

On 1 March, the cargo of flax burst into flame, probably a spontaneous combustion. All efforts to control the fire over the following days failed, so on 9 March, the captain called for the ship to be abandoned. The passengers and crew took to the lifeboats, and one week later, the German barque *Pyrmont* rescued nine survivors from one of the boats. Fortuitously, they had with them the gold that had been aboard *Blue Jacket*.

The other sixty-two souls perished. However, there was an eerie reminder of the tragedy nearly three years later when *Blue Jacket*'s figurehead, a representation of an old sailor wearing a blue jacket with yellow buttons, was washed up on Rottnest Island, off Fremantle, Western Australia, after having drifted some 10,000 nautical miles. Despite being encrusted with barnacles and weed, it was still easily identifiable.

*

One of the worst tragedies involving fire in the era of the clipper ships involved the emigrant ship *Cospatrick*, a 190-foot, 1200-ton Blackwall frigate. On 11 September 1874, she departed London with her longtime commander, Captain Elmslie, in charge. She was bound for Auckland with 429 migrant passengers aboard – 177 men, 125 women, fifty-eight boys, fifty-three girls and sixteen infants aged under twelve months. The crew comprised forty-three officers, able seamen and boys. Four other independent passengers making the voyage took the total number on board to 476.

At 12.30am on 18 November, when *Cospatrick* was 350 nautical miles south-west of the Cape of Good Hope and heading into the southern seas, the bosun's locker in the forward section of the ship erupted in flames. It was later presumed that the cause of the fire was spontaneous combustion among stored paints, oils, rags and coal dust, although it was also speculated that a crew member might have dropped a lantern or candle in the locker while trying to break through the bulkhead and into a cargo hold with the intention of stealing rum, brandy or wine, which were stowed there along with flammable goods, including turpentine.

While passengers rushed to the deck in their night attire, the captain and crew made desperate efforts to turn the ship downwind so that the smoke and flames would be contained in the forward section of the ship. This manoeuvre was unsuccessful, so all on deck could only watch in horror as the inferno burst through the deck and started moving aft.

In less than an hour, it was obvious that *Cospatrick* was doomed, and with that realisation, passengers – mothers, fathers and children – began rushing to the ship's boats, which were already suspended from their davits and hanging over the side. People leaped into them with no consideration for numbers or safety.

One boat, which was thought to have as many as eighty people crammed into it, was so overloaded that the davits buckled under the weight of the panicked passengers. The boat crashed into the boiling sea and capsized immediately, and all were drowned.

The flames spread so rapidly that lifeboats located towards the bow were either aflame or destroyed when the blazing foremast came down. This disaster immediately sealed the fate of those remaining on deck: there were no boats left to give them any chance of escape.

It appears that only two boats were successfully launched, with a total of just sixty-two people on board. Those fortunate few could only watch in a state of shock as the flames continued to spread throughout the ship, their horror turning to dread as they heard the panicked screams of terrified people facing certain death.

It is known that Captain Elmslie, his wife, their son and the ship's medico, Dr Cadle, remained on board until the very end, which came within forty-eight hours. By then, *Cospatrick* was little more than a flaming hulk almost from stem to stern, with some sections of her topsides burned to near the waterline. All three masts, blackened and broken, were hanging over the sides.

When it was apparent that his ship would soon be consigned to the depths, Captain Elmslie was seen to throw his wife over the side and leap into the ocean after her, while Dr Cadle jumped overboard at the same time with the couple's four year old son in his arms. In preference to being burned alive, they all drowned together.

Considering how far *Cospatrick* was from land, those aboard the two boats that managed to clear the ship were no doubt convinced they too would die. But they were determined not to give up hope, even though they had no food or water with them.

Despite their best efforts to stay together, a storm swept in a matter of days later and separated the two boats. One, containing thirty men and no women, had three experienced sailors on board: the second mate, Charles Macdonald, the quartermaster, Thomas Lewis, and ordinary seaman Edward Cotter, aged eighteen. If they had any good fortune, it was that there was one oar on the boat, and that a girl's petticoat had somehow found its way on board. This enabled them to create a makeshift sail and steer in the general direction of land to the north-east.

It was possibly because of this 'sail' that the British ship *Sceptre*, which miraculously came over the horizon seven days later, spotted the small boat and rescued the survivors. By then, only five of the thirty were still alive, the rest having died from hunger, thirst and exposure. In their desperate last-ditch bid to survive, those five had resorted to cannibalism: they had drunk the blood of some of the deceased and eaten their livers for nourishment.

With those five men aboard, *Sceptre* then changed course towards Cape Town, but sadly, during this passage, two more of the survivors died. Of the 476 men, women and children who had sailed from England aboard *Cospatrick*, Macdonald, Lewis and Cotter were the only ones who lived to tell the story of the ill-fated voyage.

*

By no means all of the conflagrations that destroyed the great clippers occurred at sea.

On 4 October 1853, the day when the fateful *Tayleur* was launched as 'the largest merchantman ever built in Britain', a similarly significant maritime event took place on the opposite side of the Atlantic. As many as 50,000 people took advantage of what was declared a public holiday and crowded around Donald McKay's shipyard in Boston to view the launch of the largest wooden clipper ship ever constructed: *Great Republic* – a vessel that was expected to help meet the seemingly insatiable need for passages out of England to the Australian gold rush.

Great Republic's dimensions were gargantuan: 335 feet in hull length – as long as a Boston city block – and a mighty beam of 53 feet. Because she was so large, her rig was unique for a clipper: instead of three, she had four masts, which between them could carry fifty sails. Her rig configuration was that of a barque, meaning that the three forward masts – the tallest of which speared nearly 250 feet skywards – were square-rigged, while the mizzenmast carried fore and aft sails.

McKay, not only had built her but was also responsible for her radical design, was taking a huge gamble with this project. *Great Republic*, with a Gross Registered Tonnage (GRT) of 4555 tons, had cost well in excess of $300,000 to build – some estimates go as high as $450,000 – and had taken a year to complete. Her construction costs reflected the enormous escalation in McKay's ambitions over a period of just three years: *Stag Hound*, 1534 GRT, had cost $45,000 to build in 1850, *Flying Cloud* (1782 tons) $50,000 in 1851, and *Sovereign of the Seas* (2241 tons) $100,000 in 1852.

Not surprisingly, because of her incredible size, *Great Republic*'s construction consumed more timber than any other clipper: 1,500,000 feet of hard pine, more than 2000 tons of white oak, 336 tons of iron (for cross-bracing the hull structure) and 56 tons of copper (primarily fastenings). The crew, to comprise 100 men and thirty boys, were to have the benefit of steam-driven winches mounted on deck to assist with the raising of yards and sails, as well as the lifting of cargo and the anchor.

McKay had no buyer committed to *Great Republic* at the time of her launch. Yet he remained undaunted. Through this new ship, he was determined once again to confirm to the world that he stood at the forefront of clipper-ship design and construction.

There was an element of panic in the lead-up to the ship's naming ceremony and launch when it was discovered that the Champagne that was to be smashed across the bow had apparently been consumed the night before, at an impromptu pre-launch party involving McKay's eldest son and some of the shipyard's leading hands. So, at midday, according to an observer, 'amid the roar of artillery, the music of bands and cheers of the multitude', backed by the peal of church bells, a bottle of pure water from nearby Lake Cochituate was smashed across the ship's bow by the shipyard supervisor, Captain Alden Gifford. As the bottle exploded and the water ran down her topsides, Gifford declared her name would be *Great Republic*.

McKay's inspiration for this name came from the poem 'O Ship of State', written by one of his great admirers, Henry

Wadsworth Longfellow. Its words metaphorically related the construction of great ships to the powerful expansion of the United States of America on land and sea:

> Thou, too, sail on, O Ship of State!
> Sail on, O Union, strong and great!
> Humanity with all its fears,
> With all the hopes of future years,
> Is hanging breathless on thy fate!

Over the next six weeks *Great Republic* remained in Boston so her fit-out could be completed and her rig made ready. Her design featured four decks, the lower decks being for cargo and the remainder to cater for all classes of passengers, and the first-class accommodation included two large and superbly appointed cabins on the main deck. One of these was described by an observer as 'beautifully wainscoted with mahogany' and decorated with 'recessed sofas on each side, ottomans, marble-covered tables, mirrors and elliptical panels ornamented with pictures'.

By the time *Great Republic*'s fit-out was finished, McKay had negotiated a charter deal for her in Liverpool with the Black Ball Line. She was not scheduled to sail from New York to Liverpool until later in the year, but already the Black Ball Line was promoting her as 'the largest, finest and fastest vessel to sail to Melbourne'.

Yet disaster would soon interrupt that boast.

On the night of 26 December 1853, when *Great Republic* was docked in New York and being loaded with cargo destined for Liverpool, an intense fire broke out in a nearby bakery, sending embers high into the sky. *Great Republic* and four other ships – the clippers *White Squall*, *Red Rover* and *Whirlwind* and the packet ship *Joseph Walker* – were lying directly downwind of the fire, and in little time the embers set fire to sails, masts and rigging.

The firefighters did not have equipment that would allow them to spray water high enough into the rigs of the ships to douse the flames. Before long, blazing canvas sails and timber were crashing down onto the ships' decks, setting their hulls on fire. *Joseph Walker*, *White Squall* and *Whirlwind* were burned to the waterline and *Red Rover* was badly damaged. *Great Republic* was declared a total loss by insurers after the fire was extinguished. Inspection of her smoking hulk confirmed that her entire top deck and rig had been destroyed.

Great Republic would never see Australia. The blackened hulk was sold and subsequently rebuilt minus the top deck, then later re-rigged with only three masts, all shorter than the originals. Even so, under this new configuration she made some impressively fast passages across the Atlantic to Liverpool, and from America to Japan.

*

While raging tempests, fire and icebergs were the greatest threats to the safety of those aboard sailing ships as they crisscrossed the world's oceans, disease also took a terrible toll on many occasions. The combination of poor hygiene, unsanitary conditions and claustrophobic confinement in damp, dingy and poorly ventilated accommodation – especially among steerage-class passengers – could fuel this problem faster than it could be contained.

One of the primary sources for the spread of disease and illness was the toilet facilities provided for the lower-class passengers. They generally consisted of an open bucket and a vinegar-soaked rag hanging on a peg behind a door; the already unhealthy environment became extremely odious when the contents of the bucket spilled over in rough weather.

Taking a bath was not permitted on the majority of ships, as it consumed too much precious fresh water. This meant that those with any desire for personal hygiene made do by occasionally using a damp cloth to wipe themselves over while lying under a blanket on their bunk. The limited access to fresh water also meant clothes could not be washed, so in many cases passengers were known to have worn the same attire for the entire voyage.

When, in 1851, the British Government voted to relax the rules regarding the number of children allowed to migrate to Australia, there was an immediate surge in applicants wanting to venture to the colonies. To meet this demand, the Colonial Land and Emigration Commission undertook to partially, if not completely, fund the fares of poorer families and individuals wanting to start a new life. The commission also chartered a number of ships to carry them to their new homeland, and in 1852, one of the ships chosen for the task was the 169-foot New York clipper *Ticonderoga*. One of her more appealing aspects when being considered for charter was the fact that she had twin accommodation decks, which meant far more passengers than usual could be carried, effectively doubling the ship's carrying capacity. However, this very feature was the reason why she soon became known as 'the fever ship'.

When *Ticonderoga* sailed from Liverpool on 4 August 1852, there were 795 migrants on board, the majority being Highland Scots. Commanded by Thomas H. Boyle, the ship's crew comprised forty-eight men, including Dr J.C. Sanger, the surgeon superintendent, and his assistant Dr James Veitch.

Within days of departure, it was apparent that the health of all on board was being compromised by the cramped conditions. Second-class passengers were complaining that there was barely room for one person in cabins intended to accommodate four people. It was so bad for some that they chose to sleep elsewhere on boxes and bags of produce, instead of having to endure the stifling proximity of other passengers in their tiny sleeping quarters.

But it was the design of the ship's interior that was the root of the problem: each time the decks were washed in a bid to maintain some level of hygiene, there was not sufficient circulation of air to dry out the accommodation areas. Water would constantly drip through the gaps in the planking, so that the atmosphere remained moist and damp: the perfect breeding ground for disease.

Two weeks into the voyage, there were signs that typhus – with its debilitating symptoms of fever, red rashes, diarrhoea and ultimately delirium bordering on insanity – was taking hold. Unbeknown to the medical world at the time, the disease was spread by lice.

Within a month, it was approaching epidemic proportions among the almost 800 passengers on board *Ticonderoga*. One passenger later described how ten of the deceased were bundled together in a fabric shroud and buried at sea as one.

With so many falling ill, the ship's medicos – both of whom succumbed to the disease at some stage – were quickly running out of the necessary medical supplies. However, Captain Boyle pressed on regardless.

After ninety horrible days at sea, *Ticonderoga* was finally in sight of Port Phillip. A crewman went to the mainmast and hoisted to the masthead the yellow flag signifying that there was a serious medical emergency on board. By then, 100 passengers and crew – men, women and children – had contracted typhus and died; another 300 were still suffering from it, which meant that more than half of all on board had been infected by the disease.

Once inside Port Phillip Bay, Captain Boyle turned his ship to the east and anchored off Point Nepean, which he deemed to be a safe anchorage and suitably isolated for quarantine requirements. He immediately sent a boat ashore so crew members could mark out a not-to-be-entered quarantine area by setting up yellow flags on stakes and painting white marks on trees. He also had makeshift tents erected using some of the ship's spars and sails.

The moment news of *Ticonderoga*'s plight reached Melbourne, the colonial government organised for doctors, medical supplies and food to be rushed to the area by boat. Two privately owned homes at Point Nepean were also requisitioned and placed under government control until the crisis was over. Despite these efforts, another eighty-two passengers died onshore.

Subsequently, a report prepared for the Immigration Board in Melbourne relating to conditions aboard *Ticonderoga* stated:

> The ship, especially the lower part, was in a most filthy
> state, and did not appear to have been cleaned for
> weeks, the stench was overpowering, the lockers so
> thoughtlessly provided for the Immigrants' use were full
> of dirt, mouldy bread, and suet full of maggots.

Another report, prepared by the Port Health Officer, Dr Hunt, confirmed that the mortality had been occasioned by the crowded state of the ship's decks and want of proper ventilation, particularly through the lower deck. A report in the Melbourne *Argus* on 5 November 1852 declared: 'this case clearly exhibits the cruelty and ill-judged policy of crowding such a number of people on board a single ship, no matter her size, for a lengthened voyage'.

Around this same time, passengers on two other ships sailing from England to Melbourne were also ravaged by typhus. When the news of *Ticonderoga*'s fate and the loss of life on the other ships reached England, the Colonial Land and Emigration Commission announced that it would no longer use twin-deck vessels for its voyages to Australia.

*

As is evident above, whether it was fire, ice or fever that claimed so many vessels, at least their destruction could be put down to a tangible cause. But in the era when the clippers ruled the seas, there were many occasions when only the unfathomable hand of fate could account for a ship's mysterious disappearance, or the miraculous rescue of her passengers and crew in the face of seemingly certain death.

CHAPTER 7

Miracles and Misadventure

Strange disappearances and extraordinary rescues

It is safe to say that through misadventure, or the *force majeure* that comes when the weather is in its foulest mood, thousands of passengers and crew disappeared without trace during the period of mass migration to the Antipodes in the mid- to late nineteenth century.

To peruse historic documents detailing ships lost sailing to or from Australia during the days of the clippers can seem like reading an abridged horror story. All too often the references make it clear that the ship simply vanished: 'not seen again', 'did not arrive', 'lost without trace' or 'believed to have foundered off Cape Horn'.

The disappearance of *Blervie Castle* – a wooden ship of 616 tons, built in 1857 for Duncan Dunbar – fell into this category. She sailed from London in late 1859, bound for Adelaide with fifty-seven passengers and crew aboard. Her first port of call was to be Plymouth, just 300 nautical miles south of London, but she didn't arrive. It wasn't until wreckage, and some personal possessions belonging to passengers, washed up on the coast of France some time later that it became apparent the ship had foundered somewhere in the English Channel.

Then there was *Ariel*, a 197-foot, 853-ton clipper ship that had achieved international fame in the 1860s for her remarkably fast passages when carrying tea between China and England. On 31 January 1872, she set out from London bound for Sydney with a load of cargo but never reached her destination. The only clue to her fate was the discovery in August 1872 of a wooden lifeboat on King Island that featured a brass mounting marked with the letter 'A' in gothic script.

There were two theories as to what happened: she either struck an iceberg and sank, or foundered when pooped by a marauding and monstrous wave while running down her easting, having rounded the Cape of Good Hope. The latter possibility seems more likely bearing in mind what Captain Keay wrote of his experiences in the southern seas when in command of *Ariel*:

> Running east, about 42° S latitude, carrying main topgallant sail, gale and sea quarterly with a turbulent confused swell she began to sit down aft and the sea, curling over both quarters, filled the decks to the rails [the top of the bulwarks]. I quickly took in the main topgallant and all sail off the mizzen, and she rose kindly to her work like one relieved of a load.

He went on to elaborate the challenges he faced as captain when sailing a clipper through the night in a bitterly cold gale in which he and his men were soaked to the skin:

> ... the gale burst forth from the south. I called all hands and we struggled for fully two hours to furl all [sails] except fore and mizzen topsails, but had to let the foresail hang in the gear ... and call the men down from aloft. To see – as well as the dismal darkness and blinding seas and spray would allow us – how she went into and over the mountainous nor-west seas as we steered about N.N.W. was a caution. The log was hove after the men came down from aloft, and she was going 10 knots, with only her lower topsails at fore and main [masts], into a howling gale against that fearful sea.
>
> I was secured near the helmsman, and he had a rope round him with scope enough for his arms. The binnacle light was washed out several times, but the splendid man at the wheel kept her going all right. He steered with the feel of the wind on his back and his neck and a little help [from a standby helmsman] now and then till we could see the compass again.
>
> When the first green seas came along the deck, the hen coops, which, under the monkey poop close aft, were snug enough in most weathers, were in an instant all swept overboard; and the piteous, loud screams of the fowls was like a human cry in agony, tough hushed in a moment.

'Twas very eerie, I assure you, and never to be
forgotten.

*

The vanishing of *Madagascar* is a mystery that has led to great
speculation for more than 150 years – almost as baffling, in fact,
as the famous disappearance of *Mary Celeste* two decades later.
Madagascar, a large Blackwaller launched in 1837 for the trade
to India and China, set sail from Melbourne on 12 August 1853
bound for London, and was never heard of again.

When she reached Melbourne with a nearly full
complement of migrants on board, fourteen of her sixty crew
members had immediately jumped ship and headed for the
goldfields. By the time she had been prepared for her return
voyage – with 110 passengers and a cargo of wool, rice and
more than 2 tons of gold, valued at £240,000 – only three of
the absent crew had been replaced.

When *Madagascar* failed to arrive in London, speculation
abounded relating to her fate. Some suggested that
spontaneous combustion had set aflame the wool she was
carrying in her cargo area below the lower deck, while others
were sure she had hit an iceberg. The most controversial
theory of all, however, is that she was seized by criminals
disguised as legitimate travellers; after murdering all on board,
they sailed to land, removed the cargo of gold then scuttled
the ship.

Popular legend has it that this mutiny was connected with an extraordinary event that delayed *Madagascar*'s departure from Melbourne. The captain, Fortescue William Harris, had planned to leave two days earlier than when the ship eventually departed – but as he was preparing to sail, Victorian police went aboard and arrested one of the passengers, John Francis. They returned to the ship the following day to arrest another passenger, and a third man who was preparing to board. They were soon identified as Francis's brother, George, and friend George Wilson.

These three men were wanted in connection with what became known as Australia's first big gold heist: the McIvor Gold Escort Robbery. On 20 July 1853, a horse-drawn dray laden with gold from the McIvor diggings (modern Heathcote) was attacked by bushrangers. At the time, it was on a trip of about 80 miles along rough dirt roads from Heathcote to Kyneton then south to Melbourne. A report of the incident in the *Goulburn Herald* read:

> The Private Gold Escort in charge of a sergeant and three constables left McIvor Diggings for Kyneton en route to Melbourne. About 20 miles from the diggings they encountered a log over the road. As the escort slowed, a volley erupted from nearby cover. The driver, Thomas Flookes, received a mortal wound. The police galloped off, three of them injured. The robbers seized 2223 ounces of gold and £700 in notes. The larger part

was not recovered, nor were those responsible identified at the time.

Initially it was considered to be the perfect crime, one that would never be solved ... until one of the perpetrators turned traitor.

Following their arrest aboard *Madagascar*, the Francis brothers and Wilson were to be transferred to a lockup in Melbourne, but during the journey from the docks a very aggressive George Francis broke free from the police on two occasions. Each time, he was rearrested, and eventually he was put into a cell at the police station. It appears that the police then negotiated an amnesty for him should he turn Queen's evidence and provide all the proof needed to convict the others – an offer he readily accepted, even providing evidence against his brother John.

In a follow-up article, the *Goulburn Herald* informed its readers that George Francis 'went with Chief Detective Officer Ashley, Sergeant Simcock and Detective Murray from Melbourne to McIvor to the Goulburn Diggings, looking for William Atkins, George Melville, Edward McEvoy, Robert Harding, George Shepherd, one named Billy, boarding at the Bush Inn, Joe Grey (alias Nutty) and George Elson (fighting man who had one tooth out)'.

Most of them were eventually found by the police, but George Francis gave them the slip. He was arrested again at Maiden's Punt.

It appears that guilt overtook him at this time. While in police custody on the way back to Melbourne, he was allowed to 'visit the water-closet'. Instead, he went around to the rear of the convenience, took out a razor he had somehow managed to obtain and cut his own throat from ear to ear.

Atkins and Melville, along with their respective wives, were also arrested in Melbourne aboard ships bound for England. They and their fellow felons were committed to trial. Atkins, Melville and Wilson were all sentenced to be hanged, which occurred on 3 October 1853. This event would change the laws relating to the entitlement of relatives to the bodies of executed felons. The *Tasmanian Colonist* newspaper reported:

> The execution was not entirely successful, the hangman
> being compelled to draw the legs of Melville down
> with considerable force before life was extinct.

Until that time, relatives of executed felons could claim the body. Mrs. Melville claimed her husband's cadaver and took it to an oyster shop in Bourke Street which she was evidently leasing. She placed the body on public display, enticing customers into the shop. Thereafter such bodies were, as a matter of policy, buried within the gaol wall.

In an ironic twist, by being arrested the Francis brothers and George Wilson avoided being aboard *Madagascar* when she disappeared to a fate unknown. George Francis and Wilson would end up dead, but John Francis and his wife were given free passage out of the colony, and went on to a better life elsewhere.

According to folklore, some of their fellow bushrangers were still aboard *Madagascar* when she departed, and could have been responsible for her fate.

In 2014 three researchers, two French and one Australian, claimed to have discovered the wreck of *Madagascar* on an island in French Polynesia, but while they presented evidence of a shipwreck more than a century old, it was deemed unproven that it was *Madagascar*.

*

The clipper era also featured an ongoing litany of amazing survival stories, in which passengers and crew given up for dead after their ship failed to arrive at its destination were found alive through a miraculous series of events. One such miracle involved the 1005-ton, 179-foot-long clipper *General Grant*, which was built in Maine and launched in 1864.

On 4 May 1866, the ship sailed away from Hobson's Bay near Melbourne bound for London, under the command of Captain William H. Loughlin, with sixty-three passengers and crew on her manifest, including about twenty children. Her cargo hold was filled to capacity with wool and hides, and there was also a considerable amount of gold on board, though no one would say how much.

Once out of Bass Strait her course was to the south-east so she would clear New Zealand's South Island. From there it was an almost 4500-nautical-mile charge into the Roaring Forties and across the southern seas to Cape Horn.

A week into the voyage, the westerly wind began to fade and a dense fog closed in. For two days there was no opportunity to take a sextant sight to aid navigation, so the captain ordered that a lookout be kept from aloft.

At half past ten on the second foggy night, when the ship was barely making headway in very light winds, the lookout shouted that land was just visible off the port bow. The course was changed to starboard and the sails and yards trimmed to suit so the land would be cleared. But then there was a most alarming call: land was obvious off the starboard bow, between 3 and 4 miles away. A passenger, James Teer, later provided a narrative of what followed:

> The wind was fast falling away, and in a few minutes it
> was dead calm, the ship was totally unmanageable.
> The captain did all in his power, with every flaw [gust]
> of wind from the flapping sails, but his attempts were
> useless. The yards were hauled in every possible
> direction that might enable the getting his ship off the
> shore, but all to no purpose, as the heavy S.W. swell
> was constantly setting her nearer and nearer the fatal
> rocks.

By 1am *General Grant* was at the mercy of the current and the thrust of the seas, drifting haplessly and helplessly just a few boat lengths from vertical cliffs about 400 feet high. Then came one mighty thump that sent earthquake-like shocks through the entire ship. Seconds later, an agony-laced shout came from the man at the wheel: another impact had caused the rudder to turn so violently that he had been hurled to the deck and suffered broken ribs.

It was quickly realised that the backdrop to the drama was the uninviting western shoreline of Auckland Island, 250 nautical miles south-west of the southern tip of New Zealand's South Island. But what *wasn't* known, until the very last moment, was the existence of a cavernous opening in the cliff-face – an enormous cave towards which the ship was being washed.

It was as if the massive opening in the cliff-face were a gigantic monster that had its mouth wide open, waiting to catch and swallow its prey ... and that was exactly what happened. The cave was so large – 250 feet deep and with an entrance higher than the mainmast and a downwards sloping roof – that the entire ship was swept into it by the relentless surge of the seas. It was a situation that almost defied belief.

The foremast was the first to strike the roof of the cave, and within seconds it came crashing onto the deck, along with huge pieces of rock, some of which smashed through the top of the forecastle. Seconds later, the main topgallant broke and also crashed to the deck, along with more large chunks of rock.

The captain saw their predicament as being too dangerous for the ship's three boats to be launched before first light. Inside the cave, the night was as black as bitumen, and the backwash coming from the waves rolling in would almost certainly have capsized a small boat. Everyone could only hope that *General Grant* – which was then aground at the bow and floating in 25 fathoms of water at the stern – would remain intact until morning. However, with rocks, rigging, masts, sails and yards still thundering to the deck, Captain Loughlin ordered that everyone congregate at the stern.

It was an agonisingly long wait for the day to dawn, so the moment there was sufficient light two boats were launched and navigated safely out of the cave. James Teer, who had been ordered into one of those boats, later explained what followed:

> The longboat, then lying on the quarter-deck, was
> filled with passengers, and the ship was sinking rapidly
> (the heel of the main-mast having evidently been driven
> through the ship's bottom by contact with the rocks
> above), till the boat with its cargo [of passengers] was
> floated off her deck, [but once] the longboat was quite
> clear of the ship, the sea breaking over her filled her
> with water, and she was swamped when about 100 yards
> from the ship. We then went as near the boat as it was
> safe to go, and saved three of the passengers, being all
> who were able to swim through the surf to us.

One of those pitched into the sea from the longboat was Mary Ann Jewell, wife of crew member Joseph Jewell. On seeing the boat capsize then go upside down, Joseph jumped from the ship into the wild water, swam to his wife and succeeded in getting her aboard one of the two boats that were nearby but were not able to execute a rescue of the victims of the capsize because of the dangerous surf.

By this time *General Grant*'s entire hull was submerged and sinking deeper, taking those who had remained on board with her. The captain was last seen clinging to the mizzen topmast crosstrees, waving his kerchief to the few who had managed to escape the ship.

These few, who were aboard the two remaining boats, numbered fifteen – nine crew and six passengers, among them James Teer, and Joseph and Mary Ann Jewell. It was obvious to them that there was nowhere to land along the adjacent coast, so they decided to row 6 miles offshore to Disappointment Island. They arrived there late the next day, after what Teer would describe as a testing twenty-four hours:

> We had more trouble than we anticipated to get there; our boat having such a quantity of beef and pork and bouilli [stewed meat] tins in her and seven men. It was only with incessant bailing we could keep out the water which from time to time she lifted. Once or twice she was all but full ... [we headed] towards the north end of the island ... and seeing a large rock about one and a

half miles distant … we pulled for it, and reached it just
at dark.

They remained there for a few days, then, when the weather
was favourable, the two boats were rowed 15 nautical miles
around the northern end of the largest island to Port Ross,
where they established a camp.

There was considerable anxiety for all soon after they
arrived when they realised they had only one match
remaining. Teer later noted:

> From this one match we obtained fire, which, by
> constant care, we never allowed to go out … Boiled
> one or two birds obtained on Disappointment Island,
> and one tin of bouilli. Gathered some limpets, which
> were cooked with the birds in the empty bouilli tins.
> This was our first meal after three days and two nights
> of suffering, and never did sumptuous repast taste better
> to a king than this frugal meal to us.

They were fortunate to find a derelict whalers' hut that
provided some shelter, and providence again smiled on them
when it came to finding food: they were able to catch and
slaughter pigs and goats, which had been left on the island for
that exact purpose, as a food source for shipwrecked sailors.
Seal meat, wild birds and shellfish brought the occasional
change to their diet.

Their only clothing was what they had been wearing when *General Grant* sank, so they set about making clothing from the skins of seals – shirts, trousers, vests, caps, moccasins, even underclothing. Still, they would suffer greatly during the winter months, when the island was lashed by snow, rain, sleet and frigid westerly gales, conditions so brutal that one man died.

A lookout roster was established so that during daylight hours someone was always watching in case a ship – more than likely a whaler – might happen by. They also kept a large fire burning around the clock in the hope that the smoke might be sighted by day, or its flames by night.

After nine frustrating months of looking, hoping, praying that a ship might come their way – and just trying to survive – four of the men elected to try to reach New Zealand and raise the alarm. They prepared one of the boats by decking it with seals' skins, then loaded it with food and water. The four men 'carried about 30 gallons of water in seals' gullets, and some seals' meat, and the flesh of three goats, and about two dozen eggs – all cooked', wrote Teer. However, they had no compass or navigation instruments, and could only hope that New Zealand would be, as they thought, to the east-north-east.

But it was actually slightly west of north. Sadly, the four men were never seen again.

After eighteen arduous months in extreme circumstances, there came a brief hope of rescue: 'The man on the look-out sighted a sail to the eastward of the Island, which afterwards proved to be the *Fanny*,' Teer's story read, 'but as she passed on without seeming to notice the smoke we made as a signal to her we began to give up all hopes.'

Within forty-eight hours, though, the survivors had real cause for joy:

> On the 21st November sighted the brig *Amherst*,
> Captain P. Gilroy, of Invercargill, running along the
> land from the southward. The boat was launched, and
> we pulled and got on board. We were very kindly
> received by both officers and crew. On the following
> morning, after nearly nineteen months of the severest
> hardships, all of us were taken aboard.

Some six weeks later, *Amherst* sailed into port in Invercargill, at the southern tip of New Zealand's South Island, carrying nine men and one woman, all of whom had come back from the dead.

*

One of the most remarkable stories of a wreck and survival on the Australian route came in late 1853. It involved the English-built 900-ton, three-masted, barque-rigged clipper *Meridian*, which measured upwards of 150 feet in overall length. She had been launched the previous year in Sunderland, on England's east coast near the Scottish border. Her captain, Richard

Hernaman, described his ship as 'the most beautiful barque that ever left the port of London'. He had already commanded her on one return passage to Australia, her maiden voyage, taking government-funded emigrants to Brisbane's Moreton Bay. Hernaman was considered to be a capable and experienced navigator, and he had four return passages to Sydney to his credit. In a career spanning fifteen years, he had never lost a man.

Meridian's second voyage to Sydney, which was expected to take around 120 days, departed Gravesend, on the Thames downstream from London, on 4 June 1853. The event occurred amid the usual wave of heavy sadness melded with excited anticipation of a new life in another part of the world. Eighty-four passengers were aboard: twenty-six men, seventeen women and forty-one children under the age of sixteen, including a seven-week-old baby girl named Fanny. Fifty-eight of those on board were crammed into steerage-class accommodation. The ship's crew numbered twenty-three, which was considered the absolute minimum for such an undertaking.

Among the few first-class passengers was Londoner Alfred James Peter Lutwyche, a forty-three year old judge and writer, who would go on to become prominent in political circles in New South Wales, and later the yet-to-be-proclaimed colony of Queensland. Having retired from the bench in London because of ill health, he accepted the casual role of Sydney-based colonial reporter for London newspaper the *Morning Chronicle*.

He was never expecting, however, that his first major report would be a detailed and dramatic fifty-two page account of how, against incredible odds, he and others survived the wreck of *Meridian* on a desolate and remote island in the southern seas. His story was built on his conviction that no one except those aboard the ship could have any real appreciation of the emotions faced by those 'who have been snatched, by what may almost be termed a series of miracles, from the jaws of a triple death – drowning, cold and starvation'.

It was a fast and uneventful sail south in the Atlantic, where there was 'merrymaking', music and dancing on the deck most evenings – a passage that Lutwyche described as among the finest he had ever made. *Meridian* then rounded the Cape of Good Hope and headed on a great circle route deep into the southern seas towards Australia. The only disconcerting aspect of the voyage at that point was that the ship's doctor – who, according to one passenger, Mrs M.W. Moore, 'was a drunkard and often caused uproar' – behaved so appallingly that the captain threatened to put him in irons.

When they were nearly 3000 nautical miles beyond the cape, the captain suspected there was an error with his chronometer – the only one on board. Because an accurate time was essential for the calculation of longitude in such a remote part of the world, he decided to alter course slightly to the north with the intention of sighting St Paul's Island. This would give him a precise position on his chart from which he could plot a safe course towards Bass Strait.

However, what Lutwyche described as a 'strong gale' descended on the ship. Because of the new wind direction, *Meridian* could not sail the desired course towards the island, so the captain changed his plans. He directed the helmsman to bear up a few degrees and hold a course so that the ship would be on a heading towards the extremely remote, uninhabited, 22-square-mile Amsterdam Island, a speck in the Southern Indian Ocean that was potentially an active volcano. It was 50 nautical miles to the north of St Paul's Island, 1800 nautical miles north of Antarctica, and the same distance south-west of Western Australia's Cape Leeuwin. The captain expected to see the outline of the island and its collar of white water around midnight, and once that was achieved he could confirm the ship's position on the navigation chart and check the accuracy of the chronometer. He would then call for a change of course towards Australia, or more specifically Bass Strait, which was 3000 nautical miles away.

Lutwyche, who noted that no lookout had been positioned atop the forecastle at the bow, explained what followed:

> I was looking for something or other in my cabin,
> which was on the port side, when suddenly a smart
> shock made the ship quiver from stem to stern, and
> nearly threw me down on the floor. At first I was under
> the impression that we had run foul of another vessel,
> but after the lapse of a few seconds, five or six more
> violent shocks made *Meridian* stagger from side to side

like a drunken man, and obliged me to cling fast to my cabin ... The piercing screams of the children testified the extremity of their alarm, though they knew not, poor things, the nature of the calamity which had befallen them, but the peculiar grating sound of the bottom by which the shocks were accompanied left little room for doubt, in my mind, that the vessel was striking against rocks ... for a time all was confusion, terror, and despair.

Instead of sighting Amsterdam Island, Captain Hernaman had guided his ship straight into the south-western corner of it in a gale at 7.15 on the night of Wednesday, 24 August. Lutwyche continued:

As the captain gained the quarter-deck the terrible truth flashed upon him, and with another exclamation of 'my God! it is the island,' he seized the wheel, and tried to put the helm a-starboard. The vessel again struck violently, and he then shouted, 'now, every man for himself,' stripped off his coat, waistcoat, and trowsers, and bade one of the hands, named Snow, assist him in casting off one of the hen-coops. While they were thus engaged, a heavy sea burst over the poop and swept him and Snow overboard, but Snow caught a rope as he fell, and climbed up again into the mizzen rigging on the port side ... The captain was never seen again ... the

vessel ... was now fast upon the rocks, and the sport of
the breakers.

Two others died within minutes of the loss of the captain
when they, too, were washed overboard by the might of a
massive wave cascading along the deck. They were the ship's
ageing cook, Thomas George, and a Swiss steerage-class
passenger.

Rev. James Voller, who was travelling to Sydney to take up
the position of minister at the Baptist Chapel in Bathurst
Street, would write of a 'furious battering', in which wave
after wave was 'striking the ship with violence and rapidity
until a great wave of water swirled between decks and down
hatches into the hold'.

In less than five minutes, the hull planking on the port
side proved no match for the force of the sea and the
pounding on the rocks. It was stove in, and the hull, which
by now was leaning heavily to port towards the shore, rapidly
filled with water. Most of the terrified passengers remained
below 'tween decks in pitch darkness, all the time clambering
awkwardly towards the high side so they remained above the
rising water level. Parents were frantically grabbing their
children and dragging them hurriedly towards any area in
the cabin deemed safe. Lutwyche wrote that one youngster
asked innocently 'whether the voyage was over', while
another was heard to say, 'Aunt Sarah would have a good
fire. It's very wet.'

Amid this mayhem and confusion Rev. Voller struggled through the darkness to rescue the captain's wife from her cabin, then suddenly realised he was on the verge of losing one of his own children. 'The cabin was half filled with water, and the furniture tossed around and broken', he wrote later. 'I felt under the bed to find my little girl, dreading almost to feel what I expected to find − her lifeless and mangled body. By what seemed a special mercy, however, she was entirely unhurt.'

In prose typical of the day, Lutwyche put the situation into perspective:

> … the portals of Death alone were open to receive the voyagers. Every instant the dreadful summons was expected, but in the meanwhile, clinging to every projection that offered itself; the second cabin families remained in the 'tween decks comforting one another with the assurance that they would soon be in a better place, and that when death did come, they would at least die together.

For two hours the passengers remained at death's door, huddled together in the accommodation area while the dying ship writhed and heaved on the rocks in unison with the surge of each mighty wave. There was no reason at that time to go on deck: it was impossible to reach the shore in such treacherous conditions, and there was every chance they would be washed over the side amid the white water of a wave breaking over the ship. Even so, their circumstances below deck were becoming increasingly perilous: cargo that had broken loose in the ship's hold was now 'floating about in the 'tween decks, threatening destruction to all with whom it came in contact'.

The break-up of the ship was now imminent, and heavy timber hull frames and deck beams were giving off a terrifying sound as they fractured and splintered. Two crewmen went below and directed the majority of passengers up the companionway, onto the deck and aft, where the only protection to be had was in the cuddy cabin, normally the domain of first class passengers. One young woman was doing everything possible to shelter her newborn baby – born aboard *Meridian* after departing England – while young children, drenched through, cried with fear and cold. However, efforts by the passengers to glean information regarding the predicament being faced were met with stony silence.

'No eye could pierce the surrounding darkness, and nothing was heard without but the roar of the tempest and the groaning of the ill-fated vessel', Lutwyche would recall. 'Under these circumstances, being appealed for my advice, I recommended that no attempt should be made to leave the ship, but that we should remain by the wreck as long as she would hold together, and endeavour when she broke up, to reach the shore, as each might best, on the floating pieces of timber. Our position, however, appeared so desperate, that I believe very few cherished the hope of escape, and for my own part, I exhorted all around me to think no more of this life, but to implore God's mercy and forgiveness, while there was yet time vouchsafed for repentance.' Rev. Voller then began praying aloud, and Lutwyche noted there was immediately a 'calmness and composure which showed that they were prepared to meet death'.

Salvation was tormentingly close – huge boulders were sitting fortress-like at the base of a high, sheer cliff just 50 feet away – but the raging, white, storm-driven surf that was boiling so violently between the disintegrating ship and the shore put them beyond reach. The churning seas spelled death instead of deliverance.

Lutwyche would pen a reference to what he saw as one of the 'disgraceful exceptions' to the courage and acceptance shown by most of the passengers:

> Indignation finds no place in the bosoms of men on the verge of eternity. But while human beings have human feelings, it will be impossible to recall, without exciting emotions of measureless contempt, the figure of a man in the prime of life, six feet high, and stout in proportion, with an air-bed fastened round his middle, shouting out that he 'must be saved', and forcing his way first to this part of the ship and then to that through the throng of helpless women and children in order to find some means of escape for himself.

Thomas Henderson, travelling with his wife Margaret and their eight children, gave his version of the unfolding drama:

> Under the advice of one of the mates, Leonard
> Worthington, whose bearing and cool judgement were
> beyond all praise, we remained between decks about
> two hours and a half, supporting as many of my infants
> in my arms as I could grasp, and holding them up to
> windward out of the way of the wreck[age] that was
> washing about between decks, the water at times
> reaching my shoulders, the ship reclining over at forty-
> five degrees or thereabouts. Mother and children calm
> and still; never dreaming that we should live the night
> through.

Some crew had already considered chopping down the mainmast, hoping that it would fall towards the shore and form a bridge, but that idea was abandoned because it had no guarantee of success. If the downed mast missed its mark – which was highly probable – it would then thrash around in the raging surf and accelerate the demise of the already badly damaged ship.

Incredibly, fate would provide the very means of deliverance that the crew had dared not risk. Lutwyche would recall:

> … about half-past one o'clock [am] the mainmast fell,
> and the vessel parted in two. The fall was a gradual

one, and it descended with all the rigging standing, athwart the breakers, till it touched the boulders above, thus forming the means of communication with the shore, of which the sailors were not slow to avail themselves.

Some of the nimbler passengers followed, but amazingly, there was no effort at all from the crew already standing on the rocks to rescue those who remained aboard the still-heaving ship – in particular the women and children.

However, the ship's third mate, the aptly named Mr Worthington, did have the courage to remain aboard. He quickly reassured the passengers that the poop (aft section) would hold together till daylight, and he 'would not leave the vessel till every woman and child had quitted it'.

He kept his word.

With the gale still raging and the ship breaking up further each time a thundering wave smashed into her, Worthington, with the aid of crewman Charles Snow, began assisting passengers brave enough to venture onto the downed, constantly moving mast and make the precarious journey towards the shore. The two men held on to each passenger who committed to the perilous undertaking, at times handing them a piece of rope rigging or a timber spar to hang on to for balance. On more than one occasion, gasps went up, as the rescuers 'were knocked down several times by heavy seas'. Lutwyche's account continued:

The passage across occupied a considerable time, for it
was necessary to watch for a favourable moment, and it
was difficult to induce the women to expose themselves
to unknown dangers. But finding about three o'clock
in the morning that the water in the saloon was
beginning to rise – coming in, in fact, faster than it
went out – I warned all who were willing to make the
effort to save life that the time was come when they
must quit the cuddy.

Lutwyche was certain that if the seas generated by the gale had
been any larger on the night, no more than ten of all the
people aboard *Meridian* would have survived.

However, as Rev. Voller would later write, there was still
no guarantee of survival once the shore had been achieved:

The moon, which had just made its appearance, gave
sufficient light to expose the dangers and terror of the
place. Before us the cliffs rose like a perpendicular wall,
to the height of at least two hundred feet while at their
base, the margin between the rocks and the sea was
very narrow, and it was my thought and that of others
that, if the weather did not subside, we must soon be
washed away.

By dawn, the 105 passengers and crew who had survived the
wreck were safely onshore. They had been extremely lucky to

escape, but the emerging light of day quickly revealed how inhospitable was the environment that they had now entered.

'The dawn was just breaking, and oh, what an appalling sight presented itself!' wrote Lutwyche. 'Before me lay huge boulders piled up irregularly till they reached an altitude of 40 or 50 feet, where they were hemmed in by a perpendicular wall of black ferruginous rock, rendering a further advance from the sea in that direction impossible. Turning round, and facing the sea, a small portion of the forecastle of the *Meridian* was still visible above water to the left, while on the right lay the after-part of the vessel, with the mizen still standing, pointing towards the shore. The rest of the vessel was completely broken up, and pieces of the wreck were dashed by every sea on the rocks.'

Many of the children, shivering because they had been wearing only their night attire when the ship thundered onto the rocks, remained either huddled together for warmth or in the arms of their parents until daylight. Fortunately, enough shattered timber from the wreck was then recovered and a fire lit.

Soon afterwards, the survivors made a discovery that would prove to be a remarkable stroke of good fortune. Large bales containing 'Hundreds of yards of excellent new flannel, perfectly dry, and some hundreds of red and blue serge shirts' had been extricated from the broken bowels of the ship and washed ashore. 'But for this providential supply, half the women and children, and probably some of the men, must have perished from wet and cold the very first night', wrote Lutwyche.

Yet this lucky find was small consolation for the survivors as they began to realise the magnitude of their predicament, and how remote their chances of survival were. Experienced crew members confirmed that Amsterdam Island was well outside the route taken by ships sailing from Europe to Australia, so there was virtually no chance of their being found. The only maritime activity that might occur in the region was whaling, but it was known that in the previous year, only two whalers had worked the waters around the island, and even then, it had only been for a matter of days. The precipitous and craggy nature of the island's shoreline added to the survivors' dilemma, as it was near-impossible for any small boat to reach the shore except in the most benign of weathers. The survivors soon became aware that there was no timber available that might allow them to build any type of small vessel capable of reaching the outside world.

No food had washed ashore from *Meridian*, though several of the crew had salvaged some of the wine and spirits that had been on board, and, wrote Lutwyche, they and some of the passengers 'gave way to a temptation which they found irresistible'. The survivors' only hope for sustenance would be shellfish gathered off the rocks; they had no fishing equipment. They did, however, have some guns with them, and 'a very scanty supply of powder and shot', which might allow them to shoot seabirds.

Though the top of the island might prove fertile, a safe ascent seemed nigh on impossible. Lutwyche took it upon himself to try to find a path up the escarpment so that everyone could reach the plateau above. He said he 'crawled along the rocks, painfully and slowly, for half a mile to the westward, in the hope of finding some path by which we could ascend the face of the cliff, but as far as the eye could reach, I could discern nothing but a beetling precipice, which not even a goat or a monkey could have scaled'.

When he returned to the wreck site, there was a modicum of good news: some crew had managed to reboard the ship and recover some of the stores, while other foodstuffs had been washed up on the shore. The ration for that first day was a biscuit for every adult and half a biscuit for each child, but as there was no water to be found, 'half a glass of port wine per head was served out among the women and children'. A sail and some timber were also recovered and used to create a shelter for the women and children that second night. Still, it was a miserable existence, so much so that four year old Charles Henderson was heard to remark to his mother: 'Mamma, is this place Sydney? Because if it is, I don't like Sydney.'

The following day there was positive news on two fronts: a supply of water was discovered about one and a half miles along the rocky shoreline from the site of the wreck, but better still, a path to the top of the 200-foot-high cliff was found, and there was fresh water near its summit. Their food supply was also improving: a sow had swum ashore from the ship and been captured, and the floating carcass of 'an old boar pig' had been recovered from the water. Lutwyche wrote: 'this addition to our stock we looked upon as a veritable godsend. It enabled me to issue on the Monday and Tuesday a ration of half a pound of pork, over and above what otherwise would have been each day's allowance, viz., a small handful of raisins, half a mouldy biscuit, a little tea, and some brandy.'

On Saturday, 27 August, the decision was made to quit the wreck site and establish a camp at the clifftop. It was a difficult ascent: the women and children had to be hauled to the top by rope over the final 15 feet. The sow was also dragged up the cliff by rope.

With a camp established by converting whatever material was available into makeshift tents, all survivors were reconciled to an unknown fate, but feeling it was more than likely that they would perish in this harsh and hostile environment. While an ample water supply had been found, their food supply was extremely limited and there was little prospect that any other sustenance would be forthcoming in such a desolate location. The winter cold, exacerbated by strong winds, was another life-threatening difficulty that had to be overcome.

Incredibly, though, just twenty-four hours later, a far-from-expected air of excitement swept through the camp. Some of the survivors who had ventured off to a nearby clifftop rushed back with the news that they had sighted a ship close to the island!

Their frantic waving of two red serge shirts and some white flannel had been seen by the ship's crew, who had twice lowered the ship's ensign in response. The castaways had also set fire to some nearby grass to confirm their presence on the island. Lutwyche explained, 'Very soon after the heart-stirring intelligence had reached me, I saw the vessel myself. She was a whaler apparently of about 300 tons, and still kept her ensign flying.'

But unimaginable frustration and fear soon followed. On two occasions the captain tacked his ship and tried to lay a course towards the island, but both times the strong offshore breeze prevented this. Instead, the whaler was driven away from the shore until she disappeared into the misty distance, 'and we saw her no more'.

The survivors were hopeful that when the weather turned in the ship's favour she would return, and that was what happened only forty-eight hours later. Just as the castaways were preparing to send a search party to find a landing place for a vessel, one of *Meridian*'s crew came running towards the camp shouting with great excitement: 'A boat, a boat!'

With that, everyone rushed towards the clifftop to see for themselves. Lutwyche wrote:

> I distinctly saw a whale-boat rowing near the shore, at a
> safe distance from the surf. The steersman waved a flag
> in his hand, and pointed it two or three times towards
> the quarter from which the boat had come; a loud shout

from the top of the cliff, and a pointing of hands in the same direction, showed those below that the signal was understood; and then the boat, turning its head round, pursued its way back again. All was now hope, joy and activity.

Time would reveal that the ship they had seen was the American whaler *Monmouth*. This small whaleboat had come from her, but had only been able to land on the other side of the island. The exploring party set off in that direction, followed by the rest of the survivors, including women and children. Little did they know at this point what an arduous and perilous journey it would be.

Meanwhile, on the side of the island where the ship had first been sighted, a gale had swept in, and the whaleboat had barely managed to rejoin the mother ship before she was driven downwind some 80 miles from the island. 'Happily for us we were spared the knowledge of this misfortune', wrote Lutwyche. 'I doubt that otherwise many would have laid down on the road to die.'

Unbeknown to the survivors, the whaleboat had already put ashore William Smith, a member of *Monmouth*'s crew, so he could make contact with the castaways. Surprisingly, the captain of the whaler, Isaac Ludlow of New York State, had taken command of the whaleboat so he could coordinate the rescue.

Two days into their slow and precarious trek along the cliffs at the island's edge, Smith managed to find the half-starving survivors. He led them to the island's north-eastern side where the boat had left him, and where a patch of wild cabbages had been planted by shipwrecked sailors. Raw cabbages would be the survivors' only food until the ship could return.

Eight days after *Meridian* smashed into the island, and two days after William Smith reached them, Lutwyche noted that the survivors were on the verge of giving up all hope of being rescued: 'Unless God should send us immediate aid, it was clear that two or three days would put an end to the sufferings of many amongst us.'

But within hours, at daybreak on Monday, 5 September, 'our deliverers were at hand. A long and tremendous shout of "ship, ship," from the stentorian lungs of Smith, aroused the whole encampment, and fervent thanks were offered up to Almighty God for this renewed proof of His mercy.'

With *Monmouth* holding station close to the island on the lee side, four of her whaleboats were launched to carry out a rescue. Women and children went first, and by midday everyone who had reached shore from *Meridian* was treading the decks of *Monmouth*, except for two men and a child who had not yet reached the rescue site and who were taken off the island the following morning.

'With three hearty cheers for Captain Ludlow and his brave men,' Lutwyche wrote, 'we now left Amsterdam and made all sail for the Mauritius.' Ludlow's crew had risked their lives and their livelihoods to deliver the castaways to safety.

It took *Monmouth* seventeen days to cover the 1500 nautical miles north-west to Mauritius. While the survivors spent two weeks there recuperating, local authorities arranged for the charter of the 500-ton ship *Emma Colvin*, so the passengers could complete their passage to Melbourne's Port Phillip, then on to Sydney.

Finally, after a voyage from Mauritius of seven weeks, much to everyone's relief, the towering, honey-coloured sandstone cliffs dominating the entrance to Sydney Harbour came into view on 30 December 1853. It had been seven months since the survivors had set sail from London aboard *Meridian*, and for much of that time Sydney had been a sight they thought they might never see.

Lutwyche's dramatic account of the shipwreck on Amsterdam Island was published in Mauritius (in French), then in Sydney and London. Once he had settled into his new environment, he decided his health was such that he could happily enter the legal and political arena in New South Wales. In a very short time he was making an impact on both fronts. In 1855 he married widow Mary Ann Jane Morris; she and her deceased husband George had also survived the sinking of *Meridian*.

His rise continued, until in 1859, at the age of forty-nine, he was named the first Supreme Court Judge for Moreton Bay (Brisbane). The appointment came just prior to 10 December, the day when Queensland was declared a self-governing colony.

Soon after arriving in Brisbane, Lutwyche bought a tract of land four miles north of the town centre and donated it to the Church of England so a place of worship could be built there. The area around that church is now the suburb of Lutwyche.

*

Not even the stories of death, destruction and unimaginable privation at sea could stop the steady march of the clippers across the world. But there was one threat these mighty ships could do nothing to counter – and it was one that had been with them from the very start.

CHAPTER 8

'Screw v. Sail'

The threat of the steamships

Even in the early 1850s, as the clipper era was just beginning, steam-powered commercial vessels were ringing the death knell for sailing ships on some routes across the world's oceans. But they were having little impact on the longer voyages, such as the American east coast–west coast route, and the run from England to Australia and New Zealand.

Steam power had been pioneered on the seas as far back as the late eighteenth century, but until the mid-nineteenth century, vessels designated as steamships were actually auxiliary steamships: they relied on sail and steam for propulsion at different times.

One debate that has lasted for well over a century relates to the rightful claimant of the honour of being the first true steamship to complete a crossing of the Atlantic. It appears the first vessel to be fully reliant on steam power for a crossing of the Atlantic was *Sirius*, a 703-ton paddle wheeler that sailed from London to New York via Cork, Ireland, in 1838 with forty passengers on board. However, the voyage was certainly not without its dramas. *Sirius* was going well until her coal supply ran out when New York was just beyond the horizon. Undeterred, and determined not to use the sails, the captain ordered his men to chop up the wooden spars and feed the timber into the furnace so a full head of steam could be maintained. *Sirius* then continued on to New York without a stitch of sail having seen the light of day.

Unreliability, inefficiency and an inability to carry the desired tonnage of coal to keep the boilers burning, while still having the capacity to carry a commercial cargo, were the major problems that steamships of the clipper era still had to overcome. And on long trips they were particularly ineffective, not just because of the distance but also because of the lack of ports where coal could be obtained.

It was on these long routes, where the clipper ships could harness the forces of nature – particularly in the tropical trade-wind belt and in the Roaring Forties – that the clippers came into their own. By 1852, clippers were generally completing the passage from New York to San Francisco in 90 to 120 days, while the steamers were taking around 150. Such was the speed of the clippers that they remained superior on long voyages to the steam-driven paddle wheelers, and then the single-screw ships, until well into the 1860s. When conditions suited them, they were charging past the emerging threat and disappearing over the horizon in a matter of hours.

*

Not even the introduction of the world's largest commercial steamship, *Great Britain*, to the Australian run in 1853 had much influence on the transport preferences of travellers to the Antipodes. Interestingly, even though she was steam-powered, many would refer to her in years to come as a clipper ship because of the shape of her hull and the fact that she carried sail on six masts. Only her second mast aft from the bow – the mainmast – was square-rigged, with a single yard. All her other masts were schooner-rigged: they carried large fore and aft sails set from gaffs, a concept that would allow the ship to gain benefit from the sails over the widest possible wind angle, from forward of abeam to well aft. This reduced *Great Britain*'s reliance on her steam engine for propulsion, which in turn minimised her consumption of coal.

Great Britain was a vessel of mind-boggling proportions. Costing a staggering £117,000 to build (£47,000 over budget), she was the brainchild of English engineer Isambard Kingdom Brunel, a man recognised as one of the world's greatest engineering geniuses, and a seminal figure of the Industrial Revolution. Such was his brilliance that wealthy men across England clamoured to back his schemes, so much so that by age twenty-nine, Brunel was estimated to be worth £5.3 million – more than £600 million today.

Brunel's unique talents were visible in every facet of *Great Britain*, which at the time of her launch in July 1843 was dubbed 'the greatest experiment since the Creation'. At 322 feet over all and weighing 1930 tons, she was by far the largest ship afloat from when she went into service in 1845 until 1854. As well as being the largest iron ship ever built at the time, she was the first passenger ship to be fitted with a screw propeller, a feature Brunel devised after originally planning for her to be a paddle wheeler. He also chose a unique 1000-horsepower steam engine for propulsion.

Great Britain's maiden voyage in 1845, across the Atlantic from Liverpool to New York, was completed in an impressive fourteen days. History also recorded this as being the first passage across the Atlantic by an iron-hulled steamer.

*

Before *Great Britain* went into service on the Atlantic run, Brunel's ever-inquiring mind caused him to replace the ship's six-bladed windmill-type propeller with a four-bladed design, which he further modified by adding an extension to the tip of each blade. Unfortunately, it was an idea that failed: on her second crossing of the Atlantic, *Great Britain* ran afoul of a storm that delivered conditions so rough that the propeller lost a number of its blades and one of the ship's masts went crashing over the side.

Making matters worse for the owners, their colossal vessel held little appeal for trans-Atlantic travellers. There were only twenty-eight paying passengers on board – seventeen fewer than on her maiden voyage.

Still, the owners went ahead with a second season of Atlantic crossings in 1846 – but again, it would prove to be an ill-fated endeavour. After departing from Liverpool on his third round trip of the season, *Great Britain*'s captain, James Hosken, made a series of navigational blunders on the first night at sea and subsequently drove the ship hard aground in Dundrum Bay on Ireland's east coast, just 110 nautical miles due west of Liverpool. It is thought that the captain was using outdated charts for navigation, and that he mistook St John's Light on the Irish coast for the Calf Light on the Isle of Man, 30 miles closer to Liverpool. This led him to call for a change of course towards the coast – which could not be seen in the darkness – instead of towards the Atlantic Ocean. Soon afterwards, *Great Britain* steamed straight onto the beach at full speed. Conditions were apparently calm, and no one was reported to have been injured.

Brunel visited the site soon after the calamity occurred and saw that his beloved ship had grounded at a good rate of knots, as she was high and dry. He subsequently wrote of his feelings in a letter to a friend, Christopher Claxton, who had published a book about the ship in 1844:

> I have returned from Dundrum with very mixed
> feelings of satisfaction and pain, almost amounting to
> anger, with whom I don't know. I was delighted to find
> our fine ship almost as sound as the day she was

launched, and ten times stronger in character. I was grieved to see her lying unprotected, deserted, and abandoned by all those who ought to know her value and ought to have protected her. The result, whoever is to blame, is that the finest ship in the world, in excellent condition such that £4,000 or £5,000 would repair all the damage done, has been left lying like a useless saucepan, kicking about on the most exposed shore you can imagine, with no more effort or skill applied to protect the property than the said saucepan would have received on the beach at Brighton.

It took almost a year of skilful planning and great effort to refloat *Great Britain*. Initially, to lighten the ship, all heavy items that could be dispensed with were either thrown from the deck or lowered onto the beach. After that, a huge pond was dug around the hull so that she could float on a high tide. When everything was in readiness and the tide at its peak, the ship was dragged off the beach then towed back to Liverpool.

The cost of the salvage – £34,000 – could not be covered by the financially strapped owners, the Great Western Steamship Company. The company declared bankruptcy and *Great Britain* was sold for just £25,000 to Gibbs, Bright & Co, who had acted as shipping agents for the previous owners.

The new owners had big plans for the ship. They saw her as perfectly suited to meeting the rapidly escalating demand from emigrants and gold seekers wanting to travel to Australia.

Some modifications were made, the most important being the addition of a new accommodation deck so passenger numbers could be doubled to 730. Additionally, two of *Great Britain*'s six masts were dispensed with and a second funnel added.

Amid great fanfare, *Great Britain* sailed from Liverpool on her maiden voyage to Melbourne and Sydney on 21 August 1852, with 630 passengers and a crew of 143 aboard. Obviously it was not known to the ship's owners or the captain, Barnard Robert Mathews, that the clipper ship *Marco Polo* was, at that moment, only four weeks from reaching Melbourne and establishing an impressive record of just sixty-eight days for the passage from Liverpool.

Great Britain's backers had visions of covering the 13,000 nautical miles in a remarkable sixty days, but that was not to be. They had badly miscalculated the amount of coal the steam engine would consume.

It was not until *Great Britain* had covered around 4500 nautical miles and was deep in the South Atlantic that this error was realised. The only solution was to turn back and sail almost 500 nautical miles north to St Helena Island, where coal was available. The voyage to Melbourne was extended by three weeks to a total of eighty-one days. It was a deviation that brought a riotous response from some passengers, because the delay was costing them valuable time and money. It was also rumoured that when *Great Britain* reached St Helena a number of the ship's stokers from the boiler room stole a boat and jumped ship.

*

Everyone travelling on *Great Britain* received a copy of the 'Rules for Passengers', laid down by the British Government, prior to departure. Among the most salient points were:

Every passenger to rise at 7am ...

The Passengers to be in their beds at 10pm ...

The Passengers, when dressed, to roll up their beds, to sweep the decks ... and to throw the dirt overboard.

Breakfast not to commence till this is done.

The beds to be well shaken and aired on deck ...

Mondays and Tuesdays are appointed as washing days, but no clothes on any account to be washed or dried between decks ...

On Sunday the Passengers to muster at 10am, when they will be expected to appear in clean and decent apparel. The day to be observed as religiously as circumstances will permit ...

All gambling, fighting, riotous behaviour or quarrelsome behaviour, swearing and violent language to be at once put a stop to. Swords and other offensive weapons, as soon as the passengers embark, to be placed in the custody of the Master.

No sailors to remain on the passenger deck among the passengers except on duty.

No passenger to go to the Ship's Cookhouse
without special permission from the Master nor to
remain in the Forecastle among the sailors on any
account.

There was much written by many of the 630 passengers on
this voyage, and all gave interesting insights into life on board.
It is evident passengers thought that paying some 33 per cent
more to sail to Australia aboard *Great Britain* than on one of
the smaller clipper ships would see them enjoy superior
service, food and accommodation. But that was not always the
case, as some diaries revealed.

The most common observation by passengers was the
amount of livestock taken on board to provide fresh food for
first-class travellers. *Great Britain* departed Liverpool with a
virtual farm on her main deck. Housed there were 550
chickens, 250 ducks, 150 sheep, fifty-five turkeys and geese,
thirty pigs, two lambs, one ox and a milking cow and calf.

The boundaries of the class system were clearly defined on
the ship. Those travelling second class were fed salted meat on
most days, while the steerage-class passengers, who were
located in horribly cramped quarters along the entire lower
deck, more often than not had to cook their own meals in a
tiny galley. Their usual fare consisted of ship's biscuits, a
porridge-like dish called gruel, and soup. Making their life
even worse was the fact that quite often their travelling
companions were rats and fleas.

One young steerage-class passenger, seventeen year old Glaswegian Allan Gilmour, described in his diary the accommodation they endured during the passage:

> Our berths are pretty well ventilated, but very confined
> and dark. The State Room (as they please to call it)
> allotted to us holds four persons. The distance between
> our berths for the purpose of dressing is 2ft broad and
> 6ft long, so confined that only one can dress at once,
> and even in this small space we have to build [store] part
> of our luggage.

First-class passengers expected a form of behaviour consistent with what they experienced at home – in the words of historian Andrew Hassam in *No Privacy for Writing: Shipboard Diaries 1852–1879* (1995), 'modelled on a polite social gathering at an English country house, protected and predictable'. One diarist lamented that shipboard manners were not always present, especially when it came to 'wishing good morning' to others. Everything possible was done to enable the upper-class travellers to exist in a manner similar to what they were accustomed to: they were able to participate in activities like sketching, dancing and sewing, as well as lectures and concerts in the evenings.

The meals that these privileged few enjoyed were little different from those they would have eaten at home, most comprising up to twelve courses. One of the first-class passengers, J.M. Hardwick, made a diary entry on 26 August 1852 that outlined the menu for the main meal that day:

> Dinner ... was first rate, quite such as you would get at the best hotels: soup, grouse, pigeon and veal pies, pork, ham and other meat dishes, sundry puddings and tarts and jelly, blancmange, cheese, celery and after all, a dessert.

Dining in rough weather, for all classes of traveller, was a challenge: each time the ship lurched heavily in response to the power of a mighty wave there was every chance that the plate of food being consumed opposite you at one of the long bench tables would finish up in your lap.

Another passenger, Edward Towle, made special note of the cross-section of people aboard the ship:

> There seems to be a great mixture of characters on board, men who had been gambling the night before now appeared at church with a most devotional demeanour, and others who appeared to be very steady and sedate never went to church at all ... We have French, Germans, Poles, Jews, Italians, Scotch and Irish on board.

*

When *Great Britain* entered Port Phillip on 12 November and made her way north to the anchorage at Hobson's Bay, the word of her presence spread across Melbourne like wildfire. Her enormous size, and the fact that she was the first big steamship to enter the port, saw crowds cascade onto the bay's beaches and headlands so they could catch sight of her.

Just fourteen months earlier, they had been in awe of the 184-foot clipper ship *Marco Polo*, after her first arrival on Australian shores. Now, here was a steamship-cum-clipper measuring 322 feet overall, and built from iron, not wood. The excitement about her presence in port was so great that more than 4000 people paid 1 shilling each to tour *Great Britain* while she was at anchor.

After leaving Melbourne and clearing Port Phillip Bay under the guidance of the local pilots, *Great Britain* was turned east into Bass Strait on a course that would take her to Sydney. This would be her only visit to the harbour city in all the voyages she made to Australia.

By April 1853, she was back in England and destined for another major refit based on the experiences of her inaugural voyage into the southern hemisphere. Her owners had decided that far greater emphasis should be placed on the ship's sailing ability, so that she stood a better chance of reaching Melbourne before her cargo of coal was expended. Her coal-hungry engine was replaced by a more modern, more efficient and lighter model. Also, to minimise drag when under sail, a new propulsion system was fitted that allowed the drive shaft and propeller to be lifted above the water when not in use. And the ship's forever-changing sail plan was modified yet again. She had been launched with six masts; now, the decision was for her to have only three, and they were to be increased in height so that her sail area was maximised and made more effective.

Great Britain's second voyage to Australia left no doubt that the modifications had been worthwhile. She arrived in Melbourne on 15 October 1853 after having been at sea for just sixty-five days. Her best run of all came on the considerably longer return voyage from Melbourne around Cape Horn and back to Liverpool: an astonishing fifty-four days, the same time as her fastest outbound passage, which was recorded on her last ever voyage to the Antipodes, from London to Melbourne. During her career on this route her average 'out and back' was 120 days.

Her regular schedule to Australia was interrupted between 1854 and 1857, when she was chartered by the British Government to act as a troopship during the Crimean War. After moving 44,000 troops during that conflict, *Great Britain* was rebuilt then chartered by the government to rush two dragoon regiments to the 1857 Indian Mutiny.

On returning to the Australian run, *Great Britain* went on to complete a total of thirty-two return trips down under. There were many historic moments associated with these journeys. In 1861 the first English cricket team to tour Australia travelled on board. The players arrived in Melbourne on 24 December and returned home in March 1862. The popular novelist Anthony Trollope wrote one of his books, *Lady Anna*, while travelling to Melbourne. Another emigrant of note to come to Australia aboard *Great Britain* was police superintendent John Sadleir. He was aboard for the first ever voyage and went on to become famous for his role in the capture of the notorious Kelly Gang.

Great Britain was finally retired from the service to Australia in 1876. By that time she had transported some 16,000 migrants to the colonies. It has subsequently been estimated that half a million Australians today can trace their ancestry back to this particular ship. She now sits in her home port of Bristol, a museum ship visited by hundreds of thousands every year.

*

Great Britain might have stolen *Marco Polo*'s honour in 1852 as the largest vessel to enter Port Phillip, but the lightning-fast clipper would soon have her chance at revenge against the upstart steamers.

It so happened that as Bully Forbes was preparing to skipper *Marco Polo* again on her second voyage to the Antipodes, a screw steamer, *Antelope* – owned by Liverpool's Golden Line – was being readied to make the same trip. Confident in the superiority of steam technology, *Antelope*'s Captain Thompson publicly challenged Bully Forbes to a race to Melbourne and back.

When promoting *Marco Polo*'s forthcoming voyage, the Black Ball Line certainly took aim at their steamer competitors – no doubt with *Antelope*'s challenge in mind. The company posted this advertisement:

> For passengers, parcels and specie [gold bullion and cash], having bullion safes, will be despatched early in February for Melbourne.
>
> THE CELEBRATED CLIPPER SHIP 'MARCO POLO.'
>
> 1625 tons register; 2500 tons burthen; has proved herself the fastest ship in the world, having just made the voyage to Melbourne and back, including detention there, in 5 months and 21 days, beating every other vessel, steamers included.
>
> As a passenger ship she stands unrivalled and her commander's ability and kindness to his passengers are well known.
>
> As she goes out in ballast and is expected to make a very rapid passage, she offers a most favourable opportunity to shippers of specie.
>
> Apply to James Baines & Co., Cook Street.

Before *Marco Polo* was towed away from Salthouse Dock and went to anchor in the Mersey so final preparations could be implemented, a well-attended pre-departure *déjeuner* was staged on board to honour Forbes and his second-in-command, Charles McDonald. The tributes flowed to an extent that Forbes found embarrassing – still, when he took the floor, as reported in a Liverpool newspaper, he got straight to the point:

> As regards his recent voyage, he had done his best and he could not say he would do the same again, but if he did it, he would do it in a shorter time. (Laughter). He was going a different way this time, a way that perhaps not many knew of, and the *Antelope* must keep her steam up or he would thrash her (referring to the challenge of a race round the world sent him by Captain Thompson, of the steamer *Antelope*). Captain Thompson only wanted to get outside Cape Clear and he could make a fair wind into a foul one. (Laughter.) That he [Forbes] would do his best for the interests of his employers and while the Black Ball Line had a flag flying or a coat to button, he would be there to button it.

Clearly, Forbes's reference to going to Melbourne 'a different way' was merely a psychological ploy aimed at his rivals aboard *Antelope*. This contest was shaping up to be the first real comparison between sail and steam over the 13,000 nautical miles to Melbourne.

Accordingly, the *Marco Polo*-versus-*Antelope* encounter intrigued the public and the press not just in England but also in Australia. This was no better reflected than in a story reprinted from the *Illustrated London News* in Hobart's *Courier* on 5 May 1853, under the headline 'Steam to Australia – The *Antelope* and the *Marco Polo* – Screw v. Sail'. It referred to the existing shortcomings of steamships while painting an exciting picture about the pending challenge. It also provided its readership with a valuable appraisal of a 'modern-day' steamer:

> Considerable disappointment has been experienced by the result hitherto of the experiments in steam navigation to the Antipodes. On both sides of the world a similar feeling has been expressed; and the extraordinarily rapid voyage out and home of the sailing-vessel *Marco Polo* has created among many nautical authorities a strong conviction that the latter class of craft may bid defiance to steam rivalry, at least of the kind hitherto attempted. The precise point involved in this question of rivalry is about to be tested in a race round the world, between the famous sailer we have just named and the scarcely less famous screw-steamer, the *Antelope*. The *Antelope* now competes for the belt with the great victor of the sailing ring, the *Marco Polo*, under circumstances that will render the test (at least, presumptively) determinative of the principle at stake. The *Antelope* is the property of the firm of Millars [*sic* – Millers] and Thompson, of Liverpool ... so that it is quite superfluous to say that whatever capital could furnish, or skill suggest, has been applied with no less

liberality than discrimination in rendering her perfect in every respect. Why she has been selected for this purpose by these gentlemen, in connection with their well-known 'golden line' of sailing vessels between Liverpool and Australia, seems to be her possession of every quality of excellence as a sea-boat ...

The story continued, stating that after setting a record time on a passage to Rio de Janeiro, *Antelope* had returned to England, where she had been lengthened 'so as to enhance her capacity for accommodation to the extent required for her new destination', Australia. The builder in charge of this work, John Laird of Birkenhead, near Liverpool, had applied 'his utmost ingenuity in the *Antelope* to secure victory for the screw'. The reporter went on to note that *Antelope*'s unusual three-bladed propeller was designed to 'obviate the disagreeable vibratory motion which generally accompanies the action of this instrument; so that in her progress through the water the *Antelope* will communicate to the passenger only such sensation as if she were in reality the clipper she looks'.

Referring to the features of *Antelope*'s accommodation, it was said that 'they are of a comparatively subdued character; and though exceedingly elegant wherever elegance is permissible, there is a total absence of meretricious glitter'. It was also suggested that the captain, H.C. Keen – who had now replaced Captain Thompson – was most suited to the task, as he had 'frequently navigated the southern seas; and his first officer, Mr A. French, is thoroughly familiar with screw steamers'. In closing, the writer declared that in preparing for the contest with *Marco Polo* and her legendary captain, '*Antelope* is apparently deficient in nothing whatever that should render her a thoroughly well-matched screw antagonist against the renowned sailer, *Marco Polo*'.

The scene was now set for the first true showdown between sail and steam over a voyage that would cover a distance exceeding half the Earth's circumference. The two contenders had little in common, except that the steamer's design was obviously based on the lines of a clipper ship. They were certainly very different when it came to overall length – usually the telling factor in the speed of a vessel. After being lengthened to 235 feet over all, the now more streamlined *Antelope* was 54 feet longer than *Marco Polo*, and carried considerably more sail. But they were figures that didn't daunt the indomitable Bully Forbes. This was shaping up to be a David-and-Goliath sailing challenge of biblical proportions across some of the world's wildest oceans.

*

It was 10.30am on Wednesday, 9 March 1853 when *Marco Polo* was hauled out of the dock and set at anchor in the river. One of her passengers was a young Englishman named Edwin Bird. His colourfully worded diary – the only shipboard diary known to exist from this voyage – told of what would be, for him and the other 647 passengers, a 13,000 nautical mile voyage through a never-before-experienced, often hostile environment to a completely different world.

His story started at the time *Marco Polo* was hauled out of the dock: 'There was a nice Band on Board and just as Her Noble Stern was Clearing the Dock Gates They struck up "The Girls We Left Behind Us".'

Once again, Forbes insisted on sailing on 13 March – a Sunday, his lucky day of the week. But just before the anchor was to be hauled up, a most *un*lucky incident occurred: the Liverpool police went aboard the ship seeking to arrest one of the passengers, Ephraim Jacobs, on a charge of burglary. His luggage was found to contain a considerable quantity of jewellery and watches, but police were forced to leave empty-handed after uncovering no evidence that the goods had been stolen.

There were very few women among the passengers, the majority being men representing the 'artisan' class. This imbalance of the sexes disappointed many of the males on board, a fact that ended up in print in a Liverpool newspaper subsequent to *Marco Polo*'s departure:

> One young gentleman, whose incipient moustache and
> budding imperial [beard] showed that he was shaping
> his course for the diggings, was heard to express his
> sorrow that there were not more ladies as they exercised
> such a humanising tendency on mankind ...

It was 10am on a superbly warm and sunny spring day when the steam tug *Independence* moved in, picked up a line from *Marco Polo*'s bow and, once the anchor had been weighed, commenced to tow her out of the river. It was at this time that Captain Forbes – whose recently wedded wife Jane was accompanying him on the voyage – made his famous declaration that it was his intention on this voyage 'to astonish God almighty'. Bird described the departure:

> She lay in the River until Sunday Morning when she weighed Anchor, Fired four Salutes and was answered by the American Mail Ship, *Niagara*, and went Beautifully down the River amidst the Cheers of Thousands of Spectators, the whole of the Pier Head for more than a mile being Crowded as well as the Birkenhead Side ... [and there were] many People going out in the River to Her Wishing their friends Farewell and a pleasant and prosperous Voyage to the Far Distant Shores of Australia.

During his address to the passengers while his ship was under tow, Forbes told the cook – a man of African descent known as Dr Johnson – to 'search well below, and if you find any stowaways, put them overboard slick'. Remarkably, in a matter of minutes, Johnson reappeared on deck with a writhing Irishman in his control – a stowaway who had been hiding in the cabin of a married couple.

Without hesitation, Forbes bellowed mockingly: 'Secure him and keep a watch over the lubber, and deposit him on the first iceberg we find in [the southern seas].'

Fortunately for the unwanted guest, *Marco Polo* was still under tow, so he was transferred to *Independence* and returned to Liverpool.

'When the tug left we gave Her two Cannons and as many Hurrahs as the Lungs of the *Marco Polo* would permit', Bird wrote, then explained that over the next few hours all passengers spent time preparing their cabins and adapting to their new lifestyle, while amid 'such Bustle and confusion, the Band on Deck played all the liveliest Tunes they could think off'.

Antelope departed England some days ahead of *Marco Polo*, but just as when he raced *Red Jacket* the following year, it didn't concern Forbes. He was confident his ship would sail the fastest time to Melbourne that season – so confident, in fact, that he is believed to have had bets with eleven other captains sailing there. But it was unquestionably the bet against *Antelope* that mattered most.

From the outset, Forbes left no doubt that he would maintain firm control over the behaviour of his passengers. But – despite the advertised claims about his 'kindness to his passengers' – some of his methods for maintaining decorum were severe by today's standards. Edwin Bird's diary did reveal that Forbes did his best to be civil:

The Captain came down on the second Deck inspecting the lights being Burnt privately after 9 O'Clock and as regards to loud singing and cards. He talked to them in the right style.

But then there was this:

The Captain went round last night at 11 O'Clock to see things all right. He found one of the Stewards very tipsy and saucy with it. He took a Lamp from a passenger's Hand and Floor'd Him with it.

By 20 March, *Marco Polo*'s passengers were getting their first taste of a full-blown Atlantic gale that lasted overnight and throughout the next day. Bird was comfortable with the experience, but a lot of the passengers weren't. His diary revealed: 'going 13 knots with the topsail and royal close reefed Ladies all Sick again, not one present at the Dinner [lunch] table'. He added that those absent had missed out on a good soup.

Eight days into the voyage, Bully Forbes had impressive news for all on board: *Marco Polo* was already 1700 miles from Liverpool, approaching Madeira ... and a full two days ahead of the ship's position at the same time during her previous record-breaking voyage. The captain was already suggesting they might be 'safe at anchor in Australia in eight weeks': a new record by far.

Contributing to this astonishing pace was the patented sail-reefing system the ship was carrying. Instead of having to send men aloft to reef the topsails each time the wind increased in strength, the sails could now be reefed from the deck in just fifteen minutes.

A few days later, when *Marco Polo* was feeling the first influences of the northern-hemisphere trade-wind belt, Bird wrote that the captain was destined to have a tough time with numerous passengers, including females, before Australia was reached:

There was a tremendous Row last night between the Irish Ladies and some of our Passengers. They came on Board as Widows of Officers and Gentlemans Daughters, But [I] was surprised at Hearing the noise so late. I jumped out of my Bunk and to my surprise one of those Ladies was Swearing away and challenged to fight any man on Board the *Marco Polo* … They are about all night long … The Captain Has, through the advice of His good Lady, for such she has advised him, put up a Notice on the Poop Cabin today that no ladies are to be on Deck after 10 O'clock without being accompanied by their Husbands which of course no respectable Female would do, and Mrs Forbes declared she would not walke the deck if such Lounging about on the Poop was not stopd.

The new rules were respected for less than two weeks. In late March, Bird wrote his next instalment:

> The Captn went below last evening rather late. He found two of the Cabin Passengers with the rest of the Gang Drinking their Wine and concockting there for plunder, I have no doubt. He took them by the scruf of the neck and sent them on Deck and after that He began with the Ladies. Swore if He caught either of them on the Poop Deck again He would throw them over Board, and if not quieter than last night He would land them all on the Cape Verd[e] Islands in the morning (which we sighted about 4 O'Clock) which would be altogether about 23 of them … One Passenger was lashed to the Rigging this afternoon for not paying His fine. There has been a fight just now in the 3rd Cabin between some of the Tipperary Boys, which are Cases.

Much to Forbes's relief, *Marco Polo* soon struck rough and wet weather – conditions boisterous enough to curtail much of the partying on board. They also prevented the ship's band from doing its evening presentation. Instead, those who weren't seasick amused themselves by playing drafts, cribbage and chess with other passengers.

Around this same time, sadness hung over the entire ship when it became known that a baby boy had died. Such tragic moments were not unusual on a long voyage like this, but it was a fitting tribute to the captain and his crew, including the ship's doctor, that by the time Melbourne was sighted, only four passengers had passed away. One man died as a result of complications from a broken leg.

By 30 March, the captain and all aboard were becoming increasingly impressed with the ship's progress. *Marco Polo*, now seventeen days out from Liverpool, caught and passed another ship that was twenty-six days out of England and also heading for Melbourne. At 10am this ship hove into view on the horizon ahead, and by 6pm she was the same distance behind: an amazing gain of 30 miles in daylight hours for *Marco Polo*. Bird's diary note explained why she had achieved this horizon-to-horizon run in such a short period: 'We are now going at a Spanking rate 14 Nots, all sails set, while our Opponent is going under Close reef top Sail.'

However, all were quick to accept that when traversing oceans, nothing is ever certain because of the vagaries of the weather. Within two days, when closing on the Equator, *Marco Polo* was glued to an oily sea in a windless tropical calm. Only occasionally, when a gentle swell rolled through, was there any motion; the ship stirred ever so slowly and the sails, hanging like heavy drapes, slatted and panted in response. The one benefit for all was that when the rain finally came, it was in torrents. Those who cared to took the opportunity to shower in the open air. These periods of calm and torrential cloud bursts persisted until 6 April, except when the occasional brief squall passed through.

Added interest came when another vessel out of London sailed into view. Captain Forbes ordered a longboat to be lowered over the side and rowed five miles to the ship so they could share information. She was a Dutch-crewed ship bound for Melbourne, with only twenty-eight passengers. The weather remained so calm that, as Bird related, 'they made up a Party and came on Board the *Marco Polo* and Dined with us and stayed until 6 O'Clock and since it was such a treat to see so many Different faces and to Hear such a nice Band as ours was, they all got pretty tight before leaving and Had to pul [row] Back in the Dark and many of our passengers got a little on.'

Alcohol obviously flowed freely among all, because Bird noted that 'One Cabin passenger, Mr Gardener, Got put in Chains for the Night. He threatened to Shoot the Captain and insulted Mrs Forbes and several of the passengers. We are [still] Nocking about in a Dead Calm.'

The light and variable winds persisted, right through to 12 April, a steamy and very hot day, when, at 1pm, *Marco Polo* glided across the Equator in near-glassy conditions. It was a milestone that called for a celebration among the passengers: 'Spring Music and Shampagne and Wine was the order of the Day.'

The following day, again hot and rainy, Bird recorded that the celebrations the previous day had gone on for so long that '90 per cent well Drunk and we are expecting a rough night'.

For much of the time that the ship was ambling through the equatorial regions, the majority of passengers escaped the rank, stifling conditions in the accommodation areas by sleeping on deck. However, whenever a cloud burst descended on the ship at night there came a highly entertaining spectacle as passengers panicked, grabbing their bedding and scrambling down the narrow companionways to their sleeping quarters.

On 22 April, *Marco Polo* was abeam of the Cape of Good Hope and the signs in the sky indicated rough weather was on the way. Still, dramas continued on board, most of them alcohol-infused and revolving around the Irish men. Bird's summation was simple: 'Rows with the Irish. One got in Chains for threatening the life of Mrs McDonald [the wife of the first mate]'.

Four days later, *Marco Polo* was powering into the southern seas. Her average speed, which came with the assistance of large and powerful swells and a howling westerly wind, was beginning to convince the captain that his already famous ship was within reach of her second consecutive record time for the run from Liverpool to Melbourne. But there were still thousands of nautical miles to cover before the goal was achieved.

As had been the case on *Marco Polo*'s first voyage to Melbourne the previous year, Forbes did not take a backward step when it came to maintaining maximum speed at all times. If he had to consider reefing or furling a sail because of the wind strength, then it stayed as it was until he was certain the change had to be made. When it came to navigation, he ensured that the ship was benefiting at all times from the current and wind patterns that Matthew Maury had plotted.

Now that they were in the zone of the Roaring Forties, charging ahead on the face of the powerful westerly winds, the ship's course was south of east – as close as possible to the great circle route. Few, if any, passengers dared venture onto the deck, which all too often was awash with a surging mass of icy-cold white water. The ever-present danger was hard enough for highly experienced crew to deal with, and the last thing they needed was the sight of a passenger being bowled along the deck on the face of a wave that had come cascading over the leeward bulwark.

During this particular storm, even life below deck was punishing, as Bird noted:

Sometimes ½ a Gale and a Heavy sea which made us Roll awful. Breaking Plat[e]s upsetting forms [benches] giving Young Ladies Black Eyes by being thrown from their births, upsetting Soup, Breaking Legs, Heads and so forth. Passengers tumbling from one end of the Deck to the other and sometimes flowing with Soup ...
Fights and Rows are the order of the day. All through Whiskey ... We have Had 4 extraordinary days Sailing in succession averaging nearly 300 miles per day going 14 Nots now. Therm[ometer] stood 52 [degrees] on Deck this morning which made a change of 80 degrees in 16 days ... Now we are getting so cold ... Great Coats and Shawls are in great request. The 2nd May we Had a severe Hail Storm Here while you Had a

Beautiful May day in England. The next time I wright
my log I expect Snow will be on the Deck ... We are
going on so nicely I should say we must be in
Melbourne the latter part of May.

The tempest hammered *Marco Polo* and created havoc for
passengers and crew for more than a week. Much to Forbes's
frustration, four heavy canvas sails blew to shreds when savage
squalls arrived unannounced. Worse still, it was too rough and
dangerous to haul down the wildly flaying remnants of those
sails and have crew go aloft and replace them with new ones.

Eventually Forbes – great seaman that he was – had to
accept that it was time to apply common sense and prudent
seamanship. The conditions were continuing to deteriorate
and become treacherous; there was no option but to furl or
lower the sails that were still set and lay to until the weather
improved.

During the next twenty-four hours, *Marco Polo* was pitched
and tossed by gigantic and often breaking seas. The few crew
members remaining on deck became horrendously cold and
wet, while below deck the majority of passengers – most never
having been to sea before – remained cowering in their often
damp bunks, all wondering how much punishment the ship
could absorb.

When the worst of the storm had disappeared over the
horizon to the east, the conditions quickly improved. The
moment it was considered safe to proceed, Forbes called for

the appropriate number of sails to be set, at the same time advising the helmsman, standing at the wheel on the poop deck, what the new course would be.

The loss of a day when lying a-hull was deemed expensive, particularly when *Marco Polo* was racing to secure the fastest time to Melbourne against almost a dozen other ships. But in conditions like those just experienced, only a logical and practical approach to seamanship could have been applied. Now, with all sails set, *Marco Polo* was back at full clip, covering 300 nautical miles in one day, and 342 in another: an impressive average of 14.25 knots.

Though the ship was making good speed, everyone on board had to endure bitterly cold weather delivering snow, rain and sleet from leaden skies. Bird's diary revealed that life on board was still miserable:

> There is not much going on Deck now, it's so cold.
> Music and singing, reading and such like is the order of
> the day, with concerts in the evening. We stay in our
> Births all day and Burn 2 Lamps to heat it and read and
> write.

The weather began to improve – but temporarily:

> From May 11th to Wed. May the 18th we Have Had a
> lovely week of weather as fine as a Sailor can wish for
> and as good a Breeze ... We sighted the Island of

Desolation [Kerguelen Islands] on Saturday about 4 in
the afternoon, the exact time the Captain said we
should, which proves that Hes a good navigator. Just as
we sighted it a tremendous Hail Squall sprung up
which lasted some time. Had we not at that time
within 10 Minutes we must Have been on the Rocks as
we were going at a precious rate. Its a long and large
Island with Mounds of Rocks laying out in the Sea,
which Has the appearance of Iceburghs at a distance ...
The thermometer stands 30 on Deck this morning.
Decks covered with Snow and Bitter and cold this
morning. Snowballing the order of the morning.
A man put in chains for Striking the Captain also the
Baker and Cook in Limbo ... I hope we shall sight
Land this day Week.

Then, approximately 1200 nautical miles to the south-west of
Albany in Western Australia, *Marco Polo* was confronted by
another danger. Bird chronicled:

From Wed 18th up to Wed 23rd May this has been a
very rough week of Weather. We Had Had one Sharp
Gale of wind this Week taking away more of our Sails
which we are very short of, which detained us again a
little. We saw a very large Ice Burgh on Sunday about
10 times as big as the *Marco Polo*. A grand sight it was.
Just at day break with the Breakers flying again ...

315

By now everyone was becoming anxious about reaching Melbourne – and the goldfields. Adding to this unease was news that 'All the live stock is used up, the last of the Mutton and Pork [was eaten] today with the exception of a Sow and a few Half Starved Fowls'. But most of all, everyone wanted to know if *Marco Polo* would win the race against *Antelope* and the others, in a contest where none of the opposition had been sighted.

They did not have to wait long to find out. At eight o'clock in the evening on Saturday, 26 May, a light appeared on the horizon ahead, off the port bow. It was the lighthouse at Cape Otway, at the entrance to Bass Strait. Once the lighthouse was abeam, Forbes called for sail to be reduced so the ship would slow down and reach the entrance to Port Phillip Bay in daylight.

In the middle of the night, the ship's lookout, positioned high in the rig, shouted to those on deck that he could see the outline of a ship ahead. *Marco Polo* sailed up to her, and as soon as she came alongside, much jubilation filled the air. Bird explained what followed: 'She proved to be the *Hallifax* from London 116 Days out and the Dutch Captain was quite flabbergasted when He was informed we were out only 73 days.'

With the assistance of a Port Phillip pilot who had come out from the shore, Forbes guided his ship through the swirling and treacherous waters at the entrance to the bay at 8am and continued north to the anchorage at Hobson's Bay. Before long this anchorage was easily identifiable to those on board as countless masts came into view. They resembled a forest of dead conifers, all entwined by a web of vines.

Here, having noted that 'the bay is full of ships', Bird made his last diary entry relating to the voyage:

> Melbourne is now in sight and quite a sight to see the
> tents pitched along the Beach. The Country appears
> very level and very green considering its now within
> 3 weeks of the Midst of their Winter. We all go ashore
> to Morrow in Hopes of getting hold of some Dust as
> there is good news from Melbourne and the Diggings.

Not long after the anchor was cast, and the bosun had confirmed that it was set, first a ripple of excitement, then a tumultuous roar, erupted among the hundreds of passengers and crew on deck. Deafening cheers went up when it was announced that *Marco Polo*'s time for the 13,000 nautical miles from Liverpool was faster than all other rivals – including *Antelope*, which, despite having steamed away from Liverpool before *Marco Polo* set sail, was yet to be seen.

While everyone celebrated the win and the fact that *Marco Polo* had bettered her previous record by some hours, Bully Forbes could take pride in his achievement and look forward to collecting the heavy bets that had been placed with him by rival captains.

Within twenty-four hours, though, Forbes received tragic news relating to a close friend, Captain Mackay, who was the master of the ship *Sea*. Not long after *Marco Polo* had arrived in port, Mackay had guided his ship away from Hobson's Bay at the start of a voyage to Callao in Peru. Early the following morning, Mackay ignored warnings from pilots not to exit through the reef-riddled entrance to Port Phillip Bay because a fast-flowing ebb tide and storm-driven seas offshore were making conditions extremely dangerous.

When *Sea* was halfway out to the open ocean, a tacking manoeuvre went horribly wrong: she stalled head-to-wind – stopped making headway – and would not respond to the helm. *Sea* was then at the mercy of the powerful, ugly seas and churning tidal eddies. In a very short time, she was beyond help, and being driven beam-on towards the surf-covered rocks at Point Nepean, on the eastern side of the entrance to the bay. Inevitably, one giant wave loomed onto the scene and hammered the ship onto those rocks.

Despite efforts by the brave crew aboard a whaleboat that had been launched from the pilot schooner *Boomerang* in the hope of reaching the stricken vessel, there was nothing that could be done. At nightfall, men could still be seen clinging to the forward section of the ship, but by morning they were gone: Captain Mackay and his entire crew had perished.

It was reported later that the captain possibly had some of his crew locked in irons while at anchor in Melbourne to prevent them from jumping ship and heading to the goldfields. He apparently intended to release them when the ship was in Bass Strait and well away from the coast.

*

Meanwhile, the sail-versus-steam race between *Marco Polo* and *Antelope* turned into a non-event. The steamship limped into Port Phillip Bay after an embarrassingly slow voyage of 163 days – a time due mainly, it is believed, to a series of mechanical failures.

By the time *Antelope* entered the port, *Marco Polo* was just four weeks from arriving back in Liverpool, after recording some impressive twenty-four hour runs while crossing the southern seas. A boisterous welcome awaited Forbes when he guided his ship back into the Mersey on 13 September – exactly six months after departing for Melbourne.

A month earlier, *Great Britain* had set off on yet another voyage to Melbourne, a passage that *did* confirm the potential of steamships on such a long journey. Despite experiencing some rough weather in the Roaring Forties and Furious Fifties, she reached Melbourne in sixty-five days: eight days quicker than *Marco Polo*'s best time over the same course. Her return voyage was even more remarkable: while the distance back to England was considerably greater than the outbound route, *Great Britain* was home in just sixty-two days.

Following the near-embarrassing performance of the much-touted *Antelope*, the rapid round-the-world run by *Great Britain* reclaimed a considerable amount of respectability for the coal-burners. But the swiftness of the considerably smaller *Marco Polo* on her second run to Melbourne had left no doubt that for the time being, the long-haul course was still very much the domain of purebred sailing ships. The fast-flying clippers that carried emigrants drawn by the magnetic appeal of that non-magnetic metal, gold, were the reason why the power of sail remained dominant in the marketplace.

However, there was one telling factor when it came to these great ships: the ability of captain and crew to drive their charges at full clip while remaining safe. And once again, Bully Forbes had proved just that as master of *Marco Polo* on her second circumnavigation of the globe.

Sadly, it would only be another fifteen years before a great engineering feat amid the sands of Egypt heralded the final downfall of these beautiful birds of the sea, and ensured that the steamers would finally triumph. Still, the last hurrah of the great clippers would be their most spectacular phase of all.

CHAPTER 9

Triumph of the Steam Kettles

The end of the clipper era

It was late 1861. More than 10,000 peasants – forced labourers – were hacking their way through Egyptian sand dunes using crude picks and shovels, and with each blow they struck and each spadeful of sand they heaved, the death knell of the clipper ships was being sounded ever louder.

These were the beginnings of one of the world's engineering masterpieces: the Suez Canal. It was a project that would see 75 million cubic metres of sand removed over the next eight years so that the Mediterranean Sea and the Red Sea could be linked by a canal that was wide and deep enough for the largest commercial vessels to pass though. The canal would be a mere 104 nautical miles long, but its existence would mean that the voyage from Europe to South Asia – which had previously meant rounding the Cape of Good

Hope and sailing into the Indian Ocean – was reduced by more than 3750 nautical miles.

This, coupled with the improving speed and reliability of steam-powered ships, would also have a direct impact on passages from Europe to Australia. For the Suez Canal would be the domain of the steamers alone: sailing ships would not be able to pass through because the prevailing winds did not suit. Yes, they could be towed through the canal by a steam tug, but that would be a costly and difficult exercise.

The Suez Canal could have been built many years earlier. Napoleon Bonaparte, who became the Emperor of France in 1804, had contemplated its construction. However, the plan had been abandoned after French surveyors and engineers incorrectly calculated that the surface of the Mediterranean Sea was 33 feet below that of the Red Sea: a circumstance that would require expensive locks to be built into the canal system. Later, it would be proved that the sea levels of the two waterways were identical.

It was another Frenchman, Ferdinand de Lesseps, who finalised a ninety-nine year agreement with Egypt and Sudan in 1856 to construct and operate a canal that would be 'open to ships of all nations'. The project would take fifteen years to plan and complete. Initially, the construction was by hand, and a workforce of some thirty thousand forced labourers was used to carve the canal into the desert sands.

The use of what was effectively slave labour was strenuously opposed by the British Government, which had expressed its opposition to the project from the outset. However, the underlying reason for this sentiment was probably Britain's fear that the French – with whom they were frequently at war – would gain a distinct advantage over the Royal Navy through the canal's construction, particularly in the eastern Mediterranean, where some of their more recent conflicts had occurred.

With no chance of a negotiated agreement between the two adversaries regarding the use of peasants as a workforce, the British took matters into their own hands: they sent armed Bedouins among the labourers to start revolts. It was a ploy that delivered the desired result. In 1863 the Khedive of Egypt and Sudan, Isma'il Pasha, bowed to this and other international pressure and abruptly banned the use of forced labour.

While this was a major setback for Lesseps's company, it eventually proved to be a windfall. The use of the labourers for the construction of the canal had proved to be agonisingly slow and expensive. So, with manpower no longer available to him, Lesseps built specially designed steam-powered dredges and shovels that could quickly and efficiently transfer the removed sand onto the adjacent shores.

*

At the official opening of the canal on 17 November 1869, the celebrations were upstaged – once again, by the British.

The honour of opening the canal was bestowed on Isma'il Pasha, and he invited Empress Eugénie of France – the wife of Napoleon III – to join him aboard the imperial yacht *L'Aigle* (*Eagle*), which was to lead the fleet and become the first vessel to officially pass through the canal.

However, on the night before the opening ceremony, Captain George Nares of the Royal Navy decided it was time to fly the British flag in the face of the French. He guided his ship HMS *Newport* into the canal and, in complete darkness, navigated his way through the fleet of ships waiting to be part of the next day's celebrations, to a position in front of *L'Aigle*.

It was a mortifying sight for the French when they awoke the next morning: not only was HMS *Newport* positioned at the head of the fleet with her British ensign flying proudly, but they also knew that the narrowness of the canal would prevent *L'Aigle* from passing her at any point once the parade of ships got underway.

The French immediately lodged a terse complaint with the Royal Navy. Captain Nares's superiors served him with an official reprimand – then unofficially congratulated him on his excellent night-time navigation skills, and on promoting British interests to the eyes of the world.

The opening of the canal brought a rapid and dramatic change to international trade. With the world's first transcontinental railroad between America's east and west coasts finally having been opened just months earlier, it was now possible to transport passengers and cargo right across the northern hemisphere without having to sail around either Cape Horn or the Cape of Good Hope.

*

On 22 November 1869, just five days after the opening of the Suez Canal, a clipper that was to be hailed the fastest ship that ever left the ways was launched in Dumbarton, at the eastern end of Scotland's Firth of Clyde.

Just before she slid down the well-greased slipways at the Scott & Linton shipyard and into the chilly waters of the River Leven, a bottle of red wine was broken over her bow, and with that, she was given a most unusual name: *Cutty Sark*. Before long, as the sea miles lying in her wake increased dramatically, this ship became legendary among seafarers and the public in England, China and Australia.

Her launching came just two decades after the first of the true clippers was seen under sail, and while she was not the largest ever built, she epitomised how dramatically the clipper concept had advanced. Famed English maritime author Basil Lubbock, in his 1924 book *The Log of the Cutty Sark*, extracted a quote from an old seaman who had previously sailed on clippers considered to be among the best, including 'what was probably the fastest four-mast barque ever launched, *Loch Torridon*'. The seaman's letter to the author read in part:

I served on board the *Thermopylae* on her maiden voyage, 1868–9, when she made the quickest passage ever between London and Melbourne, 60 days from pilot to pilot, and 61 port to port. I also served on board *Ariel, Cutty Sark, James Baines, Lightning, Serica, Taeping* and *Loch Torridon* and haven't the slightest hesitation in saying that the *Cutty Sark* was the swiftest of the lot.

Lubbock unearthed two other strong endorsements: 'During the whole time I never saw anything pass her, steam or sail' and 'I never sailed a finer ship. At 10 and 12 knots an hour she did not disturb the water at all. She was the fastest ship of her day.'

Everything was different about *Cutty Sark* – her shape, dimensions, even her name. The owners of the Yankee clippers had used *Glory of the Seas, Flying Cloud, Eagle Wing* and so many other classic monikers, while the British at this time were excited by mental images engendered by the names of ships on the Australian emigration run: *Champion of the Seas, Queen of the Colonies, Chariot of Fame, Dawn of Hope* and the like.

However, Jock 'White Hat' Willis, the head of the family company John Willis & Sons shipping line – founded in 1791 by his father, John 'Old Stormy' Willis – would have none of these fanciful traditions when it came to naming his exciting new cargo clipper. Instead, he turned to a work by Scottish poet Robbie Burns, 'Tam o' Shanter', published in the same year as the company was established.

The poem related the story of Tam, a farmer who had a regular habit of getting drunk after attending the village markets in the Scottish town of Ayr. One particular night he was in his usual state of inebriation, riding his horse Meg towards home, when he passed a well-illuminated church that was known to be haunted. Intrigued by this sight, and still drunk, Tam turned Meg towards the church, and on reaching the edge of the halo of light coming from the building, he was able to see witches and warlocks inside, dancing merrily while the devil played the bagpipes.

He was struck immediately by the sight of Nannie, a remarkably beautiful and lustful young witch – 'ae winsome wench' – wearing a short, see-through linen sark (chemise). She was reeling and dancing erotically in an entirely carefree mood. Tam was overcome by this sensuous scene, so to voice his approval while not knowing her name, he shouted: 'Weel done, cutty-sark!' (Well done, short chemise!) Realising the witches and warlocks were then aware of his presence, Tam immediately turned Meg and high-tailed it towards home with the witches and warlocks in pursuit. He made it to safety across the bridge spanning the River Doon, but not before the winsome wench – his 'Cutty Sark' – had caught Meg's tail and ripped it off.

The image of the seductive witch Nannie, reeling around in her short and flimsy sark, was the inspiration for the ship's name and her famous figurehead. Nannie's barely covered breasts were consistent with the widely held belief of superstitious sailors that a figurehead featuring a woman's cleavage pacified the seas (unlike another maritime superstition that said it was bad luck to have a woman on board). However, setting the figurehead of Nannie apart from all others was her outstretched arm, the hand of which grasped a horse tail made from rope.

The skill of the figurehead maker was one of the least recognised talents in shipbuilding. He was an artisan as much as a woodworker, a man who could take a large balk of knotless timber and, using everything from the smallest razor-sharp knife or chisel through to a similarly sharp adze, deftly carve then paint a remarkably lifelike creation that would stand proudly beneath a ship's bowsprit. Here, *Cutty Sark*'s figurehead maker excelled.

Having been impressed by the hull shape and performance of a sailing ship-cum-steam paddle wheeler, *Tweed*, John Willis had no hesitation in having the lines of her hull virtually replicated in the drawings for his soon-to-be-ordered ship. For that, he went to a promising young Scottish designer, Hercules Linton, who had recently established a shipyard in Dumbarton in partnership with a man named Scott.

Before the design process began, Willis took Linton to see *Tweed* when she was in dry dock, and this experience, along with consultation with two of *Tweed*'s captains, enabled the designer to decide on the final shape of the latest addition to the Willis fleet. His theory was that it would be difficult to improve on the shape of *Tweed*'s forward sections: she was particularly fast to windward, easily driven, and not difficult to tack. But it was his firm belief that the stern sections should be broader and more buoyant than those of *Tweed*, so that the new ship stood less chance of being pooped in heavy seas, and would surf down waves faster while being easier to handle.

Willis's contract for the building of the 212-foot 6-inch hull was a tough one: construction had to be completed within six months, the maximum weight would be 950 tons at a cost of £17 per ton, and there was a £5 penalty for every day late beyond the designated launch date.

Captain George Moodie, who was to be the commander for the ship's first three voyages, supervised the construction. He was considered the finest of all captains at the time, described by Basil Lubbock as 'a careful navigator, with a great deal of Scotch caution, which made him disinclined to take risks in the China Seas like some of his rivals, he knew how to carry sail, and he was a magnificent seaman and a good businessman'.

Cutty Sark's composite construction saw East India teak used for the topside planking and American rock elm below the waterline, all fixed with Muntz metal fastenings to wrought-iron frames and diagonals.

A month after she was launched, when the finishing touches to the hull and cargo area below deck were completed, *Cutty Sark* was towed a few miles downstream from Dumbarton, where she was rigged and masted. Like *Tweed*, her foremast was unusually far aft from the stem while the main and mizzen masts were conventionally positioned. It was probably anticipated that this rig configuration would make her easier to tack and safer when sailing in strong winds and large following seas. Her lower masts, lower yards and bowsprit were made from iron, while the rest of her spars were shaped from Oregon pine. She had five shrouds supporting each mast and a surprising eight backstays in all – probably a feature required by Captain Moodie so that the ship could be driven to the limit in strong winds without the fear of being dismasted. A total of 400 tons of ballast was required when she was not carrying cargo.

Accommodation for the captain and crew was above the usual standard. The captain's and officers' accommodation on the aft deck was panelled in teak and bird's-eye maple, much of which featured ornate carving. The teak furniture came from the best cabinetmaker in the region, while the captain, who on similar ships would normally sleep in a bunk, had the pleasure of reposing in a teak four-poster bed. It was said that *Cutty Sark* 'both aloft, on deck and below was fitted up like a millionaire's yacht'.

When everything was in readiness, Captain Moodie and his crew sailed the gleaming new *Cutty Sark* out of the Firth of Clyde and south to London, where she was prepared for her first commercial voyage.

*

This was a time in history when the world's oceans formed one gigantic racecourse; the two major capes were the turning points and the clipper ships were the thoroughbreds. Of all the passages these ships sailed, it was the tea route from China to England that formed the track for the major annual event. Fortunes were won and lost through wagers on which ship would be first into port with her precious load of the new season's tea. Even crewmen were known to put on the line some, if not all, of the wage they would receive for the voyage.

The Tea Race – which newspapers often referred to as the Great Ship Race – was the specific trade route for which *Cutty Sark* was designed and built. Willis was after a ship capable of winning the great race, and in his mind, *Cutty Sark*, with Moodie aboard as captain, gave him his best chance of lowering the colours of the then fastest ship on the tea run, *Thermopylae*.

It was 16 February 1870 when *Cutty Sark* sailed from London, bound for Shanghai with a cargo of wine, spirits and beer. On the return voyage, she carried a cargo of 1.3 million pounds of tea back to London. She arrived there on 13 October after a voyage taking a respectable 110 days.

It wasn't until 1872 that the much-anticipated showdown between *Cutty Sark* and the all-conquering *Thermopylae* came to pass. Heavily laden with cargoes of tea, both ships departed Shanghai together on 18 June, and by the time they were off Hong Kong, *Cutty Sark* was holding an impressive lead despite having had her fore topgallant blown to shreds. (Numerous other sails were to follow over the next three weeks.)

When the wind went light, *Cutty Sark* showed a clear superiority over her rival, and by 27 June she was hull-down ahead – a mere speck on the horizon from the deck of *Thermopylae*. Eleven days later, *Cutty Sark* was a remarkable 400 nautical miles ahead of her adversary, head-reaching in a powerful sea. Conditions were described in the ship's log as 'a hard gale with howling squalls', weather that proved too much for the fore and main lower topsails, which subsequently blew to pieces.

By the first week of August the two ships were well across the equator and sailing towards the Cape of Good Hope in conditions as cold as could be expected in the southern-hemisphere winter.

Suddenly, on August 15, as first light was breaking in the east, a massive wave slammed under *Cutty Sark*'s stern and tore her rudder from its mountings.

Captain Moodie immediately called for one of the ship's spars to be lashed to the taffrail so it could be used as a sweep oar for steering, but this proved totally ineffective.

The only person who was happy about these developments was the ailing Robert Willis – the brother of *Cutty Sark*'s owner – who was aboard the ship in the hope of improving his health. Willis, who was far from enjoying the passage, saw this situation as an opportunity to be put ashore at the nearest South African port, but Captain Moodie would have no part of it. He called for the ship to heave to and ordered his carpenter and others to make a jury rudder using a spare spar and pieces of iron.

Quite fortuitously, there were two stowaways found aboard *Cutty Sark* after she departed Shanghai – one an English carpenter, and the other a Scottish blacksmith. The carpenter helped shape the rudder, while the blacksmith formed bolts, straps and bars so the rudder could be attached to the sternpost with the use of eye bolts. It took five laborious days – during which *Cutty Sark* rolled constantly from gunwale to gunwale in heavy seas – before the job was completed in what was nothing short of miraculous circumstances.

The endeavour was not without incident, however: on one occasion the ship lurched so violently that the forge, filled with red-hot coals, was upset into the shirt of the captain's young son. He was scarred for life.

On the afternoon of 21 August, conditions had abated to the degree where sails could be set and *Cutty Sark* returned to her homeward course. The jury rudder lasted for a month. When the ship was north of St Helena Island, the eye bolts failed, as did the chains being used to turn the rudder from deck level, so the contrivance had to be lifted aboard for repairs.

Incredibly, after fifty-four days of sailing with the jury rudder fitted, *Cutty Sark* was in the English Channel, much to the plaudits of Moodie's crew. Following this superb display of seamanship, Captain Moodie went on to guide his ship into London after a total passage time of 122 days – a mere seven days behind *Thermopylae*.

*

But what is recognised as the greatest Tea Race of all had come five years earlier, in 1866, between the clipper ships *Fiery Cross*, *Ariel*, *Taeping* and *Serica*. *Fiery Cross* departed Foochow on 29 May and the other three the following day, on a course covering some 16,000 nautical miles.

After ninety-nine days at sea, *Taeping* and *Ariel* entered the English Channel and raced side by side towards the entrance to the Thames. It was only the fact that *Taeping* drew less water than her rival that enabled her to enter the river and dock in London on a lower tide than *Ariel* required if she were to avoid running aground. The winning margin was just twenty minutes. *Serica* arrived a mere two hours later, while *Fiery Cross* reached London two days in arrears.

But by the end of 1872, it was becoming apparent that the 'steam kettles' were on their way to claiming the lion's share of the tea business between China and Europe. During the previous twelve months, forty-five steamers destined for the tea trade had been launched from shipyards on the Clyde. It was soon evident to all that there was no longer any place for the clippers on this run.

It appears that, by this time, John Willis and Captain Moodie had had a falling out over what Willis referred to as Moodie's 'pigheadedness'. The owner stood his ground, and before long decided that the one man he could trust when it came to commanding his much-loved *Cutty Sark* was Captain

F.W. Moore, who had previously worked as his superintendent within the company.

Between 15 November and 2 December 1872, a heavily laden *Cutty Sark* and three other clippers, *Duke of Abercorn*, *Blackadder* and *Thomas Stephens*, departed London for either Melbourne or Sydney. Of the four, it was *Cutty Sark*'s sixty-nine day passage to Port Phillip that stood as the most impressive, especially considering the amount of cargo she was carrying.

But by the late 1870s, she was tramping for cargoes around the world. In December 1877, now under Captain W.E. Tiptaft, she sailed from London a month late after crashing into two anchored ships in the English Channel while waiting out a storm, and having to be towed back up the Thames for repairs. She arrived in Sydney with a wide variety of cargo crammed into her cargo area 'tween decks, including tea, jute and castor oil. Unfortunately there was no profitable return cargo to be had, so she took on a load of coal and delivered it to Shanghai, where Captain Tiftaft sadly died in October and was replaced by James Wallace, the first mate.

Tragedy came in 1880 when *Cutty Sark* was commissioned to take a full load of coal from Cardiff in Wales to American naval ships in Yokohama, Japan – a passage during which some of the crew mutinied and her well-respected new captain committed suicide.

This terrible event stemmed from the actions of the ship's first mate, Sydney Smith, a callous and brutal slave-driver who had no respect for the crew. During a storm in the Indian Ocean, crewman John Francis ignored the first mate's orders and threatened him with an iron bar, which Smith then used to strike Francis across the head. Francis died of his wounds days later, and Wallace had Smith confined to his quarters.

On approach to Anjer in Indonesia, it was realised that Smith was missing; the fact was that he had begged Captain Wallace to smuggle him aboard another vessel so he could escape trial. The crew immediately advised their captain that they would not sail the ship until the murderer was found – to which Wallace responded by clapping four of the ringleaders of the mutiny in irons, so that some semblance of order would return to the ship.

After departing Anjer for Yokohama, and while the ship was becalmed in the Java Sea, Captain Wallace became increasingly concerned about the role he had played in aiding Smith's escape and the consequences he would face at the inevitable investigation. The burden on his conscience soon became too much for him to endure. So at 4am on the fourth day into the journey, just as the new watch had been called on deck, Wallace walked aft, while directing the helmsman to check his compass course. He then stepped up onto the taffrail and leaped overboard, never to be seen again.

Cutty Sark eventually made her way to Singapore, and John Willis arranged with Captain Fowler of *Hallowe'en*, another ship in his fleet, to have *Hallowe'en*'s chief officer,

William Bruce, join *Cutty Sark* as captain. Fowler was only too pleased to oblige, as he 'hated his chief officer like poison and was only too delighted to get rid of him'.

Within days of Bruce's arrival onboard, *Cutty Sark*'s crew clearly understood why Fowler had encouraged his departure. He proved to be an incompetent master who claimed pay for non-existent crew and always under-provisioned the ship to save money. At one stage there was even a full-scale mutiny in protest. He was replaced after just eighteen months by Captain Moore of the clipper *Blackadder*.

In 1880 *Cutty Sark* had her sail plan reduced, and this made her safer and more manageable when charging before howling westerly winds in the southern seas and while en route to Australia. Her lower masts were reduced by almost 10 feet in height, and 7 feet were lopped from her lower yards. Despite this reduction in sail area, she remained surprisingly swift in light airs. At this time her crew numbered twenty-eight, including the captain.

In July 1883, *Cutty Sark* finally found a new vocation. That month she departed Gravesend in England bound for Newcastle north of Sydney, arriving there just 78 days later. In December that year, she departed Newcastle with 4289 bales of wool crammed into her cargo holds, along with twelve casks of tallow. In what proved to be a rapid run across the southern seas and north into the Atlantic, she was back in London in a remarkable 83 days: the best time for the year by for vessels sailing from Australia's east coast to England for that year.

Soon *Cutty Sark* had become one of the most sought-after ships for the highly profitable wool trade, delivering the finest Australian fleeces to London. She would make a name for herself as one of the four great wool clippers – the others being *Thermopylae*, *Mermerus* and *Salamis*, the latter being an iron-hulled copy of *Thermopylae*.

After that 1883 passage, the man who would be lauded as the most successful master ever to walk *Cutty Sark*'s decks, Captain Richard Woodget, went aboard along with his three collie dogs and took command. He was recognised for his ability to lead a crew through all weather conditions, his skill as a navigator and 'feel' for a ship, and the understanding and respect he held for his men.

One of *Cutty Sark*'s most famous passages came under Woodget's stewardship in 1889 – by which time the sun was rapidly setting on the age of the clipper ships. Both *Cutty Sark* and the Peninsular and Oriental Steam Navigation Company's [P&O] crack mail steamer *Britannia* were voyaging from London to Sydney at the time. *Britannia* had passed through Bass Strait and turned north to sail the final 250 nautical miles to Sydney. A fresh 'southerly buster' was blowing and *Britannia* was logging around 14 knots.

That evening, though, there came an amazing sight for all on deck. They could only watch in awe as *Cutty Sark* – which they had passed just two hours earlier – came storming towards them from astern with a real bone in her teeth: a massive bow wave. She then hurtled past the 'steam kettle' amid clouds of spray – 2100 tons of ship and cargo, with sails and rig loaded to their limits while doing a consistent 17 knots.

It was during Woodget's time as captain that a youngster identified only as C.E. Ray, from the seaside town of Hastings, England, joined *Cutty Sark* as an apprentice sailor. He would provide future maritime historians with a wealth of enlightening and insightful detail relating to life on board, as seen through young eyes, via letters he wrote to his mother while serving his 'time' aboard the famous ship.

His early letters to her spoke of his gradual adjustment to life at sea:

25 June 94

My dear Mother,

The pilot leaves tonight I expect so I am writing this short note now in case I get no more time. I am quite well and enjoying myself. The weather is beautiful but hardly any wind. We are running about 5 knots at present … I have been hauling on the t-gallant halliards and therefore the writing is very bad. We have no proper watches yet I had to stop on deck all last night. I have been aloft as far as the main t'gallant yard two or 3 times …

Sunday 15th of July 94

We have a jolly lot of fellows in the 'house', there are six of us altogether, we are divided into two watches … the old man [Captain Woodget] has got 3 dogs,

scotch collies, and when we go down in the cabin to see
the time they go for us … If we go to sleep in our
watch on deck they make us ride the grey mare, that is,
sit up on the upper topsail yard for the rest of the watch.

Now I must tell you about the grub we get coffee at
5 o'clock every other morning coffee for breakfast and
tea for tea.

Monday Wednesday Friday – pea soup and pork
Tuesday Thursday – Salt Tram Horse [salted meat]
and bread
Saturday – Junk [salted meat] and Spuds
Sunday – Leu pie …

Leu pie is my favourite dinner it is cooked
altogether in a great pot, fresh meat and spuds all in
soup like, underneath and dough on the top. Oh Lor,
I could eat 3 whacks of it now, of course, we get any
amount of dog biscuit. We shall finish the last piece of
cake today for tea. We have kept it 3 weeks which I
think is a long time … We have not had any very bad
weather yet except in the Bay [of Biscay] where she
rolled till her lee main yard arm nearly touched the
water, and shipped seas over the foc's'le head and amid
ships …

Since then we have had fine weather, it is getting
very warm I never have more than a shirt and pants on
ever at night. We get any amount of flying fish, they fly
aboard at night, then all we have to do is catch them,

cut their heads, wings, tails and fins off, clean them and then put them on a plate with some butter over them, and give them to Jimmy to cook for our breakfast. Last night I caught thirteen.

Our first job at 5.30 in the morning is to wash the pigs and closets out. I always heard that pigs were unclean animals but now I know it for a positive fact and can prove it too. Ah it is a hard life but you need not think that I do not like it for I am enjoying myself very much. Last week I had to go to the wheel and learn to steer ...

C.E. Ray's final letter to his mother was written retrospectively, after *Cutty Sark* had reached her destination of Brisbane, and was full of the challenges faced on the latter part of the voyage:

18th Sept. 94
My Dear Mother,
We have arrived hear all safe and sound having made a passage of 80 days from the Downs to the bay here ...

Now I suppose you want to know how I am. Well I am all right and getting a muscle on me like a horse and you will be glad to hear that I have not had a day's illness of any kind since I have been aboard the ship. Not even a headache. Now I must tell you something about the Passage out ... About the Line [Equator] we got 3 or 4 days doldrums. Then came heavy squalls, I used to get wet every day then, I'll go to the wheel with nothing on but pants and shirt and then a heavy squall would come and drown me but I'd have to stop the 2 hours wet or no wet. Then it began to get colder and colder till we got round the Corner [the Cape of Good Hope] then we [had] 3 weeks very bad weather during which time we never had a dry deck. Then was the time to wish you had never come to sea (if there are any boys in Hastings who want to come to sea, show them this and tell them from me to stop in a good home when they got one) hanging on to the lee wheel at night was the worst with the seas (not the little sprays you see at Hastings) washing over continually. One time we were lashed on the Poop for a day and 2 nights when daylight came the 2nd day she looked a perfect wreck on deck, The cabin was washed out, our cuddy door was burst open (we saw this in the night, but no one dare go on the main deck to shut it) all the lower bunks were washed out. Mine being a top one did not suffer much, but all the things in my chest were more or less wet.

The next Sunday the skipper's son got washed into the lee scuppers and broke his arm. He is going to have the splints off next week, the doctor says he is very lucky to have it set right at sea. Soon after this our for t'gallant and royal mast [carried] away, the royal yard went overboard, the t'gallant was hanging in the rigging, the upper topsail yard was broke in two about 18 feet from the yard arm. I was up aloft all that night with the men clearing the wreck, and I was jolly glad when day dawned and the wind lulled a bit. There was no hot coffee that morning for the galley had been washed out. For a week after this we were rigging a jury mast and yards setting up back stays etc. there is a lot of work in this although it does not sound much. Soon after this we got into the straits and fine weather … the river pilot ashore this morning he told us that we would most likely lay here till Christmas as the shearers are on strike and that reminds me please save a piece of plum duff for me. I must knock off now so expect a long letter next mail from,

    Your loving

    Sailor boy

    C. E. Ray

    P.S. … Please excuse all mistakes in spelling, and bad writing.

By 1895, *Cutty Sark* had run her race: she was no longer a profitable venture for her owners, so she was sold to a Portuguese firm for £2100 and renamed *Ferreira*. However, the great ship would not die. By 1922, she was the last fully operational clipper ship anywhere in the world.

That year she was bought by a retired ship's captain, Wilfred Dowman, and finally in 1956 she made her last ever journey to Greenwich, on the banks of the River Thames in London. Despite a devastating fire in 2007, in what is nothing short of a fitting tribute to this remarkable vessel – and clipper ships in general – today *Cutty Sark* stands restored to all her glory, the only complete clipper that exists for all the world to see.

*

Fewer than one hundred true clipper ships were built from the time *Rainbow* was launched in New York in 1845 until the last of the breed hit the water less than thirty years later. Today only three are known to exist in any form, all of which were built using composite construction (featuring a wooden hull on an iron frame).

Apart from *Cutty Sark*, the rusted iron skeleton of the 176-foot *Ambassador* – with not a hull plank nor any other piece of timber to be seen – lies on an isolated beach near the Straits of Magellan in southern Chile. And in late 2013, after a fourteen-year campaign, a group of dedicated South Australian sailors and ship lovers, with the support of the Duke of Edinburgh, saved the near-derelict clipper *City of Adelaide* from certain death. Through an impressive community effort, the weather-beaten hulk that was once a grand clipper was recovered from an existence among weeds and bushes in a back corner of a shipyard in Irvine, on the banks of Scotland's Firth of Clyde, and transported by ship halfway around the world to the city from which she took her name – Adelaide.

Unlike *Cutty Sark*, *City of Adelaide* was built primarily as a passenger ship. She offered fourteen luxurious first-class cabins, could accommodate thirty passengers in second class and up to 300 in steerage class, and carried up to 1500 tons of cargo. For the passage to Adelaide, this usually comprised products needed to support the young colony's population of 150,000, then wool and locally mined copper were shipped back to England.

Between 1864 and 1887, *City of Adelaide* made twenty-three return voyages between London and Adelaide. The majority of migrants who departed England were English, Scottish, Irish, German and Scandinavian – probably between 6000 and 7000 in all. Historians who have studied Australian migration trends have since calculated that more than 250,000 Australians can today trace their family heritage to that one ship. This figure yet again confirms that many millions of Australians have the name of at least one clipper ship somewhere on a branch of their family tree.

Fortunately, researchers have been able to locate many diaries and letters written by passengers who were aboard *City of Adelaide* on her early voyages, documents that again provide valuable detail of life on board.

On *City of Adelaide*'s maiden voyage, Sarah Ann Bray, aged twenty, travelling with her parents and sister, made notes in her diary relating to some of the social activities she and other first-class passengers enjoyed:

We danced [on deck] for a short time in the evening but
were obliged to go down on account of the rain. We
tried a quadrille in the saloon but there was scarcely room
enough, and some of the people objected to the noise.

Frederick Edelstein, on a business trip to Adelaide in 1867,
noted: 'Smoking and drinking is the most fashionable way of
spending Sundays.'

In 1871, Scotsman Melville Miller provided from-the-
heart detail of the experience he and his wife Sarah shared
after deciding to migrate to South Australia:

My wife and I having mutually agreed to leave our
native country and to try our luck in the antipodes –
with heavy heart we took farewell of my dear mother,
brothers and sisters and little nephews, on Saturday
morning.

My dear old home, too, with all my favourite haunts
around it seemed to me to be more beautiful than ever
on that memorable morning, but leave it I must, never
perhaps again to look upon the scene of so many happy
memories.

[We arrived in London] where we found the ship
City of Adelaide lying there ... the bustle and excitement
going on, in and about her, being very clear evidence of
which was the outbound ship amongst the hundreds
that towered their stalwart masts up in the air.

Having with difficulty and considerable risk got
Sarah and myself on board, and having made our way
over spars, cables and endless confusion of ropes, etc. −
we reached our saloon, and next our cabin, in which we
were to spend the greater part of the next three months.
We went on the saloon deck, from where we could see
the remainder of the cargo put in the hold and the
hatches closed.

Both Melville and Sarah suffered from seasickness in the early
stages of the voyage, but before long Melville was writing
graphic accounts of what he observed when standing on the
ship's deck at the height of a mid-ocean storm:

Plenty of wind today, rain and hail likewise, an out and
out nasty squally day. Sails all reefed except foresail, fore
lower topsail, and ripper topsail. Main, mizzen lower
and upper topsail, only sails in all instead of somewhere
about 30 which we nearly always carry. To give an idea
of the power of the wind, with this small amount of
sail, we are going over 12 knots – just plunging through
it, hurling great waves back with her mighty weight, as
if she were a rock. Tons of water came on board today,
rushing over the deck about a foot deep. There is now
never less than half a foot at all times. The bulwarks
have again been smashed in today by the rude waves ...
Very early in the morning it blew very fierce, the waves

striking her sides seemed as if a solid mass of two or three ton weight were thrown against her making her tremble from stem to stern.

During her long career sailing between the Mother Country and the colonies, *City of Adelaide* suffered only two incidents of note.

In 1874, when sailing at night near Adelaide in Gulf St Vincent, a severe storm howled in and drove the big ship ashore on Kirkaldy Beach, less than 10 nautical miles south of the entrance to Adelaide's Torrens River. All passengers were transferred safely to shore the following morning, then, to lighten ship, the cargo plus many spars and yards were offloaded onto barges. A week later, when the tide was at its highest for some time, *City of Adelaide* was towed off the beach virtually undamaged.

The other incident is of more historic interest. On 31 October 1877, *City of Adelaide* departed Port Augusta, at the northern end of South Australia's Spencer Gulf, with a cargo of copper destined for London. When only 200 nautical miles into the voyage, and while rounding Kangaroo Island in heavy conditions, a powerful wave thundered into the ship's stern and smashed her rudder.

In what was a superb display of seamanship, the commander, Captain Edward D. Alston, regained control of his vessel, then, by dragging chains over both sides of the deck at the stern and carefully trimming the sails, he managed to safely navigate his way through reef-strewn waters, around the notorious Cape Jervis and into the waters of Gulf St Vincent. Seven days later he had his ship anchored off the shoreline west of Adelaide.

Workers at a local shipyard then set about making a new rudder using strong and durable Australian grey ironbark timber. In 2005, 138 years after the event, scientists confirmed that the rudder built in Adelaide was still fitted to the ship.

By the late 1880s, *City of Adelaide* no longer had a future as a migrant ship. Between 1887 and 1893, she was used as a collier and timber carrier in England and across the North Atlantic. In 1893, her rig was removed and she became a hospital ship in England for the next thirty years.

By 1948, having been renamed HMS *Carrick*, she was destined to be broken up, but instead became a floating clubhouse for the Royal Navy Reserve in Scotland. She sank at a dock in Glasgow in 1991 and this led to her being hauled out and all but forgotten at the dockyard in Irvine.

The plan now being developed by the group that has saved her is to partially restore one side of the interior to its original style, so that the public can appreciate the life experienced below deck during the voyage of more than 12,000 nautical miles she regularly sailed from London to Port Adelaide.

*

While the period of the sweetly proportioned clippers overlapped the transition to rattling steam engines, there was to be a design grand finale for sail-powered commercial vessels: the era of the windjammers. They were as majestic as they were magnificent – vessels that, at 300-plus feet in overall length, were twice as long as the average clipper ship. The masts on the largest windjammers speared more than 200 feet into the sky – the height of a twenty-storey building – and the yards carrying the largest square sails were 100 feet long. Most windjammers could cram on thirty-five sails across four masts in ideal conditions, the total area being around 45,000 square feet – half the area of a soccer field.

But those dimensions were trifling when compared with the largest and most astounding windjammer of all: the 439-foot *Preussen*, launched in Germany in 1902. She was one of only a few five-masted windjammers and the only one square-rigged on all masts. There were forty-seven sails in her wardrobe, their combined sail area being an astonishing 73,260 square feet.

In a sense, the windjammers were considerably larger versions of the clipper ships, and they were at their most efficient on long-haul routes where trade winds prevailed for the majority of the time. Regardless, many old tars who sailed both clippers and windjammers said that the larger ships could not deliver the same speed and level of excitement as a clipper being pushed hard downwind.

*

Initially, the advent of steamships on the run to Australia was slow. In 1852 the clipper-style auxiliary steamer *Chusan*, which was rigged as a barque, became the first ship of her type to sail into Sydney on a regular basis: the start of a scheduled two-monthly mail run from Singapore on a contract negotiated with the colonial government by the ship's owners, the Peninsular and Oriental Steam Navigation Company.

However, because the ship was so costly to run, this service could only exist through government subsidies. It was also a slow procedure: the mail had to be shipped from England to Egypt then transported across land by rail, camel or horse to the Red Sea, then shipped to Hong Kong then Singapore, where it was finally put aboard *Chusan*. After that the passage from Singapore to Sydney took another fifty-five days to complete.

Regardless of their shortcomings, the large auxiliary steamers appeared destined to claim a significant slice of the clipper ships' trade in Australia – until a horrendous maritime tragedy intervened.

In 1859, the 236-foot-long auxiliary steamer *Royal Charter* – which was reported to be carrying £500,000 worth of gold specie in its vault – was on the verge of reaching Liverpool from Melbourne after a very fast passage of fifty-eight days. But within 40 nautical miles of her destination, a heinous, hurricane-force storm swept down the Irish Sea from the north-north-east and crossed the ship's course. Conditions turned from benign to brutal in minutes.

Despite heroic efforts by the captain and crew, *Royal Charter*'s steam engine was not powerful enough to provide any forward momentum. Her anchors were released in the hope they would hold, but the cables parted; then, in a desperate bid to reduce windage, the masts were cut away and sent crashing over the side. This compounded the problem as the rigging attached to the masts tangled around her propeller. *Royal Charter* then lay at the mercy of the weather and was driven ashore onto the rocky coast of North Wales, where she was smashed apart by the raging seas. The final death toll will never be known, but it is safe to assume that more than 450 lives were lost. Only twenty-seven men, passengers and crew, are believed to have survived the maelstrom, which, by the time it abated, had claimed some 200 vessels of all shapes and sizes along the coast and on the Irish Sea.

While the magnitude of the storm contributed greatly to *Royal Charter*'s shipwreck, her engine had done nothing to prevent the ship from being driven by wind and waves onto the rocks. This horrific tragedy confirmed that an efficient form of steam propulsion was still a long way off.

It was another twenty-nine years after *Chusan* first sailed into Sydney that it became apparent the end of the magnificent clipper era was nigh.

This signal came with the launch of SS *Aberdeen* in England in 1881 and, soon afterwards, the launch of SS *Australasian*. A newspaper article at the time reported that these two ships were fitted with revolutionary new engines 'of triple expansion type', which provided 2700 horsepower, and consumed considerably less coal than existing steam engines. The report added: 'The *Australasian* is intended to attain a speed of about 12 knots at sea, which will enable her cargo to be landed in Australia much faster than ordinary cargo boats.'

When the arrival of these ground-breaking vessels was coupled with the increasing use of the Suez Canal, there was no longer a future for the clippers on what was their last bastion: the route to Australia.

Still, this magnificent, history-making breed would forever hold one clear advantage over the 'steam kettles'. A clipper ship charging downwind under full sail, with everything from skysail to stunsails, spanker to flying jib, all looking buxom and near breaking point, her hull boldly pushing aside a mighty white bow wave and sending spray flying high, was a thrilling and endearing sight that could never be matched by a steamer.

Glossary

Abaft Towards the stern of a ship; 'abaft the beam' means aft of abeam

Abeam A point 90 degrees out from anywhere along the centreline of a ship

Anchor Bower, the biggest anchor; stream, the next largest anchor; kedge, a smaller anchor for special purposes, usually stored below decks

Anchor stocks The heavy timber crossbar at the top of the anchor

Athwartships Directly across the ship, from side to side

Back-winding Wind coming in from the front, or wrong, side of a sail or sails

Baffling winds An erratic wind that frequently changes direction

Ballast Any heavy material (like gravel, iron, lead, sand, stones) placed in the hold of a ship to provide stability

Beam ends The sides of a ship. 'On her beam ends' is used to describe the rolling effect of very rough seas on the ship; the ship is almost on her side and possibly about to capsize

Beat, to Sailing upwind

Belay To secure a rope

Belaying pins Wooden pins found around the mast at deck level, or at the side of a ship which are used to secure a rope

Bend / Unbend sails To attach or remove sails from their yards

Best bower The starboard of the two anchors carried at the bow of the ship. That on the port side was known as the smaller bower, even though the two were identical in weight

Bilge The curved part of a ship's hull immediately above the keel

Bitt A vertical post set on the deck of a ship; used to secure and tie ropes or cables

Bitthead The top of the bitt

Block A single or multiple sheaved pulley

Boatswain/bosun Warrant or non-commissioned officer responsible for the maintenance of the ship's rigging, anchors and cables

Bower Bow anchor or cable

Bowsprit A pole extending forward from a vessel's bow

Brace A rope or line attached to the end of a yard which is either eased or hauled in so that the sail is trimmed to suit the wind direction

Brig A two-masted square rigger

Bring to To cause a ship to turn into the wind or come to a stop

Bulwarks The planking along the sides of a ship above the upper deck which acts as a railing to prevent crew and passengers from going overboard

Buntlines Ropes tied to the foot of a square sail that keep it from opening or bellying when it is being hauled up for furling to the yard

Burthen Displacement

Cable 1. A long, thick and heavy rope attached to the ship's anchor

      2. A naval unit of distance – ten cables is one nautical mile

Capstan A large waist-high vertical winch turned by crew manning the capstan bars which lock into the head of the winch. The crew then walk in a circle to work the winch. Used to raise the anchor and other heavy objects

Careen To heel a ship over on one side or the other for cleaning, caulking or repairing

Cathead A sturdy timber projection near the bow to hold the anchor

Caulking The material making the ship watertight (such as cotton fibres or oakum) forced between the planks to stop leaks

Cay A low bank or reef of coral, rock or sand

Chains The area outside the ship where the dead-eyes, rigging and other hardware come together to support the mast

Clew The bottom corners of the square sail, or the lower aft corner of a triangular sail

Clew up To draw up a square sail to the yard by hauling on the clew lines

Close-hauled Sailing with the sails trimmed in as close as possible to the centre line. This allows the ship to sail as close to the direction of the wind as possible

Collier A cargo ship that hauled coal

Commander The next rank above lieutenant in the Royal Navy prior to the introduction of the rank of lieutenant-commander in the early twentieth century

Composite construction Construction involving multiple dissimilar materials – in this era metal frames and timber planking

Cutter A fast sailboat with one mast that carries several headsails

Dead-reckoning The method for estimating a vessel's current position based on its previously determined position then advanced by estimating speed and course over an elapsed time

Deck beams Timbers running from side to side of a ship to support the deck

Doldrums A region of the ocean near the equator, characterized by calms, faint breezes or squalls

Downs (The) An anchorage off the coast of England between Dover and Deal

Draught The measurement from the waterline to the deepest point of the vessel in the water

Driver boom The yard carrying the driver, a square sail set from the peak of the gaff on the mizzenmast

Embayed Trapped within the confines of a bay and unable to sail into safe water

Fathom A unit of measurement for depth - one fathom is 1.83 metres or six feet

Feu de joie A progressive volley of shots fired by soldiers on a ceremonial occasion

Fiferail A wooden rail positioned on the deck around the base of a mast which is used for belaying the ship's halyards

Fine off the ... bow Just off the centreline looking forward

Fore castle [foc'sle] fo'c's'le The living quarters in the bow of the ship where crew is accommodated

Foremast The first mast, or the mast fore of the main-mast

Freeboard The distance from the water to the ship's gunwale

Futtock An iron plate in the ship's topmast for securing the rigging

Gaff A spar angled aft from a mast which carries a four-sided fore-and-aft sail. The head of the sail is attached to the top of the gaff

Grog A mixture of rum and water served to a ship's crew

Gunwale/gunnel The top edge of the planking at the sides of the ship, named for the place where a crewman rested his gun to take aim

Gybe Changing from one tack to the other away from the wind, turning the ship's stern through the wind. See also 'to wear ship'

HMS His/Her Majesty's Ship

Halyard A rope used for raising or lowering a sail, yard, spar or flag

Haul up or Haul onto the wind To change a ship's course so that it is sailing closer to the direction from which the wind is blowing. At the same time the ship's sails are trimmed to suit the new course

Hawser A cable or rope used for mooring or towing a ship

Headed When the wind changes direction so that it is coming from a point closer to the ship's bow, causing the vessel to change course to leeward so that it can continue sailing effectively

Heave to Slowing a vessel's forward progress by fixing the helm and foresail so that the vessel does not need to be steered: a procedure usually applied in very rough weather

Heel To tilt to one side

Helm The apparatus used to steer the vessel by moving the angle of the rudder

Horse latitudes A subtropical region extending about 30 degrees north and south of the equator. Sailing ships were often becalmed traversing these latitudes and consequently ran out of water, making it impossible to keep horses and other livestock alive. The crew had no option but to throw the dead animals overboard.

Hove Raised or lifted with effort or force, particularly the anchor

Hull The main body of the ship

Hull-down A situation where the hull of a vessel is not visible as it is below the horizon, but the rig can be seen

Jib A triangular headsail set from the foremast which is the foremost sail

Jury-rig A temporary rig put up in place of a mast that has broken or been carried away

Kedge A small anchor used to keep a ship steady and clear from her bower anchor

Knot A unit of speed equal to one nautical mile per hour or approximately 1.151 miles (1.852km) per hour

Larboard The old name for port, the left hand side of the ship. The term 'fine on the larboard bow' refers to an area just off the vessel's centre-line, looking forward on the port side

Lead-line A sounding line with a lead weight at one end used to record the depth of water under the ship

Leadsman The man who, standing in the chains, heaves the lead to take soundings

League A unit of distance in the eighteenth century equal to three nautical miles

Lee The sheltered side

Leeward The direction away from the wind; opposite of 'windward'

Leeway Drifting sideways

Lieutenant Lowest rank of commissioned officer in the Royal Navy, prior to the introduction of the rank of sub-lieutenant in the twentieth century

Lofting floor A flat floor where loftsmen take the dimensions from a vessel's plans or half-model and scale them up to full size drawings on the floor. These patterns which are scribed using flexible battons are then used as templates

Log 1. A device for measuring a ship's speed
  2. A record of a ship's movements, the weather for navigational purposes, and general and pertinent information regarding incidents, observations and shipboard routine. Usually kept by the captain, masters and lieutenants

Luff The leading edge of a fore-and-aft sail; or to change course into the wind so that the sails flap

Lying-to / lying a-hull Waiting out a storm by lowering all sails and letting the vessel drift

Main course The lowest square sail

Mainmast The tallest mast on a vessel

Make fast To secure a line

Mal de mer Seasickness (Fr)

Marines Seaborne contingent of soldiers

Master The most senior non-commissioned officer or warrant officer in the Royal Navy at the time responsible for the navigation of the ship, subject to the command of its officers

Masthead The very top part of the a mast

Mate Assistant warrant officer to a senior warrant officer, hence bosun's mate and master's mate

Mechanical log A device for measuring a ship's speed where a four-bladed rotator is towed on a line from the ship's stern

Mizzen The sail set from the aftermost mast

Mizzenmast On a ship with three masts, this is the mast nearest the stern

Nautical mile A mathematical calculation based on the circumference of the Earth at the equator; equal to 1.15 miles

Oakum Old pieces of rope picked to shreds and tarred for use as caulking. Known as rope junk

Offing Distance from shore, land or other navigational hazards

One Hundredweight Fifty kilos

Packet A vessel that transports passengers, mail and goods between two ports at regular intervals

Painter A mooring line – usually a light line attached to the bow of a small boat

Pawl A hinged or pivoted catch on a ratchet wheel which prevents it from slipping back

Pinnace A small vessel with two fore-and-aft rigged masts; it can be rowed or sailed and usually carried men between shore and ship

Poop deck The short deck towards the stern above the quarterdeck of a ship

Pooped To have a wave break over the stern of the ship and onto the deck

Port The left-hand side of a vessel

Post-Captain An alternative form of the rank of captain. It distinguishes those who were captains by rank, from officers in command of a naval vessel who were recognised as captain regardless of rank, and commanders who received the title of captain regardless of them being in command or not

Put the wheel/helm down To turn the steering wheel in a particular direction

Quadrant A very simple instrument used to determine the altitude of a heavenly body

Quarterdeck The upper exposed deck at the stern of the ship from the mainmast to the back, usually the territory of the ship's officers

Ratlines Bands of ropes lashed across the shrouds like steps that allow crew to easily climb aloft

Reciprocal course/track To return along a course from whence you came

Reef/reefed To take in or reduce the area of a sail without furling it

Refit Repair or restore a vessel

Rhumbline The shortest distance in a straight line between two points, free of obstruction

Rigging All ropes, wires and chains used to support the masts and yards

Schooner A fore-and-aft rigged vessel, originally with two masts, but later with three or more. Designed for blockade running and as a fast naval vessel

Sextant A navigational instrument used to measure the angle of elevation of an object above the horizon

Sheave The grooved and revolving wheel fitted within a block over which a rope travels

Sheet A rope attached to either of the lower corners (clews) of a square sail, or the aftermost lower corner of a fore-and-aft sail. Also, the rope used to control the boom of the mainsail or mizzen/spanker

Sheet anchor Traditionally, the largest of a ship's anchors carried so they can be quickly dropped in the event of an emergency

Shipped on deck The situation when a large wave bursts over the bulwark and washes across the ship's deck

Shroud The standing rigging on the ship that provides lateral support to the mast

Slatted A sail flopping backwards and forwards in near windless conditions

Sloop A single-masted sailing ship usually carrying a mainsail and a single jib or headsail

Slops Ready-made clothing from the ship's stores which is sold to the seamen

Spanker A large fore-and-aft sail set from the mizzen(aft-most) mast using a gaff – a wooden spar which supports the top of the sail

Spars A general term relating to all the poles in a vessel's rig, such as masts, yards, booms and gaffs

Spritsail A four-sided sail set from a sprit which usually extends beyond the end of the yards

Square-rigger A ship using square sails as its principal form of sail

Starboard The right-hand side of a vessel

Stay A large long rope which acts as a piece of standing rigging to support the mast either athwartships or fore-and-aft

Sternsheets The stern area of an open boat

Strake A line of planking on the side of a vessel

Strike To "strike" is to remove and lower yards and topmasts to the deck

Swinging the compass A procedure where a vessel is turned through 360 degrees so that any deviations in the accuracy of the compass can be calculated and corrected

Tack A manoeuvre; and a corner of a sail

Taffrail The upper rail of the aft rail at a ship's stern

Tar A nickname for a lower-deck sailor. Derived from the fact that their canvas coats and hats were waterproofed with tar

Tender A small vessel that attends a man-of-war, primarily in harbour. Usually used to carry munitions, provisions, mail and despatches to and from the ship

Timoneer An alternative term for the helmsman

Topgallant In a square-rigged ship, these are the spars and rigging at the very top of the masts above the topsails

Topmast The second section of mast above the deck fixed to the top of the lower mast and which supports the topgallant mast

Treenails Short lengths of dowel that were wedged from both ends into holes bored through the planks and the frame using an augur

Uncleat To untie from a cleat – a T-shaped low-profile anchor point for securing lines

Waist (of the ship) The middle part of the upper deck of a ship, between the quarterdeck and the forecastle

Warp A rope attached to a ship which is used to move it from one place to another by men pulling on it when the ship is in harbour; hence warping means to move or re-position a ship by hauling on a line or anchor line

Wear ship, to A manoeuvre that comes when a square-rigged ship changes course by turning the ship's stern through the wind so that the direction of the wind comes onto the opposite side of the ship. Today it is referred to as a gybe

Windage The exposed part of a ship's hull and rig of a vessel causing wind resistance

Windlass A horizontal and cylindrical barrel used as a lifting device for a rope or anchor cable. It is turned by rods called handspikes

Yard A slender wooden spar slung at its centre on the forward side of a mast on a square-rigged ship

Yardarm The outer end of each yard from where, on square-rigged ships, signal flags were flown or men sentenced to death following a court martial were hanged

Author's Note

The Mundle family heritage embraces the sea.

For more than 150 years the oldest male member of each generation sailed the world's oceans to earn a living ... until it came to me. Even so, the sea and sailing were an integral part of my life from a very early age, and by the time I was 20 my sport and career had merged so superbly that I was set on a course through life that would prove dreams do come true.

My life under sail started as a two-year-old aboard a sandpit sailboat my father made for me in the backyard of our family home – an aging, dark and dilapidated semi-detached cottage on Sydney's lower North Shore.

The environment didn't matter to me, even though there were four adults and three young children sharing the two-bedroom residence. I had an escape.

I still hold memories of being aboard my little boat, hoisting to the top of the broomstick mast the mainsail Mum had made from a bedsheet; then setting off on my dream-laced odyssey – one I shared with the family cat and chooks, and amid chokos which were growing profusely over the rickety back fence and the ramshackle wooden chook house.

At age seven my vivid imagination had me sailing a square rigger over far-off horizons and visiting exciting ports. By this time my parents had moved my two younger brothers, Dennis and Bruce, and me to a house on Collaroy Plateau, on the northern beaches – a place from where I could see the ocean and feel the breeze.

I was very proud of the 'ship' I had built for these latest voyages. The hull was a fragile wooden tomato packing crate, little more than a metre in length. It had two masts: the mainmast was a broomstick I'd nailed to the front of the 'vessel', while the mizzen mast was a garden stake nailed to a 'bulkhead' amidships. My largest sail – the maincourse – was a Holland blind lashed by a myriad of knots to the top of the mainmast, while the square-sail on the mizzen – the crossjack – was the remnants of a colourful old curtain.

How I lived for the days when there was a strong wind blowing! That was when I'd drag my ship out from under the house and set it up on a 'course' in the backyard so that the sails would catch the wind. That done, I'd then squeeze myself into the aft part of the tomato crate, trim the sails and dream ... all the time longing for a stronger gust to descend on the scene so I could sense even more the power of the wind in the sails.

Sometimes I'd even let my brothers sail my ship...

In keeping with the family tradition, my grandfather was a professional mariner. I remember telling him one day about my 'square rigger', and he was most impressed. He then told me that my great-great grandfather had been the master of a square rigger, but details were scant.

Fast forward many decades, to recent times when I was researching this book, looking for every skerrick of detail available relating to the era of the mighty clipper ships. One can only imagine the magnitude of my delight when I found, in the 27 April 1855 edition of the *Sydney Morning Herald,* an article relating to the arrival in Sydney of the clipper ship *Commodore Perry.* It read in part *'...one of the largest and finest vessels that has entered this harbour,'* had arrived on her maiden round-the-world voyage out of Liverpool, England, and that the captain was George Mundle ... my great-great grandfather. Travelling with him were his wife, daughter Elizabeth and son, my great grandfather George Valentine Mundle (who was born aboard the ship *John Wood* in Whampoa Anchorage on the Pearl River, Canton on 30 September 1850).

Suddenly it was obvious that our family held a powerful and exciting direct link to the clipper ship era; and we were among the million–plus Australians who today can trace their heritage back to these swift and majestic thoroughbreds of the sea.

From that moment writing *Under Full Sail* became more personal: it took on an even more exciting dimension for me. The subject matter was very much in my blood.

Even so, completing this historic undertaking did not come without considerable assistance, and here I must salute the superbly professional crew of dedicated book lovers at the ABC Books division of HarperCollins Publishers. In particular I must again thank my guiding light, Publisher Helen Littleton, who has been an inspiration and a 'rudder' across all six books I have written relating to Australia's maritime history. Special mention must also be made of copy editor, Emma Dowden, who did a superb job within a very tight timeframe; Senior Editor, Lachlan McLaine; the designer of the impressive cover, Darren Holt, plus Linda Braidwood, who did a great job researching and securing the images. And, not to be forgotten are the sales and publicity teams at HCP, and the hardworking typesetter Graeme Jones, who has set all my maritime history books.

Beyond the publishing house I must also thank the booksellers who have been wonderfully supportive of my books for many years.

On a personal note my gratitude again goes out to my personal assistant, Liz Christmas. She has been an exceptional asset for me for more than a decade – my 'watch captain' and first assistant who is always on deck when needed. I must also recognise Brian McDonald for his assistance with research and Nick Burningham for his excellent technical review of the typeset pages.

Most importantly, I'm indebted to my perfect partner, Christine Power, for her resolute support and understanding during this project. She stood by me, more often than not seven days a week, as I worked to meet the publisher's deadline.

Finally there is my ever expanding crew – my readers – whom I must recognise. Thank you, one-and-all, for the inspiration you have provided me over the years. I now look forward to having you with me aboard the amazing clipper ships and enjoying this adventure *Under Full Sail*.

Rob Mundle

Index